IBO VILLAGE AFFAIRS

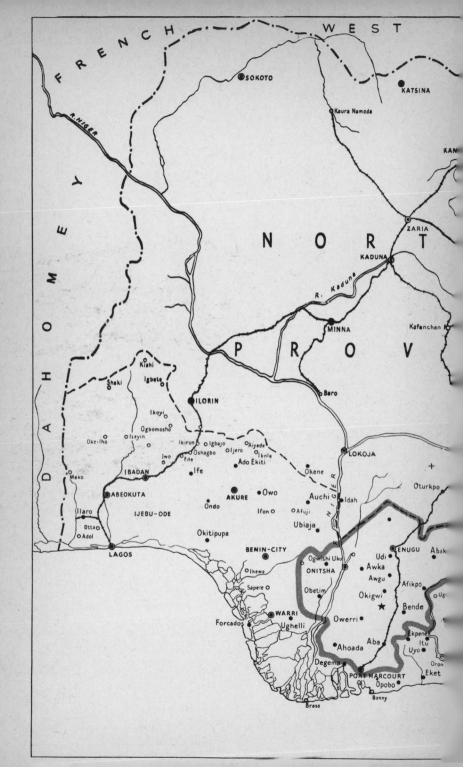

AFRICA

○ Ngura

● MAIDUGURI

H E R N

● BAUCHI

○ JOS

N C E S

● YOLA

R. BENUE

R. Temba

CAMEROONS UNDER BRITISH MANDATE

CAMEROONS UNDER FRENCH MANDATE

KURDI

Tivo ○ Gboko

R. Katsina Ala

● OGOJA   Obudu

bra

om

● Mamfe   Bamenda

Nkongsamba ○

● Kumba

● BUEA

Victoria ○   ● DUALA

NIGERIA
1935
Scale :—1 : 3,000,000 or 1 inch to 47·35 Miles.

Miles
10 0   20   40   60   80   100   120   140

REFERENCE

Boundaries, International . . . . — · — · —
     „   Provincial . . . . . · · · · · · · · ·
Boundary between the Northern and
Southern Provinces . . . — — — — —
Headquarters, Provincial . . . ●
     „   Divisional . . . •
Towns and Villages . . . . ○
Railways . . . . . ┼┼┼┼┼┼┼
     outlines Ibo-speaking area.
★ Approximate position of Umueke Agbaja.

Ibo
Village Affairs

by
M. M. GREEN

FREDERICK A. PRAEGER, *Publisher*

NEW YORK

BOOKS THAT MATTER

Published in the United States of America in 1964
by Frederick A. Praeger, Inc., Publishers
111 Fourth Avenue, New York 3, N.Y.

This is a new edition of a book first published
in Great Britain in 1947.

Library of Congress Catalog Card Number: 64-19957

Printed in the United States of America

TO
MY PARENTS

Contents

Preface to the 1964 edition

EXCEPT for corrections to the text and the addition of a short new preface this book has been left unaltered. Any value it has is in the specific picture it offers of life as it appeared to be lived in an Igbo village at a particular stage of its history.

It is twenty six years since I lived in Umueke. Eighteen months ago, when I was staying in Umuahia, I paid it a flying visit of an hour—all that was practicable at the time. Many of my friends had died but I found the one I was specially looking for, and his wife. I had been told that " progress " everywhere was such that I should not know the place. And so far as the big towns and the main roads are concerned much material improvement has taken place. But in the rural areas one wondered. No doubt " progress " is bound to be uneven, but one hopes, as many of my African friends hope, that it is not making the rich richer and the poor poorer. The people of Umueke crowded round me and my companion and urged us to help them with their agriculture or by coming and starting up a " business " of some kind among them. On the spot the significance of this was impossible to assess. But there was no mistaking the problem of unemployment in Eastern Nigeria, especially among the young people. Nor was there any doubt about the need to increase the production of home grown food. It is good to know that the present Prime Minister of Eastern Nigeria stresses the importance of agriculture.

If it were possible, one day, to live again for a time in Umueke as an ordinary individual, and to supplement scientific detachment by personal involvement, the result might be illuminating. To be a social anthropologist in the field is a severe strain both on one's own humanity and on that of the people one is among. One can but be grateful for their tolerance.

There are one or two small points that need bringing up to date. The census of 1953–54 estimates the number of the Igbo people at nearly five million. No more recent figures are yet available. (See p. 3.)

So far as the *osu* people are concerned, it is now against the law in Eastern Nigeria to call anyone *osu*. (See p. 23.)

Cowries would rarely, if ever, be used as currency now. Their disappearance is a pointer to the rise in prices which has made currency of such low value obsolete. (See p. 41.)

As to the former prohibition on carrying arms of precision, I do not know what the present position is. (See p. 65.)

Appendix

The years that have passed since the appendix was written have confirmed the importance of recognizing the factor of temperament, not least in the writings of psychologists themselves. If Janet, Freud and Jung can be seen as speaking for their temperamental affinities, and the fourth type the deliberate simplifiers, as dealt with by Dr. M. Mackenzie, it should be possible to see more clearly what in their work is of general validity and what only for those of a temperament similar to their own. How little this point is generally recognized can be seen in the generalizations of many of the followers of Freud or Jung.

Further than this, much needs to be done in relating the study of temperament to that of social groups. The light already shed on the psychology of individuals needs to be turned, with due caution, on that of social groups, It should be possible to isolate, or at least to recognize, the temperamental factor which enters into all social situations, whether political, religious, economic or other, and which bedevils understanding so long as it is unrecognized. Few things could be more misleading than to look on all social problems as psychological. But it is equally misleading to mistake for a factor of some different kind what is really an unidentified factor of temperament.

In his books, " Contrast Psychology " (Allen and Unwin, London, 1953) and " Psychological Depression " (Churchill, London, 1963) Dr. Mackenzie has clarified this question and has also made an interesting approach to the subject of temperamental types and social groups.

Orthography

The Note on Orthography on p. xi has been left standing as it refers to the body of the book and is still relevant. But it must be stressed that since 1961 there has been an official orthography for Igbo, as the Eastern Nigerian Government accepted the excellent recommendations of the Ọnwụ Committee on Orthography which met earlier that year. In the place of phonetic symbols, roman letters with diacritic marks are used, the vowel symbols now being i ị e a u ụ o ọ in place of i e ɛ a u ө o ɔ, and n being used for the velar nasal consonant.

It has not been possible to transcribe the Igbo words or passages in the book owing to the photographic technique used in the new issue, but one or two transcribed examples are given here, with the type of tone marking used now in Igbo writings for foreigners or for linguistic purposes. The high tone is left unmarked, the grave accent is for the low tone and the vertical for the mid.

p. 6. Anà m̀ àsụ̀ asụ̀sụ Ìgbò ǹke Ọ̀nị̀cà.

p. 17. onamá.

p. 61. ịlụ̀ ọ̀gọ̀.

p. 99. Ọ wụ́ òmenàlà, ọ̀ wụghí ìwu.

Throughout the book Ibo should be Igbo.

Map

The map at the front refers to Nigeria at the time of the writing of the book.

M. M. GREEN.

11 JULY 1963.

Preface

THIS book is based upon some of the material collected during two periods of field work, one of thirteen and the other of eleven months between 1934 and 1937 in South Eastern Nigeria. About six months of each tour were spent in the village here described and practically the whole cycle of the year from January to December was covered.

The writing of the book was in the first instance delayed by illness, the first draft being written in 1940-41 in the intervals of other work. Since then the first part has been more or less rewritten, also as pressure of other work allowed.

In view of administrative reorganisation in Ibo country which aimed at working more and more through indigenous institutions, and also because of the Aba Riots of the women in 1929-30, it was felt that more information about Ibo social organisation and particularly about the women was desirable. My colleague, Mrs. Leith-Ross, and I were therefore awarded Leverhulme Research Fellowships to enable us to study these questions. The area involved was so large that we did not work together, though we met at intervals for consultation.

In choosing Agbaja for special study I was guided by a number of considerations. In the first place it was required that the work should be done within the heavily populated belt of Ibo country, that is to say, where the density of population was somewhere between three hundred and about thirteen hundred to the square mile. In the second place I decided that I should be more likely to get at some of the essential features of Ibo social organisation if I studied it, at any rate in the first place, in a form that had been relatively little disturbed by European contact. Everywhere within the dense belt there has been considerable European influence, but in parts it has gone further than in others. I know that some of my West African friends think that English people delight in portraying " bush " conditions and that they wish such writers would spend more time describing sophisticated Africans. I ask them to believe that I hoped by studying the simpler forms of their society to obtain some basis of comparison from which the more complex forms might be better understood. If Europeans are to understand and help the changing conditions of South Eastern Nigeria they cannot but try to grasp the background against which these changes are taking place. It may be, too, that the time is coming when the more sophisticated of the Ibo people will be glad that something of their indigenous culture has been placed on record.

The focussing point of this book is one village—a poor and relatively unsophisticated one. How far it is typical of its kind I leave to others with greater comparative knowledge to decide. My own experience of other parts of Ibo country suggests that it has many features that are common to what I would call the interior or central Ibo of Owerri Province : but it certainly also has local variations. It is, moreover, very different from such relatively wealthy and Europeanised urban centres as Onitsha or Aba. A small-scale study of this kind clearly has great limitations, but I was anxious to avoid a composite picture and believed, as I still believe, that adequate generalisations about the Ibo people must be based on detailed investigation of particular areas. I also wanted to experience rather than to survey the texture of Ibo social life.

It was not an easy matter to decide where to settle. Accurate information was hard to come by and in the meantime one could not waste a moment in getting to grips with the language. I had spent eighteen months in Nigeria some years previously and had learned some Hausa, but it was a different matter to tackle a tone language with a multiplicity of dialects. Moreover, at that time we knew much less than we do now about the nature and geographical spread of dialectal variations. I went first to Owerri town and to Egbu Owerri for some months and worked hard at the language. When I decided to go to Agbaja because it was described by both Government officials and missionaries as a backwater, I found myself involved in a dialect which I never had time adequately to analyse and which had enough sound shifts, compared with Owerri or Mbieri, to be confusing to a European though it was intelligible on the whole to my Owerri and Mbieri staff. I came to be able to talk pretty easily with A., my Mbieri interpreter, but I used him or one of the others on most occasions in the village. I could talk with some of the

younger people, but not with the older ones ; in general
conversation or when cases were being tried in the village
I could only catch odd words. But I trained A. and my girl
S. to listen carefully, particularly to the incidentals and asides
of conversation, and also to magico-religious and other
formulæ. Some of these they were able to write down at the
time : others they memorised as nearly as possible. When,
therefore, I give texts, they are taken from one of my staff,
usually from A., and not directly from the speaker. They
therefore could not be checked, but so far as the formulæ
are concerned there is a general pattern which is in itself
something of a check.

As for taking notes myself, I soon found that among the
countless fears of these apprehensive folk, the fear of a
pencil and paper was one. When I arrived in Agbaja I went
about at first with a note-book ; but the census taking and
the introduction of taxation by the Government a few years
previously had helped to produce the Aba Riots and had
left everyone in a very jumpy condition so far as seeking or
recording information was concerned. Moreover, Agbaja
had had very little experience of Europeans apart from these
enquirers and the mere arrival of a white woman with or
without a notebook was clearly a presage of disaster. Whether
I was going to tax the women or lay hands upon the land
and the palm trees or both was a matter of opinion, but that
my coming boded no good was a subject of general agreement. I therefore gave up trying to take notes in public or
even in my own house during conversations with people
whom I did not know well, and had to write from memory,
a far from satisfactory proceeding, and there were times
when the pace made it impossible to write the same day or
even the following one. Fortunately I had the assistance of
my staff whose memories supplemented and frequently surpassed my own. As for the checking and rechecking of facts, I
have occasionally relied on an individual's opinion or account.

That the village in the first instance received me was due
to the kindness of the Roman Catholic Mission which had
at one time functioned there, and whose reinstalling of an
African teacher coincided with my arrival. This meant that
I was well looked on by N. Ɛ., the oldest man in the village
and a pagan, but with a progressive outlook. The suspicions
roused by my coming, particularly those of the women in

connection with tax, lessened with time and more or less disappeared with individuals ; but there was never a feeling of complete *sans gêne*. Perhaps there never would be in an Ibo village where rivalry between the two halves and between different extended families is part of the daily routine. If one is popular with X., one will of necessity be unpopular with Y. It is impossible to avoid intrigues. All one can hope for is to be as little involved as possible.

With all this I would like to pay my tribute to the village for its hospitality to me. Few English villages would have put up with as much from an African as they endured from me. For the many ways, avoidable and unavoidable, in which I troubled them I would like herewith to apologise. I remember with pleasure that just before I left them finally there was a moment when, in the face of external foes, the entire village was united, including the white woman.

What I owe to my Ibo staff, from my cook downwards, I cannot adequately express. They came with dark foreboding in their hearts to this bush village thirty miles or more from their own homes. " I fear we shall see no good customs here, Ma," said one of them on our first arrival ; but their loyalty and support never wavered and their interest grew till they became impassioned in the anthropological quest for knowledge. The fact that they were strangers to the village had two advantages : they had no feeling of reticence about its affairs and they were able to compare them, for my benefit, with what obtained in their own district. I may perhaps add that they learned that people in the distant bush were not necessarily "very wicked." The one who had given voice to his pessimism when we arrived came shortly afterwards and, with a look of bewilderment, reported about one of the village elders : " Ma, he is a very good old man ! " If my expedition achieved nothing else, it achieved that.

A certain lack of homogeneity in the book will be apparent to its readers. Part III is perhaps unduly descriptive : it deals, however, with women's organisations about which less is usually known than about those of the men. I have therefore let it stand. I have put into an Appendix, rather than into the body of the book, a section on temperament. I did not come upon the theories it contains until I had finished my field work, but I have found them illuminating. They are still at the stage, however, when they must, from the sociological angle, rank as hypotheses to be further tested by the facts. They are therefore better considered in a section of their own. Dr. Mackenzie has very kindly read this appendix in spite of the many claims on his time, and has passed as accurate the summary it attempts of some of his conclusions. He is not, of course, in any way responsible for the application of his theories to my Ibo material.

I would like to take this opportunity of thanking the Leverhulme Trustees for the generous Fellowship which they awarded for this work, and the Nigerian Government for their financial assistance towards publication.

I owe much to the kindness and help of Government officials, missionaries, traders and Africans in Nigeria, and I hope that they and all who have helped me in more ways than I can record will accept my thanks.

I must, however, mention Dr. Meek, who gave me invaluable information about the kinship organisation, and unfailing encouragement. He also generously gave me a typescript copy of his then unpublished book, *Law and Authority in a Nigerian Tribe* : Professor Ida Ward, who trained me in the fundamentals of Ibo language study and whose stimulating interest has never flagged : and my colleague and mentor, Mrs. Leith-Ross, whose wisdom and experience were without stint at my disposal.

Note on Orthography

For the spelling of Ibo words I have used the " new " or " improved " orthography except for the name Ibo [Igbo] itself and for place names. Such of these as appear in official maps are spelt in the old way and to alter them here might create confusion. I have therefore kept the old spelling. But there is this particular disadvantage. Many of these place names begin with Umu—as in Umuahia. *Umu* would be spelt *ɵmɵ* in the new orthography. As it denotes " children " it at once suggests, what is so characteristic of Ibo social organisation, that the local unit is also a kinship unit. This is true also of the small extended family units of which the village is made up. In recording these family names I have therefore kept *umu* and I have also written the kinship terms *umunna* and *umunnɛ* instead of *ɵmɵnna* and *ɵmɵnnɛ* in order to stress the fact that the same element, *umu* occurs in all of them.

PART I

Village Organisation

Chapter I. INTRODUCTION

THE first part of this book is an attempt to discover some of the means by which an Ibo village achieves the practical ends of government. The question has both a scientific and a practical side. The social anthropologist has the problem of discovering how, with so little, apparently, in the way of authority or of familiar forms, public business gets done. And in the search a number of interesting social devices appear. The Government official has to ask himself how indigenous institutions can not only be found and defined but also adapted to the task of indirect rule.

There are estimated[1] to be nearly four million Ibo or, more correctly, Ibo-speaking people in South Eastern Nigeria. Mainly on the left bank of the Niger, they reach from the Delta, into which some of them have filtered, up through the flat belt of tropical forest and into the rolling, orchard bush country that lies north of it. Their most immediately striking characteristic is what has aptly been called their social fragmentation.[2] This great people is broken up into hundreds of small, more or less independent, social units, the largest being, in many cases, what we may call the village-group. This is a collection of villages bound together by certain ties, but each one, at any rate in the district with which we are concerned, largely managing its own affairs.

When the British Government originally took over the administration of the country, indirect rule through indigenous institutions, which was possible with the great Mohammedam Emirates of the northern provinces, seemed impracticable among a people with so little central organisation as the Ibo. When, however, in later years it was decided to introduce indirect rule into the southern provinces it became necessary to find out the nature of Ibo institutions. They had been cut across by the system of Native Courts

---

[1] I use the word "estimated" because the Nigerian Census of 1930 was admittedly approximate in this area.

[2] M. Perham : *Native Administration in Nigeria.* Oxford University Press, 1937, p. 234.

on an arbitrary geographical basis, staffed by Warrant Chiefs, who were individuals chosen by the British with no particular reference to their position in native society. The difficult job of laying bare Ibo institutions was not, therefore, made easier by this introduction, nor by the unpopularity of the old system. But it was made far harder by the Aba riots of 1929-30 in which feeling against taxation and against the Warrant Chiefs, together with discontent at the low price of palm oil, flared into serious disturbance and bloodshed. And there can be no doubt that beneath the overt grievances lay a deep " unconscious, cultural protest."[1] The riots made the question of reorganisation on a basis of indirect rule doubly urgent and more and more intelligence reports were demanded from Government officials on the subject of the " natural rulers " of the Ibo. An enormous amount of energy and goodwill was put into the work and much information was collected,[2] though certain factors militated against a full harvest of results. Lack of time often made it inevitable that the method of questions rather than of observation should be used. Moreover, the embitterment of feeling and the atmosphere of suspicion that followed the whole question of taxation and of the riots made enquiry a matter of great difficulty, and it is surprising not that so little but that so much was achieved. One may perhaps add, in passing, that for enquirers who came later still—my own tour on this work started in 1934—the difficulty was not lessened by the fact that the people were already on their guard where investigations were concerned.

This book attempts a rather different approach from that of the search for " natural rulers." It tries to set out some of the ways in which the public or governmental affairs of an Ibo village are conducted. It does not claim to delimit the Ibo political unit. Whether or not such a delimitation is possible will depend partly on what is understood by political organisation or a political unit. It is not, I think, possible, at least among the Ibo people of the interior with

---

[1] See Perham, *op. cit.*, p. 218.
[2] Particularly by Dr. C. K. Meek, whose *Law and Authority in a Nigerian Tribe*, O.U.P., 1937, is based on his Intelligence Reports. A valuable unpublished report is that of Mr. G. Allen on the Ngwa section of the Ibo people. His command of the spoken language, rare among Europeans, was a great asset.

whom I am concerned, to point to any definite territorial unit within which there is a sovereign governmental authority. Anything of the nature of the sovereign State, which has so largely dominated the political consciousness of Europe since the Reformation, is in conception and in fact absent in this part of Africa. Power politics appear also to be absent. That there is political organisation, on the other hand, in the sense that the ends of government are to some extent secured, is an undoubted fact.[1] But political institutions are as yet largely undifferentiated and the unit within which political measures are applied will vary according to circumstances. The village largely manages its own affairs. But there are times when the larger, but far less organised unit, the village-group, or part of it, may impinge upon the doings of the village. This will be seen in the course of the following description of village organisation.

When we consider the Ibo, or Ibo-speaking people, as a whole, in what sense are they to be regarded as a unit? In the first place they occupy a common territory. They also speak a common language though with many dialectal variations. With a few exceptions these variations appear to be mutually intelligible, without undue difficulty, at least to those who are accustomed to travelling. The language is therefore, potentially, a unifying factor. How far the Ibo are culturally homogeneous it is difficult to say. Using the word culture here to include social organisation one can say that there are many factors, such, for instance, as kinship structure, which would seem to be common over much of the country. There are certain important cult symbols such as ofo [⎤] which are widely spread. There are, however, countless variations of custom from district to district and even within a small area. And peripheral or intrusive communities such as Onitsha or Aro Cuku or places bordering on other tribes will tend to show cultural features differing from those of the interior or central Ibo, particularly those of Owerri Division with whom we are concerned. But in all this matter we lack sufficient exact comparative data.

How far are the Ibo an ideological entity? To what extent do they consider themselves one people? There is,

---

[1] On the distinction between " political organisation " and " the state " see Nadel : *A Black Byzantium*. Oxford University Press, 1942, pp. 18 and 69.

as we have said, no Ibo State, no central authority which welds the people into a political whole. Thus, having no paramount chief or other organ of government common to them all, they lack what to other peoples may be powerful symbols of unity. Among the Bemba, for . instance, Dr. Richards emphasises the importance to them of their paramount chief.

As to the usage and significance of the name " Ibo," I regret that I did not go more deeply into this matter while I was in the country. I record a few points from my experience there and some from talks I have had with Ibo people in England since I returned. There is no doubt that an increasing number of educated or sophisticated Ibo-speaking people are coming to use the name both about their whole people and their language and with a more or less clear idea of the unit to which the name refers. The name, in fact, is becoming a symbol of unity. When one considers the majority of the people, however, the situation is less easy to define. The Onitsha people, who are said by tradition to be of Benin origin, would tend not to call themselves Ibo and they use the word as a term of contempt for the non-Onitsha, Ibo-speaking people. " Nwa Onyε Igbo " [‾ ‾ ‾ _ _]—" son of an Ibo "—is a scornful term. It has in this context a suggestion of " slave " in its meaning. Onitsha speaks Ibo, though its dialect is considerably different from that of the central Ibo. I asked two Onitsha men how they would answer a question as to what language they spoke. One said : " Ana m asǝ asǝsǝ Igbo nkε Ɔneca "—" I speak the

Ibo language of Onitsha." The other said that he would simply say : " Ana m asǝ asǝsǝ Ɔneca "—" I speak Onitsha language."

One of the members of my staff, A., from the interior district of Mbiεri, said that he would not call the people of Onitsha, or of Arǝ Cuku, or of Oguta, Ibo. The two former he would designate by their names. The latter he would call Nde Oru [‾ ‾ ‾ _] because they live by the waterside. He added that both Onitsha and Arǝ people have big watersides, but Ibo people are those who do not have a big water—a river, that is to say, that a steamer can go up. He also added that they are the people who are under no one else. They are not under Onitsha or Arᴓ. On another occasion we were discussing witchcraft and he said that he did not think that Ibo people have witches. People who eat εdε [¯ _]— coco-yam —do not have them, he said. It is Onitsha and Oguta and non-Ibo people like that—*oru*— who have them. How far he was using the word Ibo because he had heard me use it I do not know. But he was evidently conscious of a difference between the inland or central Ibo and certain communities which, like Onitsha and Arᴓ, lie towards the circumference of Ibo country. A sophisticated Arᴓ man to whom I have talked in London said that the Arᴓ people call themselves *Arᴓ okε Igbo*—Arᴓ, the big Igbo. An educated Mbiεri man to whom I also talked in London, where he had just arrived, said that the people of his district would not till recently have called the people of Onitsha Ibo, but nowadays they would, since they use the Ibo language. He said that his own people have always used the word Ibo about themselves. It comes into their proverbs and sayings. The old people would say, for instance : " *N'ala Igbo niilε na-eri ji ahᴓbεghe m ihε de ka nkε a*"—"In the country of all the yam eating Ibo people I have never seen such a thing." This would be true, he thought, of the people stretching from his town right down to Arᴓ Cuku. Probably at first they thought they were the only people in the world. But if they went down to Arᴓ Cuku to consult the oracle and met people there of other tribes who asked them what their language was they would say Ibo. But if they were asked near home they would reply with the name of their town.

As with most peoples, in fact, the Ibo feel the bonds between them most closely when they are confronted by foreigners. Two men from whatever part of Ibo-speaking country when they meet in Lagos or in London will call themselves brothers. Increasing sophistication is bringing a clearer notion of belonging to the whole unit of Ibo-speaking people. At home, however, people will count themselves as belonging to their village-group, will feel themselves intimately members of their village, will recognise the neighbouring village-groups as people with whom they trade and marry, and will say of the people beyond a radius of about seven miles : " The people of that place are very wicked."

We have said that these innumerable small units, the village-groups, are held together by no central or co-ordinating authority. But each one of them is linked, not by political but by social ties, to the units round it. An understanding of the Ibo system of exogamy is, in this connection, essential. Inter-marriage creates a network of ties by which the cells of Ibo society, though not united by any central governmental authority, nor arranged in any political hierarchy, are none the less inter-linked horizontally each with its neighbours by the social bonds of inter-marriage. There are also economic links, but these appear to be, in part at any rate, dependent on the fact of inter-marriage.

We are therefore concerned, in this study, first with the way in which the village, in the setting of the village-group, achieves the ends of government. In the second part we shall examine the Ibo system of exogamy and the consequent links between the villages. Only then shall we be able to come to a third point, the organisation of the women, for it is bound up with the system of exogamy.

In the Appendix we shall look at the question of temperament among these people. There can be no doubt that the difficulties of administration in this area are partly psychological. The "unconscious cultural protest" which has been said to be behind the Aba riots has its source partly in temperamental difficulties. Moreover, Ibo culture is deeply influenced by the temperament of the people and cannot adequately be understood without reference to this factor.

Chapter II. THE VILLAGE-GROUP

THE village of Umueke is one of eleven villages that together make up what may be called the village-group of Agbaja. The name " town " is sometimes given, particularly in official reports, to social units of this kind, but the designation " village-group " is preferred here for two reasons. In the first place, conditions of life are rural, not urban. In the second place, in this part of Ibo country a village is not a compact circle of houses as in and near Owerri, nor are the villages huddled together to form a town-like agglomeration of the Owerri " town " kind. They are usually scattered over a considerable area of forest, though two of them may sometimes be contiguous.

Agbaja lies about a hundred miles inland from the sea and four hundred feet above sea-level, where the great coastal belt of forested plain is beginning to rise and break up into tree-covered hills and sudden, steep-sided valleys, with frequent outcrops of rock. It is within sight—where one can get a glimpse from high ground through the forest —of the fine rolling uplands of Okigwi. The annual rainfall here is about 90 inches. This is considerably less than that of the coast, but enough to make a damp sticky heat which does not encourage energy either of mind or of body and makes more remarkable the amount of activity the Ibo people, and particularly the women, achieve. Most of the rain falls between April and November, but there is intermittent rain even in the dry season. In December and January there may be a certain amount of Harmattan, the dry, cool, desert wind. But it is unreliable and always short, and it is the only time that one's spare shoes do not grow green mould.

The forest is less lush and rank than the real tropical rain forest near the coast. There are magnificent trees which dwarf the serried ranks of palms in this, the thick of the oil palm belt. Between the trees there is dense bush which is cut down every few years for purposes of cultivation but which quickly grows up again.

Bush and forest—it is difficult to convey a sense of their

9

pervading influence. Even living in it one does not realise it till one has got away into open country and one's eyes go out to the horizon as from a prison. From the European's point of view, the forest, beautiful as it sometimes is, can none the less become stifling. For the people who live in it there is also a double-edged quality. It may hide them from the enemy, but it also enables the enemy to ambush them in his turn. Nowadays it is perhaps against the white man— or white woman—that it is most useful. The first time I walked through Agbaja on a prospecting trip, to see if it looked a likely spot to settle in, I would have thought from appearances that it was devoid of inhabitants instead of being in the " problem " population belt, so thickly is it peopled. At the sight of an unknown white woman the people had vanished into the bush—a feat they could perform with disconcerting rapidity. Not long after my settling in the village of Umuɛkɛ Agbaja, and while I was still definitely on probation, I was talking to a crowd of villagers near my house when a white man suddenly arrived to call on me. It was the first car that had navigated the bush path into the village and in my surprise at hearing it I looked round to see what was happening. When I turned again to continue my conversation with the villagers, there was no one in sight. There was just trees and bush.

One gradually becomes accustomed to the way in which even the details of existence are conditioned by the forest. The village, for instance, had the local equivalent of a telephone system. If a mother wanted her child, it was no use going to the door of her house to look for it. Ten yards away it would be invisible either in the bush or, at the right season, among yam vines or maize stems. So the village rang with the cries of parents seeking their children or friends calling to each other. Often when I was talking to one of the villagers in my house he would unexpectedly let out a shrill whoop and I would realise that he, with his trained and sensitive hearing, was answering a call that I had failed to hear.

It was largely forest and tsetse fly that kept out of Ibo country the horse and cattle-owning Fulani who overran so much of Nigeria in their Islamic Holy War in the nine-teenth century. How far the protection of the forest can be correlated with the social fragmentation of the Ibo people cannot be assessed. But that there is some connection between the two can hardly be doubted. There is also the isolating effect of the bush upon the people who live in it, which can hardly have failed to contribute to the separatist tendency that is so marked among these people. The mere fact that every village is as invisible from the next as though it were twenty miles away cannot but affect one's mental outlook. To a considerable extent the hidden neighbours seem like strangers. And the bush breeds a constant fear of ambush that is at times only too well founded. Again and again does the ambush motif make itself heard.

Before considering the nature of the village-group of Agbaja we must notice that it counts itself as descended from the same mother as the next door village-group of Umukabia, and reckons that it has kinship links with the neighbouring village-groups known collectively as Umu Ehime. Reference is sometimes made to even wider connections. But these mythical kinship links have at the present day only a limited practical significance so far as one could judge. In past times, before the British cut the country up into Native Court areas under Warrant Chiefs, the significance may have been greater. It may conceivably grow again now that the Native Courts have been reorganised with a view to bringing them more closely into line with indigenous institutions.

As to Agbaja itself, a number of different principles of social grouping enter into the make-up of this village-group, as of most other Ibo social units of this kind. In the first place it is a local unit in the sense that its inhabitants[1] occupy a common territory, the villagers being scattered through the bush over an area that is roughly speaking about three miles square. It is also a mythical kinship unit with relationship becoming genealogically traceable within, and often between, the kindreds that make up the villages. All the people born in Agbaja, with a few exceptions which do not invalidate the principle, claim descent from a mythical pair of ancestors, a man called Ngalaba and a woman called Ɔkpɛ Itɛ [_ ‾ _ _], who originated in the centre of Agbaja having been created by Ci [‾] and Ɛkɛ [‾ _], and who lived in the spot which is

---

[1] A Government Intelligence Report gives the population of Agbaja as between four and five thousand. This is probably an underestimate.

now the central Agbaja market place.[1] Near here is a piece
of sacred bush dedicated to the ancestors. This mythical pair
had eleven sons, each of whom was the original father of
one of the eleven villages of Agbaja. The eldest son founded
the family which is still the senior family of Agbaja, its
head holding the big *ɔfɔ*, the sacred, club-like symbol of
ancestral authority, of the village-group. This *ɔfɔ* takes
precedence of those of the other Agbaja villages, but apart
from this ceremonial precedence, its holder did not seem to
interfere in the concerns of villages other than his own
except in certain rare cases which will be referred to later.
The whole of Agbaja is divided, in characteristic Ibo fashion,
into two divisions, *ama* and *owɛrɛ*, there being seven villages
in Agbaja-ama and four in Agbaja-owɛrɛ.

There is also a linguistic bond between the members of
the group in that they speak the same dialect. The whole
of Agbaja is, moreover, a religious unit in the sense that
it possesses a guardian deity served by religious slaves
known as *osu* [_ ‾], with its shrine in the village of the
senior man of Agbaja. This deity has its male aspect Ɛzɛala
Ɔgɵugo, and its female aspect Lɔlɔ Ajala, and has its annual
rites. There is also a deity belonging to all Agbaja called
Ɔpara Ogugu, with its shrine in the central market place.
The whole of Agbaja performs rites in its honour annually
in the seventh month.

In the economic sphere another bond between all inhabitants of Agbaja is the possession of a central market
held every eight days. Among these people trade is second
only to agriculture as a means of livelihood and is one of
their ruling passions. Markets are the chief events of the
week and arrangements largely revolve round them. All
the villages of Agbaja have paths leading to the central
market place, and once a year, on the same day, the villages
clear their paths. This simultaneous act, performed at the
season of the annual religious rites of the whole group,
is felt to be a symbol of Agbaja unity. People talked a good
deal about it and insisted that a man could not be a real
Agbaja man if he failed to participate. All the villages will
go, they said, and each village will count its members to

---

[1] Ngalaba means forked, and can therefore be used to denote a
human being with two legs. Ɔkpɵ Ite means potter. Agbaja has
women potters and also clay. Ci and Ɛkɛ are the two creating spirits.

show how big it is. This boasting of numbers is a favourite
theme and there seemed to be a strain of rivalry as well
as of co-operation in it.

It was evident that Agbaja was an ideological unit in
the sense that its members were conscious of their membership and called themselves by the name of Agbaja. But
it also appeared that the prestige of each village was an
important factor in the eyes of its own inhabitants. From
the accounts, I looked forward with interest to seeing the
joint action of all Agbaja on the appointed day. When the
time came the difference between description and experience
was perhaps even more marked than usual. As our village
of Umueke approached the market on its path clearing
expedition, shouts and cries could be heard dying away on
the other side. I learned somewhat to my surprise that it
was another village on its way home having finished its
clearing. When our villagers got to the market place they
took possession of it alone, dancing and waving their knives
in great excitement. As another village came stamping up,
also with knives, ours withdrew. I waited, still hoping to
see the great assembly. But the elders of my village were
clearly uneasy at my lingering and finally insisted on my
going home with them and the rest of the villagers. In
some surprise I asked why the villages did not all gather
in the market place and was told that there would be much
too great a risk of their fighting. Evidently it would not
do to put an undue strain on the ideal of Agbaja unity,
a fact that emerged only too clearly later in my stay when
our village and another of the group had a bitter and prolonged dispute.

Chapter III. THE STRUCTURE OF THE VILLAGE

WITHIN the framework that we have called the village-group of Agbaja, the village of Umuɛkɛ more or less managed its own affairs, with occasional repercussions on it from part or whole of the group. Like the bigger whole of which it is a part, its members have between them the ties of kinship, locality, religion, language and economic activities. But here the ties are stronger and more intimate, and there is a greater consciousness of belonging to a real entity. There are often rivalries and disputes between the inhabitants of a village, but there is none the less a sense of belonging together.

If one takes first the local principle which is the basis of the social group we describe as a village, one finds, of course, that the people of Umuɛkɛ, who number about 360,[1] inhabit a compact piece of territory. It is not, however, strictly speaking their land which primarily gives them their identity. People living on the outskirts of the village may have their houses on land belonging to members of the next door village. This was the case of one of the men of the Umu Nwa Ɛbodim kindred and his sub-house group—*ɛbɛ ulo* [̄ _]. In the same way there were people of this next door village on land which belonged to members of Umuɛkɛ village.[2] It is perhaps misleading to speak of village boundaries. It might suggest a communally-owned village territory whereas there is only an agglomeration of lands owned by small kinship groups. But if this is made clear one may say that the inhabitants of adjacent villages may here and there overflow the village boundary to a minor degree. The important thing is to realise that a man of Umuɛkɛ living over the boundary into the next door village of Umuɔbea will none the less be unequivocally a member of Umuɛkɛ village in virtue of the kinship bond which binds together

---

[1] I made a census of the people of the Ama half of Umuɛkɛ village, including Umu Nwa Ɛbodim. They numbered 201. This was the half in which I lived. The people of the Owɛrɛ half I estimate at about 160, but there is a margin of possible error here. Any overt counting was unwise, since the counting episode which occasioned the Aba riots, and one had therefore to proceed with caution.

[2] See sketch map of Umuɛkɛ, p. 260.

14

all those who call themselves people of Umuɛkɛ. This tendency to think personally rather than territorially enters into a number of Ibo social concepts, and we shall meet it again in the judicial sphere.

In principle the people born in Umuɛkɛ are a kindred —*umunna* [¯ _ ¯ _]—claiming descent from one of the eleven sons of the ancestral founders of Agbaja, descent being patrilineal. It is clear that this rather than the fact of common locality is the primary factor on which the identity of the village rests, but its close correspondence with the local principle is of great significance in the social organisation, as we shall see later.

The fact of inhabiting a common territory, with all the daily contacts and sharing of activities that is implied in the life of neighbours, would in itself give the village a sense of identity, of common interests. But when the neighbours are also members of the same kindred the feeling of being a real unit is greatly enhanced. This does not mean that the kinsfolk-neighbours do not have sharp rivalries among themselves. The tensions in an Ibo village are many and at times acute. But it is none the less true that the village is strongly conscious of itself as a unit, particularly *vis-à-vis* other villages, and that the ties between villagers are close and effective. The name of the village is frequently used and gives expression to what is undoubtedly strong ideology. And, in terms of fact, the village is the framework within which the individual lives his daily life.

The village, together with one of the adjacent Agbaja villages which is considered closely related[1]—" we have the same *umunɛ* "—is an exogamous unit. All the married women in the village come from outside, either from other Agbaja villages or other village-groups, and all girls born in the village leave it at marriage. This fact that the exogamous unit is both a kinship and a local group is also of great importance in the functioning of the society and will be discussed in detail later.

Within the village there is the same principle of dual division that was found in Agbaja, and that is such a widespread feature of Ibo social organisation. In Umuɛkɛ it was said that the original ancestor of the village had two wives

---

[1] See page 14.

and that the children of one form the half, *nce,* known as Umuɛkɛ-owɛrɛ,[1] while the children of the other are called Umuɛkɛ-ama. Thus, while all the people born in Umuɛkɛ are *umunna*—children of the same father—those born in Umuɛkɛ-owɛrɛ are *umunnɛ*—children of the same mother—as are those born in Umuɛkɛ-ama. The working of village affairs was considerably bound up with the system of checks and balances and of institutionalised rivalry introduced by this dualism. The matter will be discussed later, but one must notice here the pluralistic principle of this arrangement and the difference of its methods from any unitary system of organisation. It is also significant as providing impetus in the absence of well-defined leadership. It is necessary to realise that the members of each half had a stronger feeling of unity, of emotional ties, amongst themselves than they had with those of the other half. This follows the normal pattern in this society by which the ties between children of the same mother are usually stronger than between those of the same father but of different mothers. Nor is this only an emotional matter. It has legal significance, for instance, in the matter of inheritance. And the fact that people will often refer to themselves or others as children of a particular ancestress may be misleading until one realises that this is not a question of matrilineal reckoning of descent. The society is definitely patrilineal, but because children of a particular wife feel themselves to be closely bound together they will often refer to their mother. But the assumption is that the listener knows that descent is reckoned through the father.

In Umuɛkɛ the division into two halves is a territorial as well as a kinship division—Owɛrɛ is one side of the village territory and Ama is the other. Again the local and kinship principles mutually reinforce each other. As so often happens in Ibo arrangements, the theoretical division of the village into Umuɛkɛ-ama, the children of one mother, and Umuɛkɛ-owɛrɛ, the children of a different mother, had had to be modified in fact because Umuɛkɛ-ama had diminished and Umuɛkɛ-owɛrɛ had increased in numbers. This had upset the balancing of the two halves for the communal work of path clearing and the big kindred known as Umu

---

[1] *Owɛrɛ* [_ _] means inside, and *Ama* [⁻ ⁻] path. The names used for this dual division vary in different parts of Ibo country.

Nwa Ɛbodim, had been taken out of the *owɛrɛ* half and joined to the *ama* half for what might be called administrative purposes. This was said to have happened about two generations ago. But everyone knew that, genealogically, Umu Nwa Ɛbodim belonged to Umuɛkɛ-owɛrɛ and in sentiment it still leaned towards them.

The kinship and local principles of social grouping correspond, in Ibo society, like hand and glove and have to be described in conjunction with one another. Just as each half of the village, like the village itself, is originally both a kinship and a local unit, so each is made up of a number of extended families. Each of these small units consists in principle of the male members of a kindred, their wives and unmarried daughters, living together in what may be called a house group, and having a senior man who holds the family *ofɔ*.

Ibo terminology is not very helpful in defining this unit. From a kinship point of view it is called *umunna* [¯ _ ¯ _], but this term, as we have seen, can be applied to any patrilineal kindred, however large.[1] The extended family is sometimes referred to as *imɛ nna*, but I am doubtful whether this term is definitive, apart from a context. Few, if any, terms of this kind are.

In its local aspect, for which the term house-group is used here, this unit is called *imɛ obi* [¯ ¯ ¯ ¯] or *ɔnama* [¯ ¯ ¯]. But *imɛ obi* can also be used about a bigger unit such as the whole of Umuɛkɛ-ama. So can *ɔnama*, but it can also be used about the smaller unit, within the extended family, of people descended from the same mother. In every case it is the context which gives precision to the term and we deceive ourselves if we think that terms like these can be defined apart from their context. The extended family is, however, known distinctively by the name of the ancestor from which its kindred members trace their descent genealogically. Descent can usually be traced further back in conjunction with one or more related kindreds, but according as these have separated into distinct house-groups they have taken distinct names. In Umuɛkɛ-ama, for instance, the extended families of Umu Nwacuku and Umu Ɛbo

---

[1] In the same way the term *umunnɛ*, lit. children of the same mother, can be applied to large or small groups of people claiming descent from the same mother or ancestress.

Durakǝ could trace their common descent, but they are now distinct units living in separate house-groups.

This fact of a common living place, or house-group, helps to give these units a consciousness of their identity which is very marked. They are often far from harmonious wholes, but *vis-à-vis* other people they have a sense of solidarity. The house-group is a collection, usually unenclosed in this part of the country, of small, one or two-roomed rectangular mud houses, *ulo* [⁻ _], with palm leaf roofs.[1] Typically, a man's house has a verandah on which he can entertain guests, and an inner room, *imɛ ulo* [⁻ ⁻ ⁻ _], or *imɛ ihɛ* [⁻ ⁻ ⁻ -]. But an older man may have an extra room across a small, walled-in yard. A woman's house has no verandah. It may have a kitchen running the whole length of the house and behind it a sleeping room and a small store room for crops other than yam. But this does not mean that a man may not sometimes live in a woman's type of house, and *vice versa*. Each house belongs to one individual, and surprise greeted my description of an English house with its many inhabitants. It was agreed that the English must have good characters to make such a system possible. It was pointed out that, on the Ibo system, if anything was missing from a house only the owner could be blamed. The sensitiveness to any matter concerning property which is a marked characteristic of the Ibo people finds its expression thus even in the nature of their dwellings.

Normally speaking, a man and each of his wives and their sons of about fifteen upwards each have a house of their own, though a newly married wife may share the house of her husband's mother or of a senior wife during the early part of her married life. By the rules of exogamy girls leave the village at marriage and before that pay frequent visits to the husband's home. They do not, therefore, have a separate house in their own village. The unit consisting of a man and his wife or wives and children may be called a household, and in its local aspect is known as *mbara ɛʑi* [_ ⁻ ⁻ - -], though again one must point out that this term may, in certain contexts, have other meanings. A house-group is a collection of households, each of which usually

---

[1] The roof consists of mats made from leaves of the wine palm, *ngwɔ* [⁻ _]. They are sewn by men and boys and placed in overlapping layers on the roof structure.

inhabits a contiguous cluster of houses. A house-group may be a fairly close collection of houses, or one or two of the households may be separated from the main group, or the whole group may have split into two or more parts though these parts are still usually adjacent. That is to say that a house-group normally occupies a common bit of territory, but varies in compactness. The variations are due partly to the size and composition of the extended family. A large family, particularly if it contains a number of adult or elderly males who are not sons of the same father but more distantly related, will tend to have a number of what might be called sub-house-groups, *mbara εzi*, each containing a branch of the extended family.

But a scattering of the house-group may also take place if there is dissension in the family. This could clearly be seen in Umuεkε-ama. This half of the village in its original form, that is to say, without Umu Nwa Ɛbodim, consists of four extended families, Umu Nwacuku, Umu Ɛbo Durakθ, Umu Ɔmθnkwθ, and Umu Duru Igwε. The house-group of Umu Nwacuku[1] was compactly built on a small piece of land, reflecting the relatively high degree of good will among the members of the extended family. One of the other house-groups, on the other hand, was scattered over a considerable area. The house of N.Ɛ., the senior man and *ɔfɔ* holder, together with those of his four living wives and of his two unmarried sons and of two widows of a dead younger brother, were clustered together. But his eldest son, S., who was married, instead of living nearby with his house turned at a right angle from that of his father, had gone nearly a quarter of a mile away to build a house for himself and one for his wife. His mother was a tempestuous woman and was not on good terms with her husband who had transferred his favours from his older wives to the youngish woman he had most recently married. There was constant friction punctuated by outbursts of strife and S. had evidently found it more peaceful to remove himself. But his eldest children, a small girl of about six and a boy of about three, spent much of their time with his mother, as is the custom in this society, the grand-children being held to replace the child who was lost by his marriage.

---

[1] See gen. table, p. 154.

There were thus close links and much to-ing and fro-ing between the two households even though they were separated by a walk of four or five minutes. A few yards away from S.'s house was that of J., a kinsman of the same extended family. Midway between S.'s house and that of his father was the house of other kinsmen, Josiah and his brothers. And away out by itself, isolated from all of them, was the sub-house-group—*mbara ɛẓi*—of A-ziɛ, a younger brother, by the same mother, of N.Ɛ.[1] He had inherited one of the widows of a dead brother and partly on her account because of disputes concerning the dead husband's land and trees, there was much ill feeling between their households and that of N.Ɛ. and his wives,[2] and finally an open breach. Moreover, A-ziɛ was not a popular character in the village and was periodically accused or suspected of misdeeds, usually of a magical order, and his living away by himself was held to be an indication of bad character. Any form of solitariness is looked on by the Ibo with mistrust.

The house-groups vary not only in the degree of their compactness but also in the distance between the groups. A cluster of houses, a group or sub-group, may stand on its own at some distance from any other houses, or the dwellings of the different extended families may be so close as to look like one house-group, though they consider themselves quite distinct. And as the size of the extended families varies greatly, so does the size of the various house-groups. The big Umu Nwa Ɛbodim family had about the same number of members as had all the four families of Umuɛkɛ-ama put together. They had increased so much that they were very short of land and their houses were jostled up against each other and against those of Umu Nwacuku. One member of Umu Nwa Ɛbodim had moved his sub-house-group, containing himself and several brothers and their families, away from the main group and had built on the land of the next door village of Umuɔbea Agbaja.[3]

This all means that the make-up of the village is not easy to grasp at first sight. It is true that each extended family

---

[1] He was born after the death of their father, whose wife took a lover. The children would be reckoned as belonging to the dead man according to Umuɛkɛ custom.
[2] See p. 108.   [3] See map, p. 260.

inhabits a house-group and that each house-group is an entity separate from the others. But short of this, the varieties of form and position are considerable. And the trees and bush and high crops that conceal one part of the village from another add to the difficulty of getting even a clear visual picture of the situation.

The two opposite processes of fission and accretion are constantly at work as slow forces of change in the village kinship, and hence local, structure. Kindreds which increase in size ultimately split into smaller units, as tradition recorded, for instance, of the now separate kindreds of Umu Nwacuku and Umu Ɛbo Durakө in Umuɛkɛ-ama.

On the other hand some kindreds, presumably from diminished numbers, coalesce into one house-group, as had happened with Umu Duru Igwɛ house-group in Umuɛkɛ-ama.

The village is far from presenting an unchanging picture from year to year. People who have had much sickness may be told by a diviner to change the place where they are living. This happened twice in Umuɛkɛ-owɛrɛ while I was in the village and considerably altered the layout of that side of the village. Or a quarrel may cause part of a kindred to go off and leave the parent stem. This had happened to a part of Umu Nwa Ɛbodim about a generation ago and this branch had gone off to live in Umuɛkɛ-owɛrɛ proper and was known as Umu Durakө when it was desired to emphasise the difference between the two branches. The common name of Umu Nwa Ɛbodim would be used in contexts where their identity was the important factor. For affairs which concerned the village as a whole Umu Durakө were reckoned as part of Umuɛkɛ-owɛrɛ, from which half of the village, it will be remembered, Umu Nwa Ɛbodim had been administratively but not geographically removed. But in kinship matters which concerned Umu Nwa Ɛbodim, Umu Durakө would participate. One saw them, for instance, taking part in the annual ceremonies of the Ala [_ _] cult of this kindred.

The village thus consists in principle of a number of small kindreds living with their wives as extended families in separate house-groups. It is also clearly divided into two halves, *ama* and *owɛrɛ*, the division being a matter both of kinship and of geography.

But the village is also spoken of as having four divisions—

ɔnama, or *ama*.[1] These were said to be Umuɛkɛ-ama, Umu
Nwa Ɛbodim, Umu Ɔfɔ Ahe and Umu Ihu Ogugu. The
last two are inter-related groups of kindreds in Umuɛkɛ-
owɛrɛ. The small kindreds of the village can always be
gathered together thus in their inter-related groups under
a common name. Or they can be considered separated under
their particular names. Umu Nwa Ɛbodim and Umu Ihu
Ogugu, for instance, were ultimately one larger kindred
known as Umu Eruru; " But when they go home," as
people expressed it, " they answer Umu Nwa Ɛbodim and
Umu Ihu Ogugu." And it is this last form that fits the theory
of the village as divided into four. There is, I think, no
doubt that, however many kindreds the village had, they
would still have them so grouped as to make four divisions.
One sees this from the arbitrary nature of the present
grouping.

Four with its multiples is the sacred number that runs
all through Ibo ritual and belief, from the four-day week
and the fourfold village to the four yams or four pieces of
yam and the four objects and four actions of every kind
that recur repeatedly in sacrifices and in magic. Again it is
the theory that is important. When my staff and I have
been watching a *dibea* making medicine, I have sometimes
counted the number of times he has performed a ritual action
and it has been either three or five. But my Ibo companions
would hear nothing of this. For them everything was done
four times.

With the fourfold division of the village we have, I think,
again a pluralistic tendency to balance sections of the social
structure against each other rather than to see the thing
as a whole. But these quarters have not the practical significance nor the permanent standing, so to speak, of the dual
division of the village. They only come into prominence
periodically. At the time of the boy's initiation rites, for
instance, certain ceremonies are performed on this fourfold
basis. One of my informants insisted, also, that the communal path-clearing of the village was done by the four
ama, two on each side. This, however, was only another
way of expressing the more usual view that each side was
cleared by one half of the village.[2]

---

[1] These divisions can also be referred to as nce, as can the two halves
of the village.   [2] See p. 12.

So far we have been dealing with the free-born inhabitants —*di ala* [⁻ _ _]—of the village. But there are also the slaves—*ohu* [⁻ _]—which may be found, generally speaking, throughout Ibo country though in greatly varying numbers from district to district. Slaves can, of course, no longer be legally acquired by purchase outright. But the word *ohu* is also applied to pawns, to those individuals, that is to say, who have pledged themselves to someone in return for a sum of money but who can redeem themselves by repayment of the original debt. The numbers of *ohu* were negligible in Umuɛkɛ. There was little wealth for such expensive luxuries in this rural community with its modest scale of living.

On the other hand there were considerable numbers of the religious slaves—*osu* [_ ⁻]—which are such an interesting element of much of Ibo society. That there are areas, such as Onitsha, where they do not occur is an interesting ethnographical matter which cannot be discussed here. But they have a considerable distribution throughout Ibo country and seem to be peculiar to this culture alone. It is not a straightforward matter to make a census of the *osu* in a village. In the first place the suppression of the legal status of slavery by the British authorities makes the Ibo secretive about this element of society which is of such importance to his religion. One will read in a Government report that the people of a certain place say there used to be ten *osu* here but they are all dead. Further investigations will show that they are not only alive but actively performing their religious functions.

In the second place, it is a gross insult to refer to anyone as *osu*. It is said that nowadays if this happened, the *osu* would take action in court against the person who had insulted him. And no *osu* would, except in the most rare circumstance, refer to himself as such. Once, at the time of an important annual religious festival, I heard a woman *osu* refer to herself as being the servitor of a particular deity— Ɔ wɵ ya nwɛ m—it is he who owns me. But this was most unusual. And I shall never forget one of my staff mistaking a free-born woman for an *osu* and letting her realise it. We were all three frozen with dismay of various kinds and it took months to restore the breach between the woman and ourselves.

The houses of *osu* people are always a little apart, on the fringe of the house-group to which they belong, for each of them belongs either to a specific individual or extended family.

Umu Nwa Ɛbodim had a large extended family of *osu* dedicated to Ɔpara Iyi, an Umuɛkɛ·deity. The ancestor of these *osu* had been bought by one of the ancestors of Umu Nwa Ɛbodim, and had married and had many descendants. There were several other *osu* attached to Umu Nwa Ɛbodim, and dedicated to other deities, and there was one attached to Umu Nwacuku and several to Umu Ɔmɵ Nkwɵ.

Originally these *osu* or their ancestors were free-born but were bought by a family or an individual at the command of a diviner, and offered as a slave to some deity whose wrath was aroused and whom the sacrifice of a mere fowl or goat would not satisfy. Henceforward the *osu* would serve the deity, taking part in the offering of sacrifices or observing the taboos of the cult. And from this time the *osu* and their descendants would become part of a class apart. It is strictly taboo for them to marry or have sexual relations with free-born Ibo, and they are subject to a number of other restrictions. They are regarded by the free-born with a repugnance which is in part at least physical and which is remarkable when one remembers that originally they were free-born themselves. And this repugnance is felt by people of very considerable Europeanisation and sophistication.[1]

In addition to *ohu* and *osu* there were a few strangers in the village. Two brothers had come to Umuɛkɛ-ama, one of whom lived by himself in a house on the fringe of the Umu Nwacuku house-group, and the elder of whom had married two wives from a neighbouring village and had a walled-in sub-house-group near the house-group of Umu Duru Igwɛ, to which extended family he had attached himself. In process of time he had become accepted as one of the elders of the village and had a considerable reputation for sagacity which expressed itself in the nickname " Teacher," by which he was known.

---

[1] An Ibo man of Mbiɛri at present in London tells me that in the old days an *osu* would be killed as a sacrifice instead of being, as at present, kept alive as a slave. And, according to him, the repugnance felt for an *osu* is partly because he is looked on as a dead man. This is the only time I have heard it suggested that *osu* people were originally put to death, but I record it as an isolated statement.

These alien elements in the population, however, modify little if at all the fact that the village consists of a kindred and their wives. They are, in fact, assimilated to the kinship group in the matter of exogamy, having to find their wives outside the village and send their daughters outside for husbands. They do not, therefore, disturb the significant pattern of the village as both a kinship and a local group.

There is, however, within the village a further and very different principle of grouping from the two we have been studying, and its full function can only be understood in relation to them. The men and boys of the village are divided into age groups, all those who have done the boys' initiation rites at the same time being members of the same age group. In Umuɛkɛ it was said that the rites were done together with half of the next door village of Umuamɛkɛ, another village of Agbaja-owɛrɛ, but the age groups themselves were on a village basis.

One sometimes sees it stated that communal work among the Ibo is divided among these groups. In Umuɛkɛ this was not so, though there were some tasks such as the carrying of a corpse to burial which could only be done by people of a certain age. Nor was this age group organisation prominent in the running of village affairs as it is prominent among some African peoples, particularly in East Africa. It sometimes took a hand in these matters, as we shall see later. But the age groups were largely social and convivial in their activities, and concerned with the interests of their own members. A man, for instance, whose son made difficulties about the wives chosen for him, would tell the son's age group that he, the father, had done his best and was not to blame. Evidently a youth's age fellows are concerned to keep the father up to the mark. I also heard it said that a man who was the permanent lover of a woman instead of marrying a wife would be laughed at by his age group. As for their convivial side, the various sets of age companions used to meet together, sitting each in a different place, at the eight-day Umuɛkɛ market, drinking and talking and entertaining their friends and with every opportunity of discussing their common interests.

It is in this bond of common interest rather than in any specific public activity that the significance of the age group would appear to consist. In the social structure of the village the age principle was a counterbalancing force to that of kinship. There might be keen rivalries between the extended families in which kinship sentiments could act as a disruptive centrifugal force of no mean strength, dividing the village into rival factions. But across what may be described as the vertical lines of division between family and family cut the horizontal lines of division of the age groups, serving as a counteracting and binding force in village life. At times one could clearly see this play of opposing forces going on.[1]

In the cult of the guardian deity of the village is a further force in the religious sphere which both emphasises the identity and makes for the unity of the village. This guardian spirit, Ɛzɛala Ogbudi in its male aspect, and Lɔlɔ Ogbudi in its female, is an offspring of the central deity of all Agbaja, just as the original founder of the village is a son of the original ancestor of all Agbaja. Human and supernatural organisation follow closely similar lines and the supernatural helps to validate and support the human.

Ogbudi is associated with a stream, the eating of whose fish is consequently strictly taboo. The spirit has a shrine in the village market place and also outside the house-group of the priestly family of the cult. A less important spirit, Ɔpara Iyi, the offspring of Ogbudi, has its shrine in a thicket near Umu Nwa Ɛbodim, many of whose *osu* are dedicated to it.

Here, as very generally among the Ibo, Ala—the earth—is sacred. In some places there is a priest of the cult but there is not one for Umuɛkɛ. There are several shrines and that of Umu Nwa Ɛbodim is the scene of an annual ceremony performed by the extended family. It is not easy to be sure of the implications of the cult of Ala. Ala is one, the people will say, in the sense that a priest of Ala can learn his functions from another priest anywhere. But when Ala is invoked, as it frequently is in prayer, it is *Ala anye* [_ ‾ - -]—our land— or Ala Umuɛkɛ, that is called upon. I used to ask my staff what they thought people had in mind in these invocations, and they said it was the local Ala and not some general conception of the land.

But it was perhaps Ogbudi that chiefly stood to the village as its supernatural protector and the guardian of its

---

[1] See p. 133.

laws. I had not been in the place a week before S. told me that Ogbudi would kill anyone who was guilty of stealing. Later on, Mgbɔkwe, a woman married in Umuɛkɛ, explained that if anyone used bad magic against a member of the village, Ogbudi would cause the magic to turn against its user. When actual cases of theft and of bad magic occurred, there were, of course, many steps taken in addition to trusting in Ogbudi. But the general references are important as indicating a frame of mind in which Ogbudi symbolised law and order, and security.

In many ways this guardian deity was a unifying force in village life. It was the central point, for Umuɛkɛ, of the annual religious rites performed by all Agbaja, village by village. Until recently the carved figures of Ogbudi, only brought out once a year for the solemn occasion, had been stood in the market place, the public meeting ground of the whole village. But since the coming of the Mission, the figures had only been placed outside the priest's house for fear of incidents.

It was Ogbudi who owned—*nwɛrɛ*—the market and it was in his or her honour that the women danced in the market place, though not on market day.

The fact that Ogbudi incarnated in the children of Umuɛkɛ was also a great bond between the people and this " spirit." And though there was, I think, no real tradition of Ogbudi as an ancestor, I have none the less heard him referred to as *Nna* [⁻ _]—father.

It would seem that in Ogbudi we have an undoubted symbol of village unity. The importance of such symbols in the political sphere has recently been stressed.[1] In Ibo society political authority is often little defined and is not centralised in any one figure like a Chief who can become a symbol of the people's unity. But it may be that in Ogbudi the village finds a personification of its identity, particularly in its legal or political aspect, that one must not underestimate.

It must also be noted that the village was something of a totemic unit in the fact that leopard was regarded as sacrosanct. In many parts of Ibo country leopard is given supernatural significance. " Tiger never come for nothing " people will say with a superb disregard of terminology but

---

[1] *African Political Systems,* Ed. Fortes and Evans-Pritchard. Oxford University Press, 1940, p. 18.

a certainty that any appearance of a leopard is a portent. But the case of Umuɛkɛ was different. They regarded themselves as having a special affinity with leopard. It was *nsɔ* [⁻ ⁻]—taboo—to kill or eat leopard, and it was believed that a member of Umuɛkɛ could fondle a leopard cub without harm. It was held that the older people of the village could transform themselves into leopard, and I met one man who said that he had seen it happen. I have also heard it said that leopard is our " father," but I could get no myth about the animal's connection with the people.

This totemic aspect does not, I think, bulk very large in the minds of the people and it has no place in village cult or ritual and is therefore not a recurring factor in their lives. But they have a song which they sing as a sign of anger and which I have also heard sung as an incitement to particular exertion—

" *Gbalaga, gbalaga, ɔnɵma abea agɵ* . . . "—" Run away, run away, the leopards are angry . . . "

The leopard is a further symbol, if not a very powerful one, of the identity of the village.

So far as factors in village unity on the economic side are concerned, we must note the existence of the village market held every eight days. When we come to look more closely at the economic aspect of life in this community we shall see how little, on the whole, the village functions as one economic unit. It is rather broken up into a multiplicity of small units and interests. But the market is the affair of the whole village and is a source not only of economic gain but of pride and prestige. It was of recent institution, having only been started about six years before my visit there, and its enlargement and aggrandisement were a constant pre-occupation. Not long after I got there the men asked if I would help them to persuade the women to use big baskets instead of small in selling their wares, " to make the market wide." Their answer to my prayer to be excused this steering between Scylla and Charybdis was a chuckle and the remark that " it is true, women are one." They also wanted a fine imposed on everyone of Umuɛkɛ who came late or failed to come at all. Not long afterwards the women asked if I would play my gramophone on market days to attract strangers. It was to be played, they said, long enough to tantalise but not to satisfy. This time I did my best to comply. A further device lay in the drinking parties of the age groups on market day. The hope was that the friends from other villages, whom they treated, would feel bound to come back another time and to treat them in return. The market, in fact, was a matter for much earnest thought. Over and above this feeling of local pride was the fact that every eight days practically the whole village came together for this economic and festive occasion, when the women traded, the men danced—and traded to some extent too—and everyone exchanged news and revelled in sociability and noise.

It was interesting to see how any village institution tended to become a matter of prestige. During my first tour the Mission authorities were persuaded by the village to give them a school on condition that they paid the salary of the teacher. An embryonic school therefore started and there was constant anxiety lest the subscriptions for the salary should fail and the village be shamed by the removal of the school to some other part of Agbaja. Even when a school for all Agbaja was mooted, Umuɛkɛ tried hard to keep it located in the village instead of having it in the centre of the village-group. It is very clear that village patriotism is a stronger force than any feeling for the whole village-group. The retort of the other villages was that as Umuɛkɛ had the white woman, they ought not to have the school too, or they would become too enlightened. Like the school, the white woman, in addition to being in many ways an incubus, had apparently also been swept into the vortex of village prestige. " Yes," they said in the intervals of enlarging upon my drawbacks : " We use you to boast with. If you go away the people outside will mock at us."

In considering the make-up of the village one must attempt to assess the place in it of the Roman Catholic Mission. Some years before my stay in the village there had been an attempt to start mission activities which had ultimately lapsed. When it was rumoured that I was descending upon them the people of Umuɛkɛ asked the Mission authorities, whose headquarters were some miles away, to send an African teacher to the village, " so that he might be able to tell them what the white woman wanted." Whether or not

he was able to fulfil that function is another story, but
from the mission point of view things went ahead to some
extent, a school was asked for, as has been said, and in my
second tour, the school, albeit a humble affair, had been
moved to the centre of Agbaja and become a school for
the whole village-group, and a new and more efficient
African teacher had replaced the original one.

Within the village the younger people nearly all came
under the influence of the mission, though among the
women it was chiefly the unmarried girls who were included.
In 1934 no one had contracted a Christian marriage, but
one couple got married in church at the beginning of 1937,
and provoked a good deal of pagan criticism as their youngest
child died almost at once. When I left at the end of 1937,
they were still the only case of a church marriage. There
were a number of baptised members of the church. But
things were in a very embryonic state as the mission authorities themselves were the first to admit.

From the point of view of village solidarity the new
religion meant that the old festivals, formerly uniting the
whole village in their performance, were now to a considerable extent, except for the women's doings, left to the older,
pagan half of the community. One would hear such comments as : " Why should I cook much food for this ceremony
since my young people do not care to come ? " But the
convivial side of a religious occasion would none the less
at times be shared in by Christians and pagans alike, thus
maintaining something at any rate of the old group cohesion.

On the other hand, festivals such as Christmas were
coming to be recognised, to some extent, by everyone even
though it might only be by sacrificing an extra fowl to the
ancestors. In the same way, Sunday was tending to become
an occasion for visits and sociability rather than for work,
and the younger girls who belonged to the Church did
not go to market on Sundays.

We have seen, also, that the mission school was a source
of pride to the village. And certainly the oldest man of the
village, N.Ɛ., though entirely pagan himself, looked favour-
ably upon the mission and had strongly encouraged its
coming, and given it land to build on. He was always in
favour of co-operation with the Europeans, and was always
saying, and I think sincerely, that he wished more would

come and live in the village, " and help our place to get up." Others among the elders might not have gone so far as that, and cases of criticism and distrust of the new ideas and procedures would crop up from time to time, as when the baby of the pair married in church died. But it is true, I think, to say that the mission was, on the whole, well looked on by the village.

Chapter IV. THE ECONOMIC SIDE OF VILLAGE LIFE

WE have been considering the nature of the village unit, the principles of grouping on which it is based and the factors which give it identity and unity both in fact and in its own conception of itself. We have seen the multiple ties holding it together and giving it a sense of solidarity. We must now consider the economic life of the community in so far as it bears on the question of the organisation of authority within the village. And we shall do well not to argue from solidarity to centralisation.

I have no adequate statistical data for estimating at all exactly the wealth of the village or for analysing its income and its expenditure. Such data is essential for any economic study of the Ibo people and in view of their land shortage, such a study is of urgent importance. It is, however, not our direct concern here, though I wish that I could present a more accurate picture than in fact I can. It did not, however, seem advisable, since it was not my main concern, to press for detailed economic information in view of the jumpiness of Ibo opinion about taxation and about such matters as their land and palm trees. Moreover the exact measurement of income in a community practising subsistence agriculture would be a whole time job in itself, if indeed it were possible.

In the absence of exact data I can only try to give some idea of the general standard of living of the village and of the distribution of wealth within it, based on the observations and impressions of myself and my staff, illustrated rather than substantiated by occasional fragments of statistical data.[1]

In the first place one must realise that Agbaja is a rural community with a very modest standard of living and using relatively few imported goods. The mere fact that no one in the village owned a bicycle is enough to suggest the difference between this area and such a place as Onitsha. A stranger, an Obowo man, had a sewing machine in the village

---

[1] For clarification in the arrangement of my economic material I am indebted to the questionnaire drawn up by Prof. Daryll Forde in connection with the Nuffield Economic Survey of West Africa.

in 1935 and did tailoring work, but he fell foul of the inhabitants and fled.[1]

All palm oil work in Umuɛkɛ was done by individuals in their homes until 1937 when one hand press for the expressing of the oil was introduced into the village, again by strangers from Obowo. This represented the extent of mechanisation in the village. Transport was a matter of head loads, agriculture a matter of hoes and knives. Clothes of any kind were scanty in 1935 though the women all wore a short cloth or kirtle from hip to knee. But in 1937, with the price of palm oil higher, clothes were more numerous and the younger men were increasingly taking to shorts and shirts or singlets. Some of the elders wore shirts and hats on gala occasions. The school children wore hideous khaki jumpers and shorts during school hours.

All the houses were made of mud with palm leaf roofs, but many of them had carpentered wooden doors of imported type and many contained carpentered chairs, or at least stools. There were a few enamel basins and a few metal spoons together with the old wooden ones.

But imported goods had only begun to scratch the surface of people's lives though there were few households from which they were entirely absent, as one realised when one called upon one of the least sophisticated families and found a Harvey Nicholls' fashion plate decorating a verandah wall. It had come *via* one of the West African French Companies with a fine heterogeneity of culture contact.

The primary occupation of the village is subsistence agriculture. The land is therefore the basis of its existence and an understanding of the land tenure system is necessary in any inquiry into village organisation. This system has been explained in detail elsewhere,[2] and here it is enough to say briefly that the village does not own communally any land except a few small pieces of bush sacred to the village deities. Ownership of the land is divided up among small groups of nearly related kinsmen, branches of the various kindreds, with the exception, here and there, of a residue

---

[1] For comparative data from a different Ibo area see J. Harris : " Some Aspects of the Economics of 16 Ibo individuals." *Africa,* Vol. XIV, No. 6, p. 302.

[2] M. M. Green : " Land Tenure in an Ibo Village." Monographs on Social Anthropology No. 6. Lund, Humphries (1941).

of land which may still be the property of a whole kindred.
This was the case, for instance, with the kindred of Umu
Nwacuku in Umuɛkɛ-ama.[1] The pressure of population on
the land is so great that every square yard of it belongs to
a definite small land-owing group which may consist of
only three or four males. Women do not own land. They
leave their native place at marriage and henceforward have
definite farming rights in the village of their husbands. But
they are not land owners.

Rights of ownership over the land are qualified by the
fact that though it can be, and frequently is, leased and
pledged, it cannot, according to native law and custom, be
sold. " Can land be lost ? " the people say. I believe that this
prohibition is widespread in Ibo country. In this important
restriction and also in the fact that the elders are called to
witness the division of land among heirs according to the
laws of inheritance, the community limits the rights of the
small land-owning groups over their land. But there is no
one individual who is looked on as holding the land in trust
for the community. This important attribute of chieftainship
which occurs in some parts of Africa is absent here.

We have said that subsistence agriculture is the chief
occupation of the village. Livestock is kept only on a restricted scale. Two or three of the rather wealthier men had
a few of the small immune native cattle, but in this tsetse
country cattle is scarce. There were a few goats and dogs,
an occasional sheep and a considerable number of fowls.
But they contributed little to the food supply except in
sacrifices or at funerals. The milk of the cows and goats
is not drunk and eggs are usually not eaten except ritually
and that rarely. Dogs are largely used as nursemaids to the
babies, licking them after defaecation and cleaning the
ground in the same manner.

It is crops, not animals, that form the food supply and
the staple food crops are yam, coco-yam, cassava and a
certain amount of banana. A considerable variety of vegetables are grown and are used in making the soup which is
the relish eaten with the main foods.

The household—man, wives and children—is the basic

---

[1] It was estimated at 450 to the square mile in this area, but was
probably more. In parts of Ibo country the population is said by
competent observers to exceed 1,000 to the square mile.

unit which co-operates for the production of these food crops, though a certain amount of outside help may be sought, as is seen below. The man normally clears the bush at the beginning of the farming season, which in this area is about February or March, and does any way part of the hoeing. But he may often call in a band of friends to help him for a day and will give them food in return. Each member of the band will be helped in turn and will provide food for the rest. There is no hiring of outside labour to help in the farm work, and particularly with bush cutting, as there is in places where land is more plentiful. On the contrary, Agbaja is in the densely populated belt from which seasonal labour is drawn for the areas usually nearer the coast where population is more sparse.[1]

The man will put sticks for the yams when they begin to shoot and will train the yam tendrils round the sticks. His farm work is then more or less over until the time for digging yams has come. The cutting of new yams in the fourth month is not of great importance in this district. Comparatively few yams are thus cut. The reason presumably is that the soil is too poor to produce a subsidiary as well as a main crop as it does in some areas.

The men also tap the oil palms[2] for the palm wine that is said to be such an important element in the diet of these people by reason of the vitamins it contains. A certain amount of it is given even to babies, but the men are the chief consumers, getting considerably more than the women. The tapping is done three times a day, early in the morning, early in the afternoon and just before dusk, and this serves as a time indicator for people wanting to make engagements. It is perhaps one of the most regular rhythms of village life, and the speedy climb to the top of the tree by means of a climbing rope round the trunk and round the man's waist is one of the most skilful techniques in the village.[3]

The woman helps with hoeing and sometimes even with bush cutting. The planting of the crops is traditionally her

---

[1] See p. 40.

[2] In this district wine is got mainly from the oil palm *nkwọ*, [⁻ ⁻], though a little may be got from the wine palm, *ngwọ* [⁻ _].

[3] I have even seen a small boy go swiftly up a tall palm tree, with no rope, to catch a lizard.

work and so is the weeding, which goes on practically throughout the farming season.

Children help with the work of farming from an early age. When a boy begins to grow up he is given yams by his father to plant for himself. But it is custom that sons should work for their father on Oriε day[1] and that on that day they should give him a gourd of the palm wine that they tap.[2]

The household is thus the main unit of production, but each wife farms independently of the others, and the crops are individually owned by husband and wife respectively. The men are supposed to be the chief yam owners, but some women also have their own. The women own coco-yam, cassava and banana among the staple food crops, and also the vegetables grown for relish. The wife is looked on as being responsible for feeding the household, though the husband helps now and then with a few yams[3] and helps with the entertainment of strangers. The household is the main unit of consumption[4] as it is of production, but there is a good deal of hospitality to kinsfolk, relatives-in-law and friends on casual occasions and on the many occasions when visits and exchange of food are required by custom. Food is thus distributed more widely than to the producing household.

Hospitality is the affair of small units, the households. There is no individual at the head of the village whose obligation it is to entertain strangers or to provide food for the villagers in times of shortage. This attribute of chieftainship which is found in some parts of Africa is here lacking, as is its converse, the right to levy tribute. There is no individual to whom tribute is paid by the village or for whom work must be done. Any such conception, so

---

[1] The Ibo week has four days.

[2] A father also is expected to pass his son through the boys' initiation rites and to give him a gun and later to provide him with a wife. Both parents give a daughter the things she is expected to take on marriage to her husband's place.

[3] He will probably help most during the months of September, October and November which come between the cutting of new yams and the digging of the main crop, but I did not collect evidence on this point. See J. Harris, "Papers on the Economic Aspect of Life among the Ozu Item Ibo," *Africa*, Vol. XIV, No. 1, p. 12.

[4] If a man has several wives, each has her own kitchen, and the one who finishes cooking first will sometimes call the children of the other wives to eat. But a mother is primarily responsible for her own children.

far as one can see, is foreign to the minds of the people. It is therefore not surprising that the introduction of taxation by the British Government in 1927 came as a shock to the Ibo people, and has never been really understood.[1]

If agriculture is the basic occupation of these Ibo people, trading is a close second. One might almost say that whereas they farm of necessity, they trade not only of necessity but also for pleasure. Their markets are one of the main features in their lives. They provide a meeting point for the discussion of common business and for the dissemination of news ; they are a social event where the spice of gossip, the recreation of dancing and the zest of a bargain relieve the almost continuous toil of hoeing, planting, weeding and harvesting throughout the year. Trading is the breath of life, particularly to the women among the Ibo, and the vigour with which bargaining and haggling are conducted is evidence of the prestige attaching to successful commercial enterprise.

In this densely populated part of Ibo country each market is normally held once in eight days,[2] and there is a market

---

[1] When I told one of the villagers that in my own country people paid tax, he was astonished and inquired to whom we paid it.

[2] The Ibo have, essentially, a four-day week, the days being Εke [⎺ ⎤], Oriε [_ _], Afɔ [_ _], Nkwɔ [_ ⎤]. It was Mrs. Leith-Ross who pointed out to me that these names appear to be names of markets rather than of days, and in those parts of Ibo country where the week has been expanded to eight days by duplicating the days, there can, I think, be little doubt that this has been done in order to accommodate the requisite number of markets. When the population is dense there will be may villages or village groups wanting to have their own market, but it is a grave offence to start a rival market on a day on which any big market is being held in the vicinity. It would lead to great disputes. If there are only four days available and each market is held every four days, there will clearly not be enough days to go round. But if the week is doubled and there are big Εke, Oriε, Afɔ and Nkwɔ, followed by small Εke, small Oriε, and so on, and if each market is held once in eight days, the congestion is considerably eased, and a district can safely have eight big markets instead of four. The overlapping of small markets does not appear to matter. The fact that a week may consist either of four or of eight days means that one must specify in conversation whether one is referring to a big week, Izu ukwu [⎺ _ ⎺ ⎤] or a small week, Izu nta [⎺ _ _⎤]. As to the days, if one's own market is held on Εke, one will call that day " big Εke "—Εke ukwu [_ ⎺ ⎺ ⎤] and the next Εke will be small. But in another district people whose market falls on what in the above context is small Εke, will call the day Εke ukwu, " big Εke." The day of the week is a matter, therefore, of space as well as of time. One will often hear the name of a day or market coupled with that of a place. Nkwɔ Umu Εzeala means the Nkwɔ day on which

somewhere within a few miles' radius from Umuɛkɛ every day. This does not mean that every individual goes to market every day, but it was considered obligatory for the whole village to turn out for its own market, known as Ɛkɛ Ogigɛ. A move was made while I was there to get the whole of Agbaja to come to the central Agbaja market, Oriɛ Ɛkpa. A high percentage of the villages used also to go to the neighbouring Umunumu market, Afɔ Ɛgbu, about a mile away. I could hear them streaming past my house on their way out and home.[1] Between these two bursts of noisy activity a calm settled on the village which told one how empty it was. Thus on three days out of eight most people went to market and a number went on one or more of the other days. Nkwɔ Umuɛzɛala was a big market about four miles away to which people went periodically if not weekly. The distances people walk with a heavy head load tend to be less here than in some parts of Ibo country, but now and then individuals would go for many miles. A stranger going round to a number of Ibo markets is apt to have the impression that thousands of people are buying and selling minute quantities of the same things. Rows of women seem to have trays or baskets with more or less the same miscellaneous collection of small objects—little leaf packets of mashed oil bean, a few red peppers, half a dozen matches, some sliced cassava. But in fact the markets are to a certain extent specialised in the sense that one is reputed good for meat or livestock, another for pots, another for yams and so on. There is a constant flow of food stuffs such as yam

---

the people of Umu Ɛzɛala hold their market once every eight days. And it is thus that people can unambiguously reckon their days and make their social engagements within a certain district. But the market may sometimes be called, habitually, by the name not of the village-group or village, but of the group deity which is looked upon as owning the market. The eighth day market for instance, of the village-group of Umunumu, next door to Agbaja, called its market Afɔ Ɛgbu, after Ɛgbu Mmiri, the tutelary deity of Umunumu. This was the generally accepted name of this day in the district. There were other naming possibilities which need not be referred to here, but the upshot was that one could only follow the local time reckoning if one had considerable local knowledge. Terminology in these, as in other matters, was firmly embedded in the social context.

[1] This market started about 4 p.m. Smaller markets started rather later, but the more important ones began about noon or soon after. People often got home after dusk from market.

from the less densely populated areas in to those with a heavy population, the return being partly in palm oil. There are, moreover, trade secrets or small specialisations in such matters as mashed oil bean. One village will possess the art, the next door village will not.

The women are the great petty traders, spending much time and energy for what must often be a very small profit. But even a few heads of cowries are worth having as a profit when life is on a modest scale, particularly when the gaining of them involves the pleasures of the market. But the time and energy involved are considerable, and already the women have much arduous work with their farming, cooking and palm oil making. It is small wonder that they are thin as rakes and often show signs of physical strain, and their frequent references to the amount of work they have to do are amply justified.

Men trade in rather a larger way than the women and in certain different classes of goods. But everything here was on a small scale compared with a trading centre such as, for example, Onitsha. No one here had a bicycle, far less a lorry with which to carry oil to distant collecting centres. It was sold by the potful usually at the nearby markets, and therefore at a lower price than it would have fetched nearer to the European depots. Young men would sometimes go as far as Umuahia to buy stockfish which they could then sell retail.

Markets are arranged according to well recognised customary rules. Some of the more important goods such as livestock will be displayed in special places, but the women with their small wares sit according to geographical principles. The women from each village sit along the path which leads from the market place back to the village from which they have come. Thus, as they say, if there is fighting in the market they can escape easily to their own homes.

A number of small objects are made in the village in people's spare time either for use or for sale locally. Men would often bring to some gathering the climbing ropes they were making and get on with them in the intervals of discussion or other business : mats, baskets and wooden spoons, chairs and bed-frames of so-called bamboo[1] were

[1] The mid-rib of the wine palm—*ngwo*—is much used for these purposes and is usually translated " bamboo."

made by the men and boys. A few women very occasionally
made a small number of pots. Only once I saw this done
and the four women concerned were all born in the neighbouring village-group of Umunumu where pot-making was
traditional, though not on a very large scale. Umuɛkɛ had
no clay suitable for pot-making : it had to be fetched from
the next door village.

But much the most important occupation of the village
after farming and trading was the making of palm oil and
the preparing of palm kernels, some for consumption, but
most for sale in the local markets where they are bought
partly for local use, but largely for export.[1]

Normally speaking, the work is done co-operatively by
man and wife, and the palm oil is looked on as belonging
to the man and the kernels to the woman, the proceeds
from the sale of them being apportioned accordingly. These
proceeds are one of the chief forms of money income and
the current price of oil and kernels can almost be guessed
from the faces of the people. A rise or fall of price vitally
affects the whole community. The labour involved in the
production of oil kernels is long and tedious, particularly
for the women, and with a low price the return is poor.

Another method of earning a modest amount of money
was that of going away for a few months in the dry season
to do farm work or odd jobs for other Africans in the
districts nearer the coast where population is less dense and
land more plentiful. This applies to the younger people and
chiefly to the young men of whom a considerable number
went, but a fair number of girls went also. The pay is small,
about $1\frac{1}{2}d$. a day, but the workers are fed and housed for
this.

I only knew of one man in the village who was away
working more or less permanently. In those parts of Ibo
country where European contacts are more numerous than
in Agbaja many men, of course, go away to work for
Europeans, chiefly in domestic posts. There was, so far as
I saw, no paid labour, or practically none, within the village.
People helped each other in return for food, but not for pay.

Since the village practices subsistence agriculture and
since it builds its own houses from local products it might

[1] See Hancock : " Survey of British Commonwealth Affairs." *O.U.P.,*
1942, Vol. II, Part I, p. 246.

appear that any money made by selling oil and kernels and
other goods or by going away to work would be available
for such things as clothes, enamel basins, school or mission
fees, medical fees either to European or African doctors,
tax,[1] bribes, to say nothing of luxuries like tobacco. But
before coming to this conclusion one would have to be sure
that the village grows enough food to support itself. So
far as subsidiary food or relishes are concerned, this of course
is not so. Salt always has to be bought and dried fish for
putting in soup. Since there is practically no game left in
these densely populated areas, meat also has to be bought
on the relatively rare occasions on which it is added to the
soup. But it is a luxury to be afforded only in small quantities.
Stock fish is also a luxury to be bought usually for festive
occasions. As for the vegetables that form an important part
of the relish or soup, some are bought but some are also
sold and it is not easy to be sure how the transactions balance.
The sums involved are very small, of course : leaf bought
for two heads of cowries, for instance, would figure in a
woman's market purchases.[2] But though small the sum is
not negligible in an Agbaja budget. What is more important
is the question of staple food crops —yam, coco-yam, cassava,
banana. There is no doubt that some of them are bought,
but some of them are also sold. Is there a seasonal exchange
or an exchange of individual surpluses in which a balance

---

[1] In 1935 the tax assessment for the village of Umueke was £8 12s. 6d.
It was a poll tax on men, but the village had decided that boys down to
about the age of 14 should also pay, to lower the rate per head. If a
boy's father were dead his tax tended to be paid by his mother. The
women were therefore by no means escaping from paying tax.

[2] Cowries are still used extensively in this area for small market
transactions. A head of cowries, *isi ego* [‾ ‾ ‾ ‾], is the smallest unit in
circulation and consists of six cowries. The value of a head of cowries
fluctuates in terms of the pennies and shillings of the West African
currency. Between May and December, 1935, the value varied between
27 and 37 heads of cowries to a penny. Between January and April, 1937,
it varied between 20 and 25.

The shilling also fluctuated, in this part of the world where there
were no banks, in terms of the penny. It was sometimes worth $10\frac{1}{2}d$.
and sometimes as much as $11\frac{1}{2}d$. A number of factors contributed to
this situation, but the low value of the shilling was undoubtedly due, in
part, to the number of counterfeit coins in circulation. One of the young
men of Umueke tried paying part of the bride price of his wife in
counterfeit in 1937. Unfortunately for him his mother-in-law was not
taken in.

between buying and selling is maintained? It would be satisfactory to be able to answer this question. It raises the whole problem of how far in some of these densely populated areas the demand for food is outrunning the home-produced supply, and of what are the alternative sources of income and the alternative supplies of food. No answer, adequately supported by facts, can be given here, but so far as my observations and impressions and those of my staff went, it seemed to me that the village bought a good deal of its food.[1] Moreover, the money women earned by the sale of palm kernels was said to be used for buying food.[2] Some men certainly sold yams, but this, I think, was not because they did not need them for food but because yam was too much of a luxury for home consumption. It tended to be sold and cassava tended to replace it as food.[3] Also, some men, if they needed money, for instance, to bribe their way out of police action, had to sell part of their yam crop.

The assessing of the standard of living of a people depends upon the criteria employed and these are not easy to decide upon. It has already been said that Agbaja had a modest standard of living in the sense that clothes were few, housing on the whole rather poor, European goods very limited and school education rudimentary. Perhaps the most convincing criterion is diet. The economic factor is of course only one of the determinants of a people's diet, but in Agbaja it was, I think, considerable as a limiting factor. Meat and fish had to be bought and were used very sparingly. To my non-expert eye there seemed to be a lack of protein in the normal diet. As for the main, starchy foods, cassava

---

[1] One of my staff made somewhat rough and ready observations : of 169 individual market transactions in March, April, July and August, 1937. Food is plentiful in March and scarce in July and August, so the period covered is fairly representative. An analysis shows that main food was bought in 72 cases and sold in 43, and subsidiary food was bought in 88 cases and sold in 28.

[2] As for the money the men earned from the sale of oil, they spoke of it as being used for paying the bride price of a wife. The bride price that is paid by the individuals in the village and that which is received may be taken as roughly balancing in the long run. But if a young man's father has died and he has no sister of marriageable age, he may often be hard put to it to get a wife. About £12 seemed to be the bride price level at this period and in this area.

[3] See M. M. Green, *op. cit.*, p. 36, *re* drawbacks of cassava as a food crop.

was constantly eaten and was, so far as we could judge, on the increase. Both here and in the case of meat the pressure of population on the land was making itself felt : land which is not good enough to carry yam will carry the inferior food crop, cassava. Moreover, cassava being grown from cuttings costs nothing to plant, whereas yam, being grown from seed yams, is an extravagant crop.

My staff, who came both from Owerri and Mbiɛri, where the standard of living is not very dazzling, were none the less struck by the low Agbaja standards, particularly as shown in their food and in the number of their yams. Allowance must always be made for local patriotism and for mistrust of food habits that are in any way different from one's own. When this is discounted, the comments probably had a considerable basis in fact.[1] The significance of all this for our present purpose is that these Agbaja people have an economic background which in addition to its influence on physique tends to produce anxiety and stresses and strains. This in its turn is bound to react upon all spheres of their life and to enter as one factor into all culture contact situations.

Another relevant economic fact is the absence of marked differences of wealth between one individual and another. This must be tentatively stated in the absence of exact calculations of individual wealth. There are, of course, variations : some people have more land than others, and

---

[1] Since any form of overt counting was liable to arouse fears I did not try an accurate or comprehensive reckoning of people's yams. But by visiting yam barns and reckoning the number of stocks—ɛkwɛ [̄] of yams, I made the following rough calculations. Of a random sample of 17 married men the average number of stocks owned was 18·6. Of a small random sample of 5 young unmarried men, the average number of stocks owned was 14·4, and of 5 lads the average was 7·3 stocks. 9 stocks was the highest recorded as belonging to a woman. She was an elderly widow. Another such widow had 8 stocks. These figures were collected in Umuɛkɛ-ama and Umu Nwa Ɛbodim, and are based on such small samples that they must be taken as a rough indication rather than as statistical evidence. On the whole the yams tended to be small. A stock—ɛkwɛ—consists of 80 yams.

I asked my cook, from Mbiɛri, one day, what he thought about yams in Umuɛkɛ as compared with those in his own and Owerri parts. He said that from what he had seen he thought about ten people in Umuɛkɛ would have about as many yams as one woman in Owerri. He reminded me of a man's yam barn we had visited in Owerri and asked if I had not noticed how big it was. It must have contained several hundred ɛkwɛ, he thought.

more trees of economic value, such as the wine palm, than others. Some are better off in respect of wives and children. A few people own several cows, but as there is little opportunity for, or habit of, the accumulation of capital, no well-defined wealthy class has yet emerged in a rural community of this kind. This must be borne in mind when anything in the nature of political organisation is being considered.

A form of economic and social organisation which exists over much of Ibo country and which was popular while I was in Umuɛkɛ was that of " meetings," known locally as *mikiri* [⁻ _ _]. A *mikiri* is a voluntary group either of men or women or both, sometimes from one village, sometimes from more than one, who subscribe to a common fund for the benefit of all the members. There might be anything up to about fifty members in the group and possibly sometimes even more. I was told by one man that these *mikiri* had only started in Umuɛkɛ about eight years previously and had come in from Okigwi way, where their object was to provide a man with money when he wanted to marry a wife. In Umuɛkɛ, he said, this idea was not so central : the money might be used for anything. This would seem to be an example of the borrowing of customs that goes on so much among these people from one locality to another. Certainly the women's *mikiri*, consisting of all the women born in Umuɛkɛ and consequently married elsewhere, was only started in 1935 while I was in the village. From then onwards " meetings " became the fashionable craze.

I went to a good many of the women's " meetings " and they are described later. The others I frequently heard about or saw or heard as I passed by. One was always coming upon people hurrying off to a *mikiri* or getting their house yard ready to receive one.

There were two main types : in one the members would meet at regular intervals, sometimes every 24 days. On one occasion, I believe, they met every Sunday. On each occasion every member would make a small subscription, usually in money—a few pence—but sometimes in kind. The whole collection would go to the member whose turn it was to benefit on that particular day, and each member would benefit in rotation. There was always anxiety lest a member, after receiving his benefit, should abscond and pay no more subscriptions at subsequent meetings. On the other hand, a member could be expelled from the *mikiri* for certain offences, theft among them, and would then forfeit all he had already paid in. Expulsion was greatly dreaded,[1] and fear of it acted as a spur to honesty.

At the women's " meeting " it was hard to know whether the hostess of the " meeting," who was also the benefit member for that occasion, gained any more in subscriptions than she spent in entertainment. It depended to some extent on the individual woman.

The economic principle of the *mikiri* seemed to be that of a savings bank in the sense of accumulating a sum of money from a number of small periodical payments. There was also a strong social and convivial side, eating, drinking and talking being important features. It may be that this does something to explain why putting money in the Post Office Savings Bank is apt to appeal so little even to a sophisticated Ibo. There is something bleak about the Post Office system when compared with that of the *mikiri*.

The following description was given me of a mixed " meeting " of men and women in the owɛrɛ half of Umuɛkɛ village. The members met at each one's house in turn, the men bringing 2*d*. each and a gourd of palm wine when the host was a man, and 1*d*. when a woman. The women brought 1*d*. each and some oil bean. The host or hostess of the particular occasion received the subscriptions of that " meeting " and was bound to continue his subscriptions thereafter on pain of a fine. The members shared the wine and oil bean, arranged the place of the next " meeting," settled cases, I was told, between members or kept the peace between any who had a case pending in the Native Court.

I was told about another mixed " meeting " in Umuɛkɛ in 1937 where the women members subscribed 3*d*. each and twenty of the men members subscribed 1*s*. each, and ten subscribed 6*d*. each.[2] In addition, the male kinsmen of a man member would each give him 2*d*. when his turn came to be host and to get the collection, and their wives would cook food for him, at any rate if he was an unmarried man.

The idea of a collection meeting could be adapted to various circumstances. For instance, I was told one day that

---

[1] See *infra.,* p. 125.
[2] I was told that in Mbiɛri considerably larger sums would be subscribed.

a young man of Umu Nwa Ɛbodim had had a baptism feast the day before. Other baptised Church members had collected 2*d.* a head for him and unbaptised members 1*d.* each.

There was another type of " meeting " in which each member put in a certain sum of money and thus formed a fund from which any member could borrow in time of need. I was told that this type had been abandoned because of the difficulty of avoiding embezzlement of the fund. I only came across one example of this type of " meeting " : the case, as described to me, throws light on methods of procedure and was as follows :

One morning in March, 1937, my garden boy, I., a man of Umuɛkɛ, came late to work and excused himself by saying that during the night he had been unexpectedly roused by members of a " meeting " to which he belonged, who said that they were going to collect outstanding debts from " meeting " members, and that any member failing to join with them would be fined a fowl. They were doing the collecting in this sudden fashion in order that the debtor members might have no warning and therefore no time to hide such of their property as might be liable to distraint.

The " meeting," said I., started seven years ago, the members being 40 men, of all divisions of Umuɛkɛ village. Each had contributed 1*s.*, after which no more contributions were made. This capital of 40*s.* was placed in the hands of one of the kindred heads who had since died. The plan was that any members wishing to borrow money could do so, paying 100 per cent. interest per annum. The interest would be divided among the " meeting " members. Incidentally, 100 per cent. interest seemed a usual rate in this part of Ibo country.

On this occasion several of the " meeting " members had gone to the widow of the man who had held the bank of the " meeting " and had asked her to hand over the fund. She had replied that far from there being any fund, people had not yet paid back the money they owed. The members knew that a certain debtor member had just married off one of his daughters and had received £7 as bride price. They decided that they had better act quickly before he could spend this money. They therefore raided his house and seized his gun and some of his yams. He had originally borrowed £1 and was said now to owe £4, but it was decided " to have mercy on him " and only demand £3. He produced 10s. It was then decided that if he produced £1 more and " wrote " an agreement—he was illiterate—to pay £1 10s. later, they would give him back his gun and yams. In addition, 1s. was taken from him " for the feet of the members " who had gone to him. Another member was visited who had borrowed 10s. and owed £1. His property was not seized because he produced 10s. and " wrote " a promise to pay the other 10s. in two or three months.[1] Another member who owed 8s. was visited. As he could not pay two of his goats were seized, also a fowl, in lieu of 1s. " for the feet " of the raiding members. But the fowl turned out later to belong to someone else, so they took a knife and a hoe of the defaulting member and gave them as compensation to the owner of the fowl.

There are perhaps two points of special interest in connection with the system of *mikiri* : in the first place, they are an example of organisation for a specific purpose which seems, among these Ibo people, to have gone further than organisation on a territorial or political basis. The *nde dihea* [‾ ‾ ‾] are another example, though they are of course a professional group. But the cow-owners' society was a non-professional group of people united by a common interest. I do not know how highly organised they were, but the members were said to come from a number of village-groups and to subscribe to a fund which was used for taking action, if necessary, in the Native Court, against people who stole or killed their cows. The strength of feeling between cow and crop owners is described in another place.[2] It is enough here to note that in 1935 a number of cows in and near Umuɛkɛ died in mysterious circumstances, and I was told that they were being secretly poisoned instead of openly killed by the enraged crop owners in order to thwart the efforts of the cow owners' society. This suggests that the society was something to be reckoned with. Its members, of course, would tend to be drawn from among

---

[1] I was not present at these raids and do not know what this "writing" means. Practically all the inhabitants of Umuɛkɛ were illiterate. I only knew one inhabitant of Umuɛkɛ, a youth, who was even partially literate, though the children were, of course, beginning to go to school.

[2] See p. 210.

the wealthier elements of the community in so far as there can be said to be such elements.

A further point about these " meetings " is that they are a rudimentary organisation for the provision of small scale credit and that in their mutual benefit aspect they are typical of one of the most marked features of Ibo social life. Title taking,[1] for instance, is, on its economic side, a form of mutual insurance. When an individual is admitted to the taking of a title he has to expend a considerable sum of money and produce food and drink, all of which is divided among those who have already taken title. Each of them, of course, had originally to make this initial expenditure, but it was in the nature of an investment on which a share of the fees of every new member is a dividend. In the same way, when a man succeeds to the *ofo* of a kinsman, he must call the other *ofo* holders and give them food and drink, and they must ceremonially present him with his *ofo*. This vested interest or mutual benefit aspect characterises one situation after another in an Ibo community. It would be worth bearing in mind in any plan for introducing co-operative enterprise among these people.

---

[1] See p. 58.

Chapter V. VILLAGE ORGANISATION AND THE SUPERNATURAL SPHERE

PRIESTS AND *OSU*

WHEN we turn to the supernatural sphere and ask what element of authority it supplies in village affairs, we find, as in the economic sphere, that there was no individual of outstanding power or authority either directly in things spiritual or indirectly in things secular.

There was indeed a hereditary priestly family, Umu Nwacuku, said to have been chosen in the old days by the guardian deity of the village, Ɛzɛala Ogbudi, for the service of his cult. The head of the family was specifically the priest, though his brothers were also involved. They performed the annual religious rites of the seventh month, done, village by village, throughout Agbaja. At this time and only this, they brought out carved wooden images of the guardian spirit, images of a man, a woman and a child, and placed them, together with a spear, just outside the priest's house, not on the ground but on a small wooden plank. During the rest of the year the priest officiated for anyone who had been told by a diviner to sacrifice to the village spirit with the help of the priest. If the diviner had not actually directed that the priest should be present, the latter might give permission to the person or persons desiring to make the sacrifice to proceed on their own. But he, and usually a brother with him, always made the sacrifice that was required each year, as well as at the time of birth, from the parents of any child in whom this village spirit had incarnated. It is, I think, a widespread belief among the Ibo people that a child is the reincarnation of some ancestor, but this belief in the incarnation in some children of a non-ancestral local spirit is of narrower distribution. It came as a new and surprising fact to my staff who were either from Owerri or Mbiɛri, about thirty miles away. The Agbaja guardian deity, Ɛzɛala Ogɵugo, also incarnated in any Agbaja child. Here again sacrifices had to be made yearly for these children and there is not doubt that the prestige of the spirit and its priest or *osu* were enhanced by this. The priest and the *osu* also acquired some degree of wealth from the offerings, though there was always an element of reciprocity, the priest providing food for those who came with sacrificial offerings.

In the case of the spirit of Umuɛkɛ village it was interesting to find that the first time it had incarnated was in a boy who was now about ten. It is a *dibea*—a diviner—who on the fourth day after birth announces the identity of the child, and one wondered, without having time to pursue the matter, why the incarnation of this spirit had suddenly been initiated. The people themselves will sometimes say : " The spirits imitate each other."

The priest of the village deity was thus a distinct personage with a hereditary position and publicly recognised position. He and his brothers also had to observe strict taboos such as sexual abstinence on two nights out of four, but he was not a holy figure set apart from daily life. He went about his farming and took part in village activities as did anyone else. Though he was respected in his priestly functions I saw no sign that he was held in special awe. I do not attach great weight to the statement of a young man who was a Christian and also of a very strong-minded disposition, but his reply to my question is none the less worth recording. I asked him whether, if he were a pagan, he would be afraid to offend the priest for fear that he might subsequently refuse to perform a sacrifice on his behalf. He replied scornfully that if the priest refused to sacrifice, his *agbara* [¯ _ _], deity, would kill him. But, he added, the person he would be afraid of was an *osu* because if he injured him he would have the expense of providing the spirit he served with a new one.

These *osu* people have already been referred to. Their anomalous position of being " horrible and holy " in the eyes of society does not necessarily make them into people of authority, but it does mean that they are or may be a part of the mechanism whereby law and order are preserved. That in some Ibo communities they have grown rich and to some extent powerful through the sacrifices made to their deity is undoubted. Sometimes they have practically ousted the priest, largely, I think, because their strict observance of taboos to some extent released the priest or the family head from his own obligations. This position of prominence, however, did not exist in Umuɛkɛ. There were a considerable number of *osu,* one of whom had been dedicated to the village guardian deity and who lived with the priestly family and helped in the service of the cult, but none of them were rich or outstanding figures in village life. It was said, though, that sometimes if a man was owed money he would send an *osu* to collect it, knowing that the *osu* would be considered inviolate as the possession of the spirit. I also noticed that a big, strong *osu* of Umuɛkɛ sometimes assumed, or was given, mild police functions.[1] The most striking case I saw of pressure exercised by an *osu* was in the land dispute referred to later. In this case one of the parties invoked the yam spirit of Agbaja, and it was the *osu* of this spirit who had to collect the fine that was levied on the other party. It was evident to the onlooker that the *osu* stood on strong ground in the negotiations. As he was also in an advanced state of leprosy he was able to levy what in effect amounted to blackmail as the mere threat of entering the house of the old man against whom sentence had been given was a potent weapon. Even so, by adroit management and a measure of good luck, the old man did in the end avoid paying the fine. The case was of great interest from many points of view, but a description of it would go beyond the limits of this chapter. All that can be noted here is that the *osu* people cannot be disregarded in an account of the management of this Ibo community's affairs.

VILLAGE CULTS

As for the beliefs and sentiments associated with the tutelary deities of village-group and village, we have seen how they contribute in a number of ways to the sense of identity of the village and village-group community, and to its stability. They also reflect the kinship and local pattern of Ibo organisation. Moreover, the lack of well-defined tribal consciousness is accompanied by the absence of a tribal deity. But just as the people of Agbaja marry and trade with the people of the village-groups near to them, so they recognise the guardian spirits of these groups though they are not directly concerned with their cults. When their

[1] See *infra,* p. 123.

annual ceremonies are performed, there is much exchange of hospitality between relations by marriage. Moreover, an Agbaja man may call on the priest of the guardian spirit of a neighbouring village-group to bring the ɔfɔ of the spirit so that he may swear his innocence on it in a case. In some instances there is a recognised order in which the ceremonies of different spirits must be performed. The new yam ceremonies which are initiated, in Agbaja, by the village of Abɔse, must be done before those of the village-group of Umu Ɛzɛala can start. In this case certain distant kinship bonds are recognised between Agbaja and Umu Ɛzɛala. The right to start any ceremony is a matter of prestige. When, in 1937, there was conflict between Abɔse and Umuɛkɛ, and the sacred spear of the yam spirit, Ajiɔkə Ji, was planted as a threat in Umuɛkɛ, the time for the new yam ceremonies drew on and they could not be done in the absence of the spear. Among other causes for anxiety in the situation was the fact that if Abɔse did not keep up to time, Umu Ɛzɛala would go ahead without waiting for them, and thus the prestige of Abɔse would be impaired.

Whether or not there is any conception of deities that are either universal or at any rate more than local, it is not easy to know. We have seen that Ala, the ground, seems to be a village or village-group conception rather than anything wider.

As for Ci, the spirit who creates people and whose name, as in Cinɛkɛ,[1] has been taken by the Christians to denote the Creator, it is difficult to know what the real Ibo significance of the word is. Ci and Ɛkɛ together create an individual, but each person is thought of as having his own Ci and whether, over and above this, there is any conception of a universal Ci seems doubtful.

Ancestor cult is an important factor in the life of the people. Apart from the performance of certain burial and second-burial ceremonies which are the concern of the whole village, its sphere is that of the individual or extended families rather than of the village as a whole, and does not therefore fall directly within our province, which is the organisation of the village. But the supernatural sanctions which stress the virtues of filial piety and mutual responsi-

[1] The meaning of this word varies according to the tones with which it is said.

bility among kinsmen so far as the dead are concerned cannot fail also to promote them among the living. This will provide a cohesive element in village life so long as it does not over-stress the particular kinship bonds of small units within the village in opposition to others. There is always, as we have seen, this tension between the separatist kinship interests of the extended families and the unity of the village as a whole.

NDE DIBEA

The two sets of people who pre-eminently deal with the supernatural side of life are the priests and the *nde dibea,* and it is important to be clear as to the marked difference between them. A priest, though he observes taboos and performs ceremonies, is yet what one might call an ordinary member of society. A *dibea,* on the other hand, though he still joins in many of the generalised activities of farming, trading, house-building and the like, is none the less a specialist, a member of a profession which entails hard and costly training and initiation, and complicated and often arduous technical activities.

The word "*dibea*" can perhaps best be translated either as "diviner" or as "doctor-magician." A *dibea* will normally specialise in one or other of these two branches of his profession, though some combine the two activities, and all seemed to have a smattering of both.

Entry into the profession is characteristically Ibo in being open to anyone. There is no question here, or anywhere else so far as I saw in Ibo society, of a closed hereditary guild system. There is probably a tendency for sons or other young relations to follow in the footsteps of a *dibea* father or senior relative, but the principle on which an individual starts on the career of diviner is that he shows signs of mental derangement. His parents then, as in all cases of sickness or misfortune, consult a diviner to know the cause and cure of the trouble, and in these mental cases they may be told that Agwǝ Nshi, the spirit of divining and of magic, is troubling the youth and that he must become a *dibea* and therefore a servitor of Agwǝ Nshi. People distinguish clearly between a man they consider mad and a man "troubled" by Agwǝ Nshi. The latter is probably, at this stage of his life anyway, psychologically unstable :

whether or not, as seems likely, his training as a *dibea* helps to stabilise him is a matter that would repay investigation. In any case, he is made socially useful and respectable instead of being regarded as an outcast and a liability.[1]

Becoming a *dibea* involves much expense and a long process of teaching and, in the case of a diviner, of initiation by other *nde dibea,* a description of which cannot be given here.

What must be stressed, however, is the part played by the *dibea* in the daily life of the Ibo. When anyone is ill or overtaken by disaster, either he or his relations will hurry to a diviner to know why, since most if not all misfortune has a supernatural cause, and it is the diviner who by the vision he has acquired during his training can see these causes. He will then prescribe the sacrifices to be made or the ceremonies to be performed. Except for the few annual occasions of more or less public sacrifice, offerings and ceremonies for the ancestors and the spirits are performed at the behest of the diviner. The diviner can also be consulted in cases of theft. In addition to all voluntary cases of consultation, if anything habitual can be so described, custom decrees that a diviner shall be consulted in the two fundamental crises of birth and of death. He must be visited on the fourth day after a child's birth by the child's kinsmen in order to ascertain what ancestor or spirit is incarnated in the baby, and therefore what name it should be given. When anyone dies, kinsmen again must go to ask a diviner, and if need be, several, the cause of death. The cause is always, so far as I have seen, held to be supernatural—an offended ancestor or spirit, or the magic or sacrifice made by an enemy.

Clearly the diviner needs a considerable local knowledge to deal with his clients, and this must extend over a wide area since a man will usually go some distance, several miles at least, to consult a *dibea*. There is, I think, little doubt that the diviners, whatever their supernatural or supernormal powers, have methods by no means supernatural of learning a great deal of what goes on, and from the very

[1] For a discussion of this whole matter on a wide comparative basis, see N. K. Chadwick : *Poetry and Prophecy,* Cambridge University Press, 1942, and " Shamanism among the Tatars of Central Asia," *Journal of the Royal Anthropological Institute,* Vol. LXVI, 1936.

nature of their clients' cases they must gain a considerable insight into the private lives of many people. They must also, particularly in giving reasons why people have died, be a considerable factor in expressing and upholding the moral code of the community, since death often comes as a result of an offence against this code.

As for the doctor-magician, he will be summoned in cases of sickness, which is regarded as supernaturally caused except in very slight cases, to make " medicine," *ɔgwɵ* [‾ _], for the patient. *Ɔgwɵ* is a compound of medical and magical substances and of ritual performances and spells. The *dibea,* too, can be invoked to make protective medicines for an individual or a group, or to make special medicine against enemies. He is the great protector against bad magic or sorcery, which is the bugbear of the Ibo mind, even in many people of European education.

Into the distinction between good and bad magic, or magic and sorcery, we cannot enter here. Ibo society distinguishes between good, socially approved magic, and bad, socially forbidden magic or sorcery, usually called *nshi* [‾ ‾], in distinction to *ɔgwɵ*, though this terminology is not invariable.[1] Magic enters into and permeates every phase of life, and the fear of sorcery is very great. It is accompanied, at least in that part of Ibo country, the interior region, which I know best, by an absence of belief in witchcraft. Peripheral communities, such as Onitsha and, so far as my limited investigations went, Arɵ Cuku, have witchcraft beliefs. The Onitsha word for witch is *amɵsu* [_ _ _]. In Agbaja both the word and the belief were absent.

From the point of view of the location or organisation of authority within the Ibo community a number of interesting points emerge from a study of the *nde dibea.* In the first place one remembers that in some African societies, as for instance among the Azande, a chief or ruler may have a special oracle of his own to which, in certain judicial cases, recourse must necessarily be had by his subjects. Clearly this will enhance his power and prestige. But among the Ibo the individual is free to consult, for the customary

---

1 When a *dibea* is asked by a client to make bad magic against an enemy, he must be told the name of the individual against whom the bad magic is to be used. This again adds to the *dibea's* store of knowledge about people's private lives and tensions.

fee, whatever diviner he may fancy, and the diviners are independent members of their profession just as is a Harley Street doctor of his. The individualistic and equalitarian character of this society is well exemplified in this, as also in the hardy scepticism with which the practitioner is regarded. Faith in the principle of magic and of divining is unlimited, but a particular diviner will often be tested before consultation. He may be asked, for instance, to divine the number of seeds in an unopened fruit. Diviners vary greatly in reputation. In the case of the doctor-magician, if he does not cure the patient within a few days he is likely to be replaced by another, with the minimum of remuneration. As for the possession of powerful magic, which may in some societies increase the prestige of a chief, among the Ibo anyone who can pay a magician can buy as much magic as he can afford.

In the second place, after wondering long about it and learning nothing, I eventually found an interesting degree of organisation and co-operation among the individual *nde dibea,* at least in the area in and around Agbaja. I had no opportunity of discovering how far it was true in other parts of Ibo country. I have only the account of one informant to rely on in this matter and I have little doubt that his descriptions were more grandiose than the actual facts. That was an almost invariable rule with informants, but I have no reason to doubt the truth of the main lines of his description. He was a young and fairly junior but intelligent doctor-magician of my own village whom I knew well and with whom I talked much about many things. He told me that the *nde dibea* from sixteen neighbouring village-groups, which he named, had meetings in the various markets in rotation, and discussed matters of common interest and drew up regulations for the whole body. It seemed that in the old days meetings of the *nde dibea* were customary but were discontinued when the British Government came. After a time the old people told the younger ones about this custom and they decided to start it again. Of the sixteen village-groups in question, eleven, said my informant, claimed descent from one mother, and five also from one mother, and because these two units were near together, or rather, geographically mixed up in the same area, their *nde dibea* had common meetings. This alone was interesting as

I knew of no other regular link, if a slight one, between such a large number of village-groups. It was made more significant by the fact that several *nde dibea* whom I knew struck me as being intelligent beyond the average and likely to be people of initiative. They also had a fund of local knowledge. It was therefore not surprising to learn that the *nde dibea* were, incidentally to their professional work, exercising powers of a more general nature, expecially of both a judicial and a law-making kind. These will be dealt with later on. Clearly in Ibo country the *nde dibea* are a force to reckon with.

RAIN-MAKERS

The rain-maker, who in some African tribes is the arbiter of their destiny, is here more in the nature of a petty trades-man.[1] In an area where the annual rainfall is about 90 inches it is clear that there will be no undue anxiety on the score of drought. This does not mean that there are no rain-makers. Instead, however, of one such figure of paramount importance there are, characteristically enough, a large number and with little or no power. The village of Umueke alone had several. They are more often called rain-drivers than rain-makers, but both titles are used, and they are, in the nature of things, more often invoked in the former capacity. Nevertheless, I found the belief that the rainy season could not happen without the intervention of the rain-makers. Like the *nde dibea*, these men undergo a training and an initiation into their calling. The rain-drivers of the village-group of Agbaja perform, though each individually, the communal function of driving rain by a magic ritual on the day of the Agbaja market, as do those of the village on the day of the village market. In return they have the right to a special portion of any meat that is divided among the village. For the rest, they can be hired by any individual for a fee to keep off rain on any occasion such as a feast or the building of a house. They were hired, though not by me, while the village was building my house, and at times they were surprisingly successful. They can be hired to ruin rival markets by causing rain to fall on them, a type of inter-village sparring that gave harmless vent to much pent-up

[1] It is interesting to note that certain features in the ritual of rain-making, such as the use of stones, are common to both Ibo and some E. African practice.

feeling. In a word, they are village charàcters, but rulers they are not.

TITLES

In many parts of Ibo country, as is well known, there are certain titles which men can take by performing a series of ceremonies and expending a 'considerable sum of money which goes to those who are already title-holders. There is thus a mutual benefit society aspect which one finds in many other Ibo arrangements.[1] The best known and most widely spread of these titles is probably ɔʐɔ [‾ ‾]. Titleholders have considerable prestige both by reason of their wealth and because of the supernatural bearing of the title. In some Ibo communities they have come to play an important part in matters of law and order, and in this they would seem to be a part of the general tendency in this society for power to fall to any group that has prestige or organisation. They will not be further discussed here because in Umuɛkɛ Agbaja there were, so far as I could discover, no living titleholders. Some had had titled fathers, but the distinction was not hereditary, though the sons sometimes were vaguely referred to as *nde nʐɛ*, titled people. This absence of living titleholders, together with the fact that in Owerri and neighbouring towns the system of title taking does not exist, shows, I think, that the system cannot be considered a pivotal position in Ibo methods of government as seems sometimes to be supposed. It may be of considerable importance in some areas, but in others it evidently is not. Nor is there, in Agbaja, any other distinction of rank. There is the distinction between free born—*di ala*—and slaves—*ohu* and *osu*, but that is a matter of status rather than of rank. If it ever had any political significance the legal abolition of slavery by the British would have undermined it.[2]

THE HOLDERS OF ɔFɔ

We have left to the last the people who hold *ɔfɔ* because

---

[1] See p. 44.

[2] A point of some interest was raised by my cook. He was a man of titled family, and he said bitterly one day that if one saw a man going about in rags, one could be sure he was a real free born man. People like the *osu* had gone into British service and were now going about in fine clothes. It would be interesting to know how far this employment of a special class leads to friction with their own people.

they are neither priests nor magicians with a primarily supernatural function but are kindred heads whose preoccupation is largely with secular matters. They are, however, supported by the supernatural sanction of their *ɔfɔ*. They will be more fully discussed when we deal with the governmental aspect of village affairs, but they must first be considered among those of the community who wield supernatural authority. The head of each kindred possesses a sacred symbol, looking usually like a small wooden club, sometimes bound with iron, and called *ɔfɔ*.[1] It is held in great awe and respect, and is frequently used. People judging an important case will be sworn on *ɔfɔ*. By it an unknown criminal may be cursed or a man suspected of crime may swear his innocence, saying let *ɔfɔ* kill him if he is guilty. A devout family head and *ɔfɔ*-holder ought daily, or at least on certain regular days, to chew pepper and spit it on his *ɔfɔ* asking the sacred symbol to spare him if he is innocent, but to kill those who seek his undoing, or conversely to kill him if he himself is seeking to injure any other human being. This will tend to be done more frequently when the *ɔfɔ*-holder is on bad terms with anyone. This ceremony, an affirmation of innocence, is known as *eto ɔgu* [‾ ‾ _], and emphasises that aspect of *ɔfɔ* in which it is a guardian of the moral code.[2] In addition to giving confidence and a sense of protection to its owner it is undoubtedly an important social sanction in this and in other respects which we shall have occasion to describe later.

Just as there is in Agbaja a man who holds the big *ɔfɔ* of the village-group, so in each village there is a senior kindred whose *ɔfɔ* is the big *ɔfɔ* of the village and is held by the head of that family. If a number of *ɔfɔ* are being used for any ceremony, this man's *ɔfɔ* will take precedence of those of the other kindreds of his village, and he has certain other rights in virtue of his position, which we shall see later. How far he also has practical power is another matter that

---

[1] The form varies in different parts of Ibo country. Dr. M. D. W. Jeffreys has much of interest about the possible origins of *ɔfɔ* in his Intelligence Report on Awka division. This Report contains much information about Ibo customs.

[2] Nearly all socially approved rites, both magical and religious, are accompanied by this type of formula, in which help is asked only if the asker is innocent. The moral code is thus continually emphasised and upheld.

will have to be considered. If we were spending a few days asking questions in an effort to discover natural rulers we might well at this point make an entry to the effect that there seems to be some kind of a town head or village head. Such entries have in fact been made ; but if we have the misfortune to live long enough in the village to observe what happens our entry is likely to lose in simplicity what it gains in correspondence to the facts. This observation will be part of our subject matter when we try to see how the practical affairs of the village are managed.

We can already see that again in the matter of this important sacred symbol, *ɔfɔ,* its possession is not limited to one family in the village, nor to one village in Agbaja. An *ɔfɔ* is held by the head of each kindred even though one kindred is senior to the others. There is again distributed rather than unified authority.

Chapter VI. The Military and Civil Aspects of Village Organisation

Military

When we come to the political aspect of Ibo organisation in this part of the country we shall see that the fruitful method of approach is in terms of activities rather than of institutions, and we shall find ourselves far from any situation in which a sovereign authority controls a well-defined territory.

If we take Professor Radcliffe-Brown's definition of the political organisation of a society as " that part of the total organisation which is concerned with the control and regulation of the use of physical force,"[1] we shall find a certain fluidity in the arrangements of the community we are studying. But if we can see something of how a relatively orderly existence is made possible, of how breaches of this order are dealt with, laws made and public business transacted, we shall get some idea of how the ends of government are achieved in an Ibo community.

As Professor Radcliffe-Brown also points out, political organisation is concerned both with external and with internal matters. " In dealing with political systems, therefore, we are dealing with law on the one hand and with war on the other."[2]

On this subject of war one is, of course, in the unsatisfactory position of having on the whole to ask questions about the past which one cannot supplement by observation ; but certain facts suggested that the difference between the past and the present is perhaps not so great as might be imagined.

It is in the military sphere that leadership has pre-eminently developed in some parts of Africa and in which political institutions can be clearly discerned. Among the people we are discussing, however, this is far from being the case. I was given several accounts of fights—*elə ɔgə* [̄ _ _], to

---

[1] *African Political Systems*, edited by Fortes and Evans-Pritchard. Introduction, p. xxiii.   [2] *Ib.*, p. xiv.

fight—some of which had been witnessed by the speakers, others of which were in their fathers' time. Of these fights, one was between Agbaja and the neighbouring village-group of Umukabia, to which it held itself to be nearly related. This was recounted by old N.Ɛ., and concerned a woman *osu* dedicated to the Agbaja deity, Ɔpara Ogugu. The *osu* belonged to the Agbaja village of Umuɛcɛlɛ, who own the cult of Ɔpara Ogugu, but the deity is a tutelary spirit of all Agbaja, and thus when the *osu* seized a goat in Umukabia and was herself seized by Umukabia in retaliation, all Agbaja was involved. They did not agree that the woman should stay and bear children for Umukabia, and therefore they went and fought.

N.Ɛ's story was punctuated with little whistles and squeals of excitement. Later in the day I was again in his house while he conducted a delicate negotiation in a case that was going badly for him. Suddenly guns were fired in the distance for a big man who had died in the next-door village. When N.Ɛ. heard them, he rocked and grunted with excitement and told me that that was what it sounded like when they fought. When they heard that sound their hearts would " shake and be strong."

I was also told, in Owerri, of a fight between Owerri and the neighbouring town or village-group of Egbu. But the other stories of fights in Agbaja were between various villages of Agbaja and not between different village-groups.

Two accounts were given me by James (Nwa Ɛbodim). One was of a fight between four villages of Agbaja-ama, who reckoned themselves descended from one mother, and were known as *nnɛ anɔ* [¯ ¯ – –], and three villages of Agbaja-owɛrɛ, including Umuɛkɛ. They fought for a day in the central Agbaja market of Oriɛ Ekpa. Another fight was between Umuɛkɛ, of Agbaja-owɛrɛ, and an Agbaja-ama village and lasted about a month. It started from a dispute about bride-price which was successfully settled by arbitration, but the winner shot off his gun in triumph and accidentally killed a man of the other side, and this started a fight.

I. told of a fight which started between two villages of Agbaja-ama while they were clearing their paths to Oriɛ Ekpa market place. A fugitive sought sanctuary with one of I.'s ancestors in Umuɛkɛ. When a man does this, his protector must not let him be harmed. In this case, however, the pursuers broke in and wounded the fugitive, whereupon an Umuɛkɛ man, father of the present priest of Umuɛkɛ, shot the aggressor. This led to fighting in which yet another village became involved, and Umuɛkɛ killed about fourteen of their opponents. This was the largest number of casualties I was ever given.

Another fight, described by J.,[1] had taken place a few years previously between Umuɔbea village of Agbaja-ama and Umuɛcɛlɛ of Agbaja-owɛrɛ, during their annual path clearing in Oriɛ Ekpa. They fought about a certain tree which each claimed. Since the fight took place in the seventh month, which is the month sacred to the deities of Agbaja, the matter was judged by all Agbaja. They seized the yams of the two villages, who then took the case to the Native Court. But the heads—*ndi ama ala* [⁻ ⁻ ⁻ ₋ ₋]—of Agbaja went to Court and said that the case must not be dealt with there as it concerned one of their customs. So they were allowed to judge it themselves and Umuɛcɛlɛ was found guilty. In the old days Umuɛcɛlɛ would have had to produce a slave to be hung in Oriɛ Ekpa. Now, since the British are here, Umuɛcɛlɛ was made to pay £10, which was taken by all Agbaja. The *owɛrɛ* half of Agbaja, to which Umuɛcɛlɛ belonged, was deeply shamed, said J., himself of this half, and sat with their hands over their faces while the *ama* half rejoiced. He added the illuminating comment that in the old days they would have fought, the shame was so great. I asked whether in the old days they never abided by a judgment but followed it by fighting. He replied that they would fight first, and when they had fought for perhaps a year—the characteristic idiom of exaggeration is probably sounding here—and people saw that too many men were getting killed, the case would be judged and the guilty party made to pay a man.

What one cannot tell from these accounts is the extent to which the whole village or village-group was involved in what usually started as a dispute between a few individuals from each side. There was apparently nothing in the way of permanent military institutions. There were traditional modes of behaviour, but no special leader and no professional

---

[1] A young married man of Umuɛkɛ of independent outlook who acted as one of my night watchmen and was a good informant.

troops. Fighting was therefore probably a rather scrappy sporadic affair. But present-day conditions suggested that in the case of a village, if not of a village-group, attack on any member by an outsider was one of the few things that made the heart of the village beat as one. While I was in Umuɛkɛ two members of the same kindred had a dispute and one invoked the sacred spear of the yam cult which was the property of another village, also of Agbaja-owɛrɛ. This meant that the second village became involved in the case, which became more and more embittered as time went on. Umuɛkɛ was at first divided in its support of the case and old jealousies and rivalries within the village flared up. When the other village kidnapped a youth of Umuɛkɛ, with intent, as Umuɛkɛ believed, to kill him, the village swung into line behind the youth's family and offered to fight. This closing of the internal ranks in the face of an external threat must undoubtedly have been a general tendency. How long or how effective village solidarity would have been is a different matter and must have varied with circumstances. It is clear from the accounts that a good many of the fights were rather of the nature of domestic brawls, though no doubt bitter ones. There was never any suggestion of fighting undertaken with the object of winning territory or of subjugating other people. Local patriotism was and is strong though variable in content, and jealousies and rivalries were keen, as they are to-day, but they did not and do not lead to territorial annexation and to a social situation of conquerors and conquered.

My questions about a military leader produced the vague and indirect answers that such questions—to these people irrelevant and barely comprehensible—were apt to produce. When I asked about the head—*ishi* [⁻ ⁻]—of the fighting, the answers bore on the man chiefly concerned in the quarrel or on the crux—*ishi*—of the dispute. It was explained that whoever was mainly concerned in the dispute would call a *dibea*—doctor-magician—to make magic for the fighters and would pay the biggest share of the cost. But those who used the medicine—it would be put into cuts in the skin—would contribute. The magic or medicine was known as *uʃɛrɛ ɛgbɛ,* breeze of guns. The projectiles of the enemy would be as though blown about by the breeze and would miss their mark, however near. Or the enemies' guns would go off with a small noise or a big noise, but nothing would come out, though if there was a big noise the gunpowder might explode.[1] The *dibea,* in addition to making war magic, would decide which people were fit to fight. This fitness consisted partly in having observed the taboo which prohibited sleeping with a woman the night before fighting. Beyond this the functions of the *dibea* apparently did not go. It seemed that he did not divine—*egba aja* [⁻ ⁻ _ _]—in order to find out the propitious day for fighting and so contribute to the military planning.

Questions as to who would lead the actual fighting were answered vaguely with : " Some of the older people." A recognised leader or chief evidently did not exist in the military any more than in other spheres. One must note here that reliance on the supernatural element introduced by the *dibea* must have helped to make well-defined practical leadership less necessary than would otherwise have been the case. The medicine would have maintained morale and generated confidence in the way that a popular general might in other circumstances achieve. We shall see again, and notably when judicial matters are discussed, how reliance on the supernatural supplements practical organisation and techniques.

As to the customs observed, and particularly their reference to the various social units involved, it was said in Owerri that guns were not usually used between members of the same village-group. Knives, bows and arrows, or spears were used in these circumstances. In Agbaja, where the constituent villages of the village-group are more scattered than in Owerri, guns were mentioned in the account of one fight between Agbaja villages. Knives were spoken of in another, and in the rest weapons were not specified. Guns were of course used against outsiders. Outsiders to the village-group who were killed could of course be eaten. As within the village-group, I am less clear. One informant said that certainly one Agbaja village could eat a man of another Agbaja village, though not one of his own village. This may well have been the case, though I did not get it adequately confirmed. Whether the theory was often translated into fact as between members of the same village-group is another matter.

---

[1] No " arms of precision " may by British law be carried. The guns used now and formerly are flint-lock Dane guns.

The same informant explained that human flesh was not eaten, as I had asked, because people liked it, but in order to boast against the enemy. When a man was killed in fighting his people would try to remove the corpse : but if they were slow in doing so, or if they ran away, the opposing side would capture the body and eat it, and they would boast of it and ask the enemy village if they called themselves men and yet allowed a man of theirs to be eaten.

Fighting might be a one day affair or it might drag on for weeks or months. If two village-groups were fighting, a third group, together with the women of the belligerent groups, might intervene to stop it. If two villages of the same group were involved, the women of the group might stop them.

In two of the accounts I was given of fighting between Agbaja villages, the whole of Agbaja, after the fighting, judged the matter. In one case the fighting had taken place on market day in the central Agbaja market, and for this offence the guilty side had to produce a man to be killed in the market place. They did not produce one of their own people, but bought a man. In the other case, where fighting went on for a month and eight people were killed, the two sides and the rest of Agbaja ultimately judged matters, and one side had to give a man, also bought, to their opponents to equalise the losses. How far any procedure of this sort was followed between two village-groups, I do not know.

In all cases of fighting, whatever the unit involved, when peace was made a *dibea* would be called in from the distant town of Umudiɔka, nearly a hundred miles away, to make a peace medicine known as the medicine of *nsɔ nri* [‾ ‾ ‾ ‾], taboo eating.[1] Both sides in the quarrel would eat this medicine.

It may be briefly recorded here that Umuɛkɛ had a man-killing society known as *nde nkwa ikɛ* [‾ ‾ ‾ _ ‾ ‾], the

---

[1] I have seen this medicine made by an Umudiɔka *dibea* for all the babies of Umuɛkɛ who were the incarnation of the tutelary deity of the village, Ogbudi.   It was made for them in case they should ever inadvertently eat the sacred fish of the Ogbudi stream which would be " as though they were eating their brothers." It was also made in case they should ever unknowingly eat with a person who in a former incarnation had been killed by Ogbudi. The medicine would keep both parties from being harmed.

members of which were people who had killed a man. They were said by my informant in this matter to be the only village in Agbaja to have such a society : only they, said he with the usual local patriotism, were so strong. The men they killed they ate. When any of their members died, or when any of them killed a man for the first time, they would dance their own special dance *egba nkwa ikε* [¯ ‑ ¯ _ ‑ ‑]. They had a drum covered with human skin and they would also bring out the heads of the people they had killed. My informant said that the older people were talking of dancing this dance again, though not of bringing out the heads, but the man who used to play for them was away from the village.

CIVIL : PERSONNEL

In the military sphere we have found little in the way of differentiated institutions, and as in the economic and supernatural aspects of village life, we have found no centre of authority. When we turn from the military to the civil aspect of village organisation the question of natural rulers is obviously of importance whether to the British official seeking to establish indirect rule or to the anthropologist arriving as a stranger in the village and looking for a channel of communication with its people. Both are likely to be confronted by difficulties.

We have already seen that within the village each kindred head holds a sacred symbol known as *ɔfɔ* and that in each village the head of the senior kindred holds the big *ɔfɔ* of the village which takes precedence over the others. Moreover, of the eleven villages of Agbaja, the village held to have been founded by the eldest son of the original ancestor of Agbaja, holds the big *ɔfɔ* of the whole village-group. At the time of the reorganisation of the Native Court system, round about 1930, the British authorities had come to different conclusions in different areas as to who were the " natural rulers " of the Ibo people and in some places had wisely come to no conclusion at all. In Agbaja they had decided that one man from each village, the holder of the big *ɔfɔ* of that village, should be a Court Member of the new Court, to which six or seven village-groups belonged. The Intelligence Report which led up to this decision had discovered the *ɔfɔ*-holders and had referred to the senior

one of them among the eleven villages of Agbaja as the
" town head."

In Umuɛkɛ, however, things had not gone according to
plan. The holder of the big ɔfɔ of the village was a weak-
witted, youngish man who had been terrified at what might
happen in all this strange white-man palaver, and had hung
back. Thereupon another man, who had no particular position in the village but was probably a pusher, had stepped
into his shoes, more or less on his own initiative, and the
fait accompli was accepted. At his death, his son had succeeded
him, with resulting friction in the village.[1]

To discover some effective channel between the village
and myself was from the first moment of my suspicious
arrival a matter of some urgency. I held a preliminary parley
with the elders about the question of my staying there. It
was at the best inconvenient, in every minor emergency, to
have to communicate with a dozen or so elders scattered far
and wide through the village. The Court Member, naturally,
pressed himself upon me as the " chief " ; but knowing
nothing about him at that stage I reserved judgment as to
his real position in the village but decided to try him as a
go-between. The stream where we all got our drinking water
was considered by my staff to be in a far from sanitary
condition. I suggested to the Court Member that the village
might, in the interests of all concerned, at least remove
some of the rotting bread-fruit from the place where we
drew water. He agreed that it should be done next day.
Next morning early I heard a noise of a kind that one comes
to associate intimately with an Ibo village, though the
inhabitants hardly notice it.[2] It appeared that the stream
ran through one half of the village, Umuɛkɛ-ama, whereas

---

[1] In many places the plan of choosing one man to represent a village
was not followed. Either representation was to be in rotation, or more
than one man could be sent. I do not know whether the Agbaja system
has been maintained there, but I think it is improbable.

[2] Now and then I would invite the women of the village to a party
at my house and the sharing of the food would produce two hours of
vociferation to which no description can do justice. On the day following
the first party I asked a friend of mine among the women whether they
always squabbled quite so noisily on such occasions. She looked at me
in surprise and said they had been particularly quiet in deference to me.
" If we had been alone we should probably have killed several people,"
she remarked with that fine, sweeping use of the verb " to kill "—*igbu*
[⁻ ⁻], that enriches harmlessly so much of Ibo conversation.

the Court Member lived in the other. It was the prerogative of Umuɛkɛ-ama to clean the stream—once a year was the modest estimate given—in return for which they might on that occasion catch any fish that they could. When the Court Member, urged thereto by the ignorant white woman, had given orders about stream-cleaning, they had been roused to furious protest at this infringement of their traditional rights. They would no doubt have protested whoever had tried to interfere, but the incident did not suggest a harmonious relationship between the Court Member and village.

It eventually emerged that the man who ought in the circumstances to have been the Court Member was, as we have said, a youngish man called N.O., who held the big ɔfɔ of the village—ɔfɔ ozuzu ɔha [_ ⁻ _ _ ⁻ _ _]—in virtue of the fact that he was the senior man of the kindred Umu Ɔmo Ukwu, of the original founder of the village. This meant that his ɔfɔ took precedence over the others in the village and was the first to be put down in any ceremonial involving the use of ɔfɔ. It also meant that N.O. had the right to the first share of food or anything else that was to be divided among the whole village, the second and third shares being taken by the senior men of the two kindreds next in seniority.[1] It meant, too, that if the eleven villages of Agbaja were each to produce ɔfɔ for some special purpose[2] it would be N.O. who would go with his ɔfɔ from Umuɛkɛ. What had to be discovered was the extent to which this recognised position of the holder of the big ɔfɔ conferred upon him any rôle of practical leadership : but it was clear from the beginning that even his position was very much that of *primus inter pares*. Each kindred—*umunna*—had its own ɔfɔ, held normally by its senior man and known as ɔfɔ ozuzu ɔha—ɔfɔ of the people. The ɔfɔ-holder of the kindred is sometimes referred to as onyɛ bi n'ama [⁻ ⁻ – – ⁻], literally, one who lives on a path, or as one who is onyɛ ishi ɔnama [⁻ ⁻ ⁻ ⁻ ⁻ ⁻], the meaning being that this man is head of the house-group (literally, head of the entrance to the path).

Accounts of the rules of succession to ɔfɔ are apt to vary

---

[1] Nwa Onyɛ Okoro of Umu Nwa Ɛbodim took second share and O. A. of Umu Nwacuku took third.

[2] See, *re* Em. swearing, p. 230.

in accordance with the circumstances of the particular informant. If he is trying to justify his own position or substantiate a claim his account will be affected accordingly and the recent tendency of the British authorities to recognise ɔfɔ as a mark of authority has probably increased the desire to qualify as ɔfɔ-holder. In any case the search for " natural rulers " had meant that everyone was on his guard in matters of this kind and that information was apt to be unreliable.

The basic rule of succession to the ɔfɔ of the kindred is that a man should succeed to the ɔfɔ of his father : but this was open to a number of interpretations. Some said that when an ɔfɔ-holder died his eldest son should hold the ɔfɔ. Others said that it should go to the brother of the dead man because it was their father's ɔfɔ. Others said that it should go to this brother if the dead man's son was a child, to be held until the child grew up.

Only two ɔfɔ-holders died between 1935 and 1937, and neither while I was actually in the village. One was N.O., the holder of the big ɔfɔ which went to his younger brother by the same father. He had in fact no male child. The other was Ibɛ Ɛgbu, the ɔfɔ-holder of one of the kindreds of Umuɛkɛ-owɛrɛ. He had a son but the kindred ɔfɔ went, not to him, but to a classificatory brother of Ibɛ Ɛgbu, younger than himself, because this man's father and Ibɛ Ɛgbu's father were born of the same father and he had originally held the ɔfɔ. Ibɛ Ɛgbu had, however, also acquired a personal ɔfɔ—that of ɔnɵ agwɵ—during his lifetime, and this passed to his son. It was said, however, that it would remain in the roof till the death of the man holding the kindred ɔfɔ and that only then would the son really hold it.

On the basis of facts relating to other ɔfɔ in the village and the accounts of principles of succession, it would seem that the case of Ibɛ Ɛgbu represents orthodox procedure with regard to the succession both of the kindred and the personal ɔfɔ. It is, however, doubtful whether orthodoxy always prevails.

The question of physiological paternity was said to be of no importance in relation to succession to ɔfɔ. A man would succeed to the ɔfɔ of his sociological father whether or not he was his natural father.

Ɔfɔ plays an important part in Ibo life and beliefs. That of the *umunna* is a symbol of family or ancestral authority and a reservoir or carrier of supernatural power. There are also *ɔfɔ* connected with the various deities such as Ala, the guardian deity of the village, or Agwɵ Nshi. A *dibea* has a special *ɔfɔ,* used for the purposes of his profession and connected with his Agwɵ Nshi, the spirit associated with magic and divining. But it is the ancestral *ɔfɔ,* that of the *umunna,* which people have chiefly in mind when they speak of *ɔfɔ.* It is held in great awe and respect, and is constantly used or invoked. " *Ɔfɔ na-ɛji ogu ɛgbu* " is said about *ɔfɔ.*

The meaning is that *ɔfɔ* never kills an innocent man.[1] *Ɔfɔ* is often brought out and placed on the ground when sacrifice is being made to a deity. It is knocked—*gɔ* [⁻]—on the ground when it is used in swearing. It is evidently in some intimate connection with Ala and must be kept from contact with the ground except when it is being ceremonially used. It is usually kept up in the roof of a man's room when not in use and is carried in his bag slung over his shoulder when he carries it with him.

I asked N.Ɛ. one day why *ɔfɔ* was such a big thing to them. He was *ɔfɔ*-holder of one of the *umunna* of Umuɛkɛama. He almost at once, with that emphasis on property that recurs again and again among these people, explained that if anything belonging to the *ɔfɔ*-holder were stolen, he would take *ɔfɔ* and spit pepper over it and ask that whoever has stolen the thing may die, and he will knock *ɔfɔ* on the ground, invoking the ground and the cloud and the *agbara* [⁻ _ _] to help him. He will avert his face, showing thus that he is angry, and the ground also will be angry.

On another occasion, he spoke of *ɔfɔ* as the thing that helps a man to get children. He also referred to the protestation of innocence of the *ɔfɔ*-holder—*etɵ ogu*—on his *ɔfɔ* and explained that if a man went against his *ogu* he would pass water and die.

A sophisticated Christian in Owerri, talking about *ɔfɔ,* made one feel the importance to these Ibo people of the concrete symbol. He said that a man will tend to get a personal *ɔfɔ* when he gets to middle age, even if his father is still alive. He must have something to hold when he prays : he cannot expect the elder to do it all. He also added that

---

[1] *Iji ogu* [⁻ ⁻ ⁻ _] means literally to hold a piece of young knotted palm frond, *ɔmɵ* [_ ⁻], while protesting innocence, *etɵ ogu* [⁻ ⁻ ⁻ _].

Church people were trying to divest *ɔfɔ* of its pagan, super-natural significance because it is awkward for a Christian not to be able to inherit it. If a man cannot hold it he may sometimes be prevented from inheriting certain property. Also it is bad for a younger man to hold it : he will probably die soon.

This last belief was corroborated by an Mbiɛri man who told of an individual who succeeded to *ɔfɔ* in place of a Christian who was the rightful heir. But it troubled him greatly, so in the end the heir reverted to paganism and took the *ɔfɔ*.

With their characteristic lack of any apparent desire to elaborate matters of history or tradition, none of the people of Umuɛkɛ who talked about *ɔfɔ* volunteered any myth of its origin. One of the oldest men, a particularly good talker, when I asked him about it, said, " Who can say how *ɔfɔ* first came ? " No one knows how the world first began, but when men first came, *ɔfɔ* came too. He went on to give a story illustrating the power of *ɔfɔ*. He said that once, very long ago, before he was born, people were in Oriɛ Ekpa and a bird called Ɛzɛ Ikɛ came and perched on a tree. They feared it was a bad omen, so they knocked *ɔfɔ* saying if it had come for any bad thing, let it die. And it died. So now they say " *Ɔfɔ* that killed Ɛzɛ Ikɛ."

As has been pointed out, N.O., though he held the big *ɔfɔ* of Umuɛkɛ, was none the less only one among the other *ɔfɔ*-holders of the village. These men, who were not neces-sarily old since a young man might be and sometimes was the senior man of his kindred, formed the bulk of what might be described as the council of elders, if that term does not suggest something too formal. The name given to this body in the village was *nde ama ala* [¯ ¯ ¯ _ _], literally—the people of the paths of the land—and meaning the kindred heads. J. explained that this was a name given by the British. In the old days, these people would, he said, have been called *nde ikɛrɛmɛ*. According to him, this was the name of the oldest age grade—*ɛbiri* [¯ _ _]. Other people gave as the name of this age grade, *nde akatakwɵ okii*. The *ndi ama ala* were rather different in composition from the oldest age grade, though one noticed a tendency towards a confusion between the two when the men of Umuɛkɛ divided themselves into their age grades to sit together and drink and chat on the village market day. On this occasion people who were of the *nde ama ala* tended to sit with the eldest age grade, the *nde akatakwɵ,* even though they belonged to a lower *ɛbiri.*

The *nde ama ala* were, in principle, the holders of the *ɔfɔ* of the kindreds—*umunna.* No one, said N.Ɛ. one day, could be *onyɛ ama ala* [⁻ ⁻ ⁻ _ _] without *ɔfɔ.* He would be *okorɔbea,* a youth. But in fact the *nde ama ala* included, beside the kindred heads, any old men of the village even though they did not hold a kindred *ɔfɔ.* There was also a stranger included who had settled in Umuɛkɛ-ama and who was elderly. He had the reputation of being of good counsel and was, as has been said, nicknamed " teacher " by the villagers on this account. The Court Member was also taken as one of the *nde ama ala* because of his official position. He was the only member of the body who might be said to belong in virtue of a political office, and his was a British and not an indigenous position. Dr. Nadel has recently pointed out[1] that in a Nupe village, membership of the council is an official political appointment even though it goes to heads of the kinship group. In this Ibo village, however, one could hardly say that the dozen or so *nde ama ala* were differentiated as a body from the kinship structure. They might exercise certain political functions, but basically they were there in virtue of their position in the kinship system. No structural differentiation can yet be said to have taken place.

It would be easy to over-emphasise the *nde ama ala* as a formal body even of a kinship order. The whole village, or such part of it as is concerned, can and does participate in any matter that interests it. " A case forbids no one," they say. Only a description of actual cases judged or laws made will give an idea of what part is played either by the elders or by the assembled village, or what part falls to quite other groups in the community. We shall see again the tendency to a dispersal rather than a concentration of authority. By dispersal we mean not only that the whole body of villagers can and do, if they so wish, take a hand in most practical affairs, but that there is often a tendency for matters to be handled in an *ad hoc* fashion by a number

---

[1] Nadel : *A Black Byzantium.* Oxford University Press, 1942, p. 47.

of different groups or sections of society rather than by one recognised centre of hierarchy.

It accords with this absence of centralisation that there is no one who can be described as a chief or headman, no one who is what might be called the chairman of the *nde ama ala*. N.O., as has been said, held the big *ɔfɔ* of Umuɛkɛ, but it soon became clear, both from what people said and from what one observed, that though every one recognised his position and his rights he cut no ice from the point of view of practical leadership. My neighbour, the priest of the village guardian deity, discussed him one day, and, lest it be thought that he was disparaging a rival among the elders —for he, though a young man, was a family head and an elder—it must be made clear that he himself, in spite of his position, carried little practical weight. He was a gentle and attractive creature, though with little claim to intellect. He was, too, vague and indifferent about money. This peculiarity if nothing else would have disqualified him as a practical leader in a society where the go-getter is above all admired. His priestly function was universally respected, but when the elders turned to the secular affairs of life he sank into a contented nonentity. From him, therefore, it was interesting to learn that in practical matters the village looked on N.O. as a child. In judging cases " he does not get mouth," said the priest, so his " brother " speaks for him. In other words, N.O. had no gift of expression any more than of intelligence. Moreover, he had no children and he belonged to a kindred that had almost died out. An elder of the house-group next to which N.O. lived would if necessary, speak for him. All this one later saw from one's own observation and cases of it will be described. It was interesting that the man's practical incapacity was openly stated, side by side with the admission that he held the traditional position of big *ɔfɔ*-holder and senior man. There was evidently no difficulty even in theory about divorcing position from power : far less was there any in practice.

It is, I think, fairly certain that if N.O. had been a man of forceful character and ability his position would have contributed to his power. As it was, his *ɔfɔ* was feared ; but with his feeble wits his hereditary position was not enough to give him weight as a leader in village affairs.

It is interesting to note in passing that when N.O. died

in 1936 one of the reasons given for his death was that his ɔfɔ killed him " for making it low," that is to say, for failing to take up the position of Court Member. It is impossible to analyse exactly the elements in this reason. The British had designated the big ɔfɔ-holders of this region as Court Members. Whatever the indigenous meaning or function of ɔfɔ this would probably have been enough to make N.O.'s refusal of the official position seem to be an insult to his ɔfɔ. But taken together with the fact that a kindred ɔfɔ-holder is supposed daily or frequently to declare his innocence on ɔfɔ, it suggests that ɔfɔ is both a symbol and a sanction of responsible citizenship.

While I was trying, both for practical and for theoretical reasons, to discover whether there was anyone in the village who could be called a " chief," I appealed to my staff. A. said he could not discover who " led the nde ama ala." People answered differently, according to their part—nce—of the village. This was probably as good a comment as could have been made. The nde ama ala were a collection of kindred heads rather than a body representing the village. There was much jealousy between Umueke-ama and Umueke-owere which I found to my cost when the village built a house for me. Neither side considered itself bound by agreements unless its particular elders had been present at the discussion, and even within a kindred there would be complaints that only the senior man was called for discussion, and why should he be singled out ? Direct rather than representative democracy was the prevailing system.

Umueke-ama did, however, look to some extent to N.E. If there is a case it seems to be he who will first come out, said one of them. He was the oldest man of the village and an ɔfɔ-holder. He was shrewd and dignified and quiet, and certainly carried weight among the elders ; but just because of his quiet, deliberate manner he was apt some-times to be overborne by others possessing the more vocal, pushing qualities that are cultivated and admired in this society. He had, however, in his youth, had some contact with the Europeans who first came to this part of the country, and later, in the days of the Warrant Chiefs, he had, according to his own account, worked with one of them and made so much money that he had married eight wives. Although he was certainly not wealthy when we knew him and had only four wives surviving, it was probably the fact that he had had some experience of the world that helped to give him a certain position in the village. His jealousy of the present Court Member was probably in part due to the fact that he himself had profited by past methods of British administration and no longer did so. He maintained a forward-looking attitude, and it was he who had given land to the mission for building. He was always telling me that he wished Europeans would come to live in the place to help it to " get up."

Another helpful staff comment was from my cook. He himself was a man of good standing in his own village thirty miles away, and in the early days of our stay in Umueke I was asking him whom he thought might be likely to take the lead there. He remarked that someone " who got open eye " was more likely to be prominent in practical matters than anyone of merely traditional position. The mission teacher, who came from a different part of the country also said, on another occasion, that in his town the people who are important when a case is tried—the people who go out to consult—are those who " get mouth."

It would, however, mean overlooking vital mechanisms in the working of this society if one merely disregarded N.O., the senior man. Negligible as an individual, he was none the less of practical as well as ceremonial importance as an institution, as the embodiment of certain rules. In this society, where a hierarchical authority is absent, institutionalised behaviour and formal rules proliferate and are an important part of the social fabric. It has already been noticed that N.O., as senior man of the village, had the right to the first share of food or of anything else that was being divided among the village as a whole. Clearly, in an over-populated and poor community, the method of sharing is of great importance, and one quickly realises in conversation that the matter bulks largely in people's minds and is the subject of minute customary regulation. I have seen a small child refuse a piece of food because it was offered out of turn. When to poverty is added an excitable nature, it is clear that the public dividing of food might, in the absence of strong authority, easily give rise to disorder. This was evident on one occasion when the elders came at my invitation to eat at my house. The food was put before them and they were asked to share it according to their own custom. Partly, no doubt, because the occasion was not a traditional one, feeling ran high and anxiety became vocal as the food was divided up into shares. The clamour increased till at last N.O., usually lethargic and silent, rose and cursed by the big ɔfɔ anyone who should snatch food out of his turn, saying let ɔfɔ kill anyone who did so. This calmed things down, the sharing proceeded correctly, and one realised the importance of a known order of precedence.

For purposes of indirect rule it is necessary not only to discover indigenous institutions but also to understand the part they play in the society which has evolved them.[1] It may be that the big ɔfɔ, though like its fellows it indicates a measure of public responsibility, should be regarded as a regulative device rather than as the mark of a ruler. This point would, however, require substantiation from a much wider area of observation than my own. I put it forward for the consideration of those who have experience from other areas.

---

[1] Since indirect rule is bound to face an indigenous community with new needs, it is certain that some modification of existing institutions or the devising of new ones will eventually take place. In any society institutions arise in answer to needs. If therefore the indigenous community is to take a leading part in the adoption or creation of institutions, a first necessity would seem to be that it should understand the nature of the new needs. The community in which I lived was profoundly ignorant on this score. Efforts at explanation had been singularly ineffective. A far more determined attack on this aspect of the problem of indirect rule seems indicated in this area. Perhaps mass educationists will turn their attention to the matter.

Chapter VII. The Law as Maintained

Before going on to discuss the part played by the elders or by other groups or by the village as a whole in the trying of cases, we must look briefly at those factors which make for the upholding of law and custom. As Malinowski has pointed out, the law in maintenance is both more important and more normal than the law in breach and must be carefully considered if the workings of any society are to be understood. From this angle the whole body of rules, customary, legal, conventional, ethical, which secure the necessary minimum of social conformity, are best considered as part of a whole series not divisible into water-tight compartments. We shall see when we consider the judicial function that in this society law is distinguished from custom in the sense that it is enforced, directly or indirectly, by the community, and that this distinction is recognised by the people. In this chapter, however, we are not concerned with this distinction.

In considering the whole question of social stability one must recognise, in the first place, that there is a general acceptance of the existing form of society. There are many personal dissatisfactions and criticisms, but they do not lead to general criticism of the *status quo* or demands for a revolution or a new order.

It has already been indicated that among these people rules rather than rulers are the essential mechanisms of social order. One learns how well-known is the formal pattern of rules and behaviour that custom decrees for all situations of importance and one resigns oneself early to the fact that a description of almost any social event will include a catalogue of the exact gifts or payments, down to the number of pieces of firewood, that should be made and the exact number of times that each ritual activity, if such is involved, should be performed. The precision with which accounts of this kind are given strikes a European as remarkable. These people evidently attach importance to detailed regulations, and have great facility in memorising them.

In order to be effective, such regulations must be a matter

of common knowledge. Here the small size and compact nature of an Ibo village community are clearly relevant. They are factors that one does not sufficiently recognise at first. I would search laboriously for the machinery, the institutionalised means, by which certain organised activities were carried out. Sometimes they existed and could be discovered, but sometimes my efforts would be met by a smile, as when I asked my old lady friend, Nwa Ori Ego, how people would be summoned to judge a case. If there is a case, will people not come out, she said, with a look of amusement at the foolish question of the white woman.

In the same way, when one seeks to discover how people know when to do the yearly communal path clearing and the religious ceremonies that follow it one finds that people can give a series of days, in terms of an eight-day week, on which various activities have to be performed. Just before the chief annual religious occasion a special sign is given by the people in charge of the deity concerned, but before this the succession of events is a matter of general knowledge. In this agricultural community the year, without any calendar, is bound together by the succession of the seasons and of their religious observances and everyone knows the order of events.

EDUCATION

The small size of the Ibo community, the fact that so many people live in such a restricted space, has its effect on the whole question of education which is, in itself, one of the bases of the maintenance of the social order. Professor Radcliffe-Brown points out that in some societies penal sanctions hardly exist. Education is enough.[1] Among the Ibo penal sanctions certainly exist. The very fact that people live cheek by jowl probably makes them inevitable : but this same fact means a general participation of young and old in most matters of public concern and children grow up immersed in the affairs of the community, most of which are enacted within a radius of a mile or so instead of at some distant centre. Moreover, children tend to be present at many of the doings of their elders and education is, on the whole, probably a matter of assimilation rather than of formal teaching. From a very early age children begin to take

---

[1] *African Political Systems*, p. xv.

part on a small scale in the work of the family. One will see a toddler clutching a few twigs of firewood or a child with a small pot going to fetch water or a group of piccins cracking kernels. In their play they build houses and share food. " See how they imitate their elders," said a woman member of my staff, one day, as we passed some children who were playing thus. I asked a woman on one occasion how children learned to carry things on their heads. She said that they taught themselves. They certainly experimented from their earliest days. I saw my neighbour S's boy of about three and a half years sharpening a knife on a stone one day and using a small knife on another occasion. He would also climb up the ladder his father was using in repairing his roof.

I did not make a systematic study of indigenous methods of education but there did not seem to be any marked system of group instruction. The question of initiation rites is not an easy one to deal with. Those of the boys have gone underground to a considerable extent from fear of European disapproval and tend now to be held in connection with the initiation of a *dibea*. None were held in Umuɛkɛ while I was living there, though when a *dibea* was initiated in the neighbouring village-group of Umunuma, we saw boys in initiation dress going to market with him in his public inception as a diviner and they had probably been passing through a period of initiation at the same time as he did his own. I obtained a number of descriptions of the normal boys' initiation rites, which used to be held every few years and through which most of the boys in the village except the quite young ones had passed. The boys of part of the next door Agbaja village also participated. The chief feature of the rites was described as being the acquiring of aggressive medicine or magic—*okɛ ɔgwθ* [¯ ¯ _]—rather than the receiving of instruction. This medicine could only be used against people who had not themselves acquired it, against strangers that is to say, and more particularly against women because the latter never acquired it. The medicine was put into the boys' eyes and into cuts in the skin over a period of eight days. In so far as they were not supposed to cry it may be said that hardihood was inculcated. It was impressed upon them that the medicine must not be used upon an innocent woman. A skull was placed upon their heads with the conditional curse that they should die if they used the medicine wrongfully. There was thus inculcation of a certain code of morality. Moreover, a number of ancestral shrines were involved in the performance of the rites and the boys would thus learn about them if they were not already familiar with them. But in the main the rites would not seem to have been much concerned with instruction. It is clear that they would, however, enhance group solidarity—the village as against strangers, the men as against the women of other villages whom they had married and who had come to live in the village. This male-female dualism was a recurrent motif in a number of different forms. The fact that all married women in the village were, by the rules of exogamy, from other villages may have had something to do with it. In this question of the medicine possessed by the men there was no doubt that the women feared it. I have heard a woman attribute her difficult labour to it, and it was a good deal talked about. In addition to increasing a sense of group solidarity, the rites would no doubt give a sense of confidence to the growing boy just at the time when he needed it most, by providing him with a weapon against strangers, an aggressive weapon, so that by attacking he could defend himself.

In the same way the girls' period of seclusion, so far as one could gather from descriptions of it, seemed to have been a time of rest and of feeding up before marriage rather than a time of instruction. It had tended, even more than the boys' rites, to be abandoned or superseded by a series of dances and of exchanges of gifts known as *eta okporoko* [¯ ¯ ¯ _ ¯ ¯], and its significance was not, therefore, easy to assess.

In so far as there is any teaching by precept rather than by example it would seem to be a matter between parents and children, and particularly between father and son and mother and daughter, rather than between the group and its members. Discussing the matter with N.E., he said that a father would call his son alone to give him advice. He would not give it in front of others. The father will advise the son and the mother the daughter. Children spend a certain amount of time staying away with relatives, and the eldest son and daughter of a couple are supposed to spend a good deal of time, as children, with their paternal grandparents, as compensation to these for the loss of their son at marriage. This means, of course, that the children come under a variety of influences. I heard S.'s wife saying, on one occasion, that she was sending her eldest child, a small girl, to stay with one of her kinsfolk until she learned some sense. But to a considerable extent the children bring each other up, small ones looking after yet smaller in a manner strongly reminiscent of Stepney or Poplar. Whether or not it is symbolic I do not know, but when a baby is born it is given, after being washed, to a small child to carry into the house where its mother will spend the next few days. Almost at once it will in part be looked after by quite small children. I have seen a little girl of about five or six carrying a newly born baby over her shoulder, or sitting down and giving it water to drink. Later on children will take the baby out with them when they go to play, or tend it while their parents go to market. The boy of about eight who lived next door to me used to speed across my compound with his baby brother hanging over his shoulder and clutched by the ankles. Though disaster frequently seemed imminent, it did not occur. On the other hand one would be struck at times by the care shown by one midget to another.

If there is no child of suitable age in the immediate family where a baby has been born people will sometimes get one from elsewhere to come for a time to " carry " the baby. I was told, though I did not actually see it happen, that payment would be given to the small nursemaid, about 10s. or £1 for the period it spent with the baby[1] : five shillings would probably be paid in advance and the rest when the baby could walk and the child went home. One would see a baby who was beginning to eat solid food being carried about by its child attendant at the time of the evening meal and being fed from a bowl or pot. One of the older women explained that it was not good for a mother to carry a child all the time as she would give it the breast every time it cried. The Owerri girl on my staff added that in her country people think it better for a child to be carried by other children rather than by its mother. It will be carried away and instead of crying for its mother

---

[1] This was one of the very few cases of paid labour in the village.

it will watch the other children playing, and by watching it will develop more quickly, walk more quickly, for instance, than if it is left with its mother. It may be, though I did not hear the theory enunciated, that this early upbringing by fellow children has something to do with the independent and equalitarian outlook of these people in later life. From their earliest moments they are surrounded by their peers rather than by their superiors. Whether or not this does affect their later attitude I do not know, and I would not like to dogmatise or to generalise about this attitude. I had little opportunity of observing it elsewhere. It did, however, seem that in this village at least obedience and respect for one's elders were not strongly marked features of the social picture. One situation or incident after another recalls itself. There were children living next door to me on either side. To the left, R. used to complain that her eldest child, a small girl of about five, was disobedient and would not crack kernels or run messages when she was told. To the right I would repeatedly hear a woman shouting for her small son and I was told that he made no attempt to obey her. Both these mothers were impatient individuals, probably for reasons of health, and treated their children more roughly than is, I think, usual among these people, who are very fond of their children. But I repeatedly saw how little control the older people apparently had over them. The strictest discipline I saw exercised was when the children used to come to listen to my gramophone. A youth would then constitute himself master of the ceremonies, and if any child showed signs not even of excitement but of normal enjoyment he was apt to receive a sharp crack on the head with a stick. It may be that there is tacit recognition of the fact that in a crowd of these excitable folk disorder must be dealt with in its early stages if there is to be any hope of quelling it.

As for the attitude of youths to their elders, examples of scant respect will occur in later chapters, but one or two may be given here. I one day heard old N.Ɛ. urgently calling my boy A. Afterwards A. and my Owerri girl, S., told me that N.Ɛ.'s son, Nwa Okwɛ, a troublesome lad of about fifteen, had cut firewood—incidentally it was for my household—and had let the wood fall on some of his father's yams, thereby damaging them. His father's youngest wife had expostulated, whereupon Nwa Okwε had set upon her and they had fought with and about the sticks he had cut, she claiming that she should have them in return for the damaged yams. She was then abused by the mother of Nwa Okwε, another and older wife of N.Ɛ. When A. arrived, the old man was trying to separate the fighters, but the lad, Nwa Okwε, turned on him and fought him, said A. The old man took his matchet and hit his son on the back with the flat of it. Thereupon another rather older son, Columbus, set upon him, he also having a matchet. A. then, as is decreed by custom, took away the matchets of the disputants to try to avert bloodshed, and gave them to one of N.Ɛ.'s wives to hold. The mother of Nwa Okwε and Columbus then rebuked them for fighting their father. The father and the wife whom Nwa Okwε had fought were then persuaded to go to their house and bystanders tried to restrain Nwa Okwε, who was evidently beside himself and who struggled with them all. After a time he went away and then returned and attacked his father in his own house, and threatened, said S., to kill him, and abused him saying he would kill him, dig his yams and use them for his burial ceremonies. The old man cried out and people came and held the lad till he desisted. S. said that his mother, who was hysterically inclined at any time, was crying and was saying that a *dihea* had told her that to-day either Nwa Okwε would kill someone or that someone would kill him. Let him not kill his father or what would people say, as S. phrased it, getting by now a little incoherent. She herself was shocked by the whole episode and said that it is very bad for a son to fight or abuse his father or fight his father's wife. A. said that in his part of the country—Mbiεri—it is forbidden for a son to fight with his father or to flog his father's wife, though, he added, it sometimes happens. He and S. were both Christians and their reaction may have been coloured by this fact.

In the same way it is difficult to know how far the cases one saw in the village of lack of respect from younger to elder people were due to the undermining of authority by new conditions brought about by European influence. Economically the younger people were less dependent now than formerly on their parents. Morally it was difficult to say whether or not new ideas were lessening respect for parents. The only case I witnessed of conscious conflict in the matter presented a rather different problem, but has its relevance. It concerned the same old man, N.Ɛ., and his eldest son, S., and happened about two years after this fight. N.Ɛ. became involved in a serious case in which his opponents had the sacred spear of Ajiɔkɔ Ji, the yam spirit, placed outside his house as a menace of disaster if he should fail to produce the fine demanded.[1] S. told me that he himself, as a Christian thought of throwing the spear away to show the worthlessness of pagan threats; but his father who was a pagan and was greatly frightened about the spear would not allow him to do so. In great perplexity he obeyed his father and left the spear, and the reason he gave was that he thought that if he disobeyed his father, he would be disobeying the laws of God. What restrained him in his own opinion was thus the new sanctions and not the old.

More than once I have come on cases of sons quarrelling or bickering with their mother. On one occasion I was told that the senior woman of Umu Nwa Ɛbodim's extended family had quarrelled with one of her sons, a lad of about fourteen, and had run away to the village of her birth in consequence. The next evening she came in to see me and said that she had had a quarrel—ɔka [‾ _]—with her son the day before. Her version was that she had told him to carry things to farm for working and that he had objected and had cursed her. In vexation—iwɛ [‾ ‾]—she had cursed him in return and had then run away to her native place. Next morning her co-wives had gone after her and begged her to return, but she had refused. She explained to us that she had just returned this evening for the village market, which happened to be on this day, but that when she had finished her marketing she would go back to her own village and not return to her husband's place for two days. She would come then as one of her co-wives was having a meeting—mikiri. Altogether she was rather on her high horse. I heard the next day that her husband's eldest son by a different wife had taken palm wine that morning and gone to the offended woman's birth place, but had found that she had gone off to a meeting. He would go again the next day.

---

[1] See p. 107-8.

The son who had quarrelled with her said, I was told, that he did not first abuse his mother. According to him he went off to a distant farm with a working party to help and later his mother came bringing food she had cooked for them. He said that as they had eaten before they started it would be better to carry on with their work and eat the food later instead of stopping at once. His mother took offence and they quarrelled, and she went to her native place. So far as I had seen, this woman was not hasty and hot-tempered like the mother of Nwa Okwε. She would preserve her equanimity except under extreme provocation. I did not witness what happened between her and her son, but the whole episode hardly suggests respect as from children to parents.

As between the young men—*okorɔbea*—of the village and the elders—*nde ama ala*—an example of the relationship between them in what might be called the law-making sphere will be given later.[1] Two further intimations of the same kind may be briefly given here.

Once, when I told N.Ɛ. that I had something I wanted to discuss with the *nde ama ala,* he begged me not to summon them openly because he said that the *okorɔbea* would make palaver as they said that the *nde ama ala* got more out of me than they did, and that they felt aggrieved. On another occasion, when the *nde ama ala* came to protest to me about something I had done I noticed that one of the younger men, a turbulent character, was with them. Their protest was very mild and N.Ɛ., who was not with them and who was angry with them for coming, told me afterwards that they had been put up to coming by the youth.

Altogether one could not say that in this village youth had apparently any great respect for age. I cannot remember that such respect was ever mentioned among the qualities that it was felt desirable to encourage among the young : nor, though this is a different matter, could one say that a dignified bearing, at least in any sense in which a European would use the word, was a marked characteristic of the elders with the exception, perhaps, of N.Ɛ., who temperamentally had a quiet manner and a certain exclusiveness. The behaviour of some of the others might at times almost

1 See p. 134.

be described as skittish. I have seen an old man chase a middle-aged one playfully, and with much laughter on the part of the latter, round the market place, not, of course, at market time. And one came to wait for the magnificent finality with which an old man, having delivered his oration to an assembly, would swing round on his heel and sweep out only to return a moment later in a perfection of anticlimax because he could not bear to forego that last word which it is everyone's ambition in this community to achieve.

As to the virtues and qualities considered desirable in this community, they emerge as various aspects of the society are described and only a few indications need be given here. There is much to show that the man of energy, the go-getter, is among the admired types. This has already appeared in people's attitude towards N.O., the ineffective individual who held the big ɔfɔ of the village. When he died the disapproving comment on the brother who succeeded him was that he seemed to be lazy. It has been seen, too, that the man who was priest of the village tutelary spirit was a gentle individual with no wife or children, and with little push or go and that outside his religious sphere he had little influence in village affairs.

The man who has not got a well-filled yam store will feel ashamed. One of my neighbours in Umuɛkɛ had contracted a debt in order to bribe the police and had had to sell a large number of yams in trying to pay it off. The buyer had allowed him to keep the yams in his store until the planting season so that he should not be shamed. S. said that in her country, Owerri, if women had big yams they would put them in front of their baskets and other people would praise them and they would be gratified.

It is desirable that a man should be " smart." Part of the funeral ceremonies for an old man is known as egba mmɛ [‾ – – – –]. A man takes a fowl and runs and touches it on the ground first at the head of the corpse and then at the feet and at both sides of the body. He then wrings its neck and it is eaten by those belonging to the oldest age grade. The man chosen to run with the fowl is one who is smart and quick and the ceremony is believed to make the dead man smart and quick—light of body for running messages or for work, it was said—when he is reincarnated. This was described to me by J. as being done for one of the family heads of Umuɛkɛ-owɛrɛ who died while I was away from the village. I asked him who had been chosen to do it. He named a notorious character who had some years previously been chased from the village for his misdeeds. He had a reputation for making bad medicine or magic, and for going after other men's wives. He had recently been allowed to return, as is the way in this society when time has softened people's memories. There was no doubt that he had a gift for being on the spot. Whatever was going on he would be sure to turn up and put his oar in, particularly if anything was being shared. J. laughed when he spoke of him and said he had seen him chosen three times to perform this ceremony.

In this densely populated country where the land is over-farmed and it is hard work to get a living, it is perhaps not surprising that there is an almost hypertrophied sense of property. Theft is execrated as one of the worst and most shameful of offences, and is considered as deserving extreme penalties.

Money, the economic symbol, bulks large in the minds of these people, inveterate traders as they are, with a skill in market transactions that amounts almost to genius. There is a song of which the burden is that children are better than money. On the other hand, the women sing of their husbands as being money-makers and of me they would sing as the white woman whose father is a money-maker. But stinginess or meanness is not admired. N. Ɛ. was thought to be rather near, to have a tight hand, and this was not spoken of with approval. On the contrary, anyone visiting a person's yam store must be given a yam. This act of generosity will please the yam spirit. Anyone dropping in when people are eating will always be offered food and a visitor at other times will be entertained with palm wine— *mmae* [¯ ¯ ¯]—and kola—*ɔje* [¯ ¯].

On two occasions a lad, the younger brother of the village priest, who worked in my compound, talked a little about the things a father would tell his son. He would correct him, by the time he could understand, if he saw him doing anything foolish, and he would give him good advice as to how to make and keep money. He would tell him to work hard and would explain to him that stealing is a bad thing. Property, money, honesty are constantly recurring motifs.

Together with emphasis on loyalty between kinsmen, they are prominent in the only long statement I collected about the qualities or subjects that would be stressed in the upbringing of children. I asked Nwa Onyɛ Okoro, the head of Umu Nwa Ɛbodim kindred, one day, how a child would be brought up and how people would want him to turn out. He replied that anyone who is born has to be trained : he himself, when he sees his own son growing up and climbing palm tree and getting sense, will show him his lands and all his properties : and he and the boy's mother will tell him who are the people and the in-laws that they go to visit and are on good terms with. They will also tell him the people they avoid and with whom they are not on good terms. I asked what sort of a person they would want their boy to grow up into. He answered that if they saw the boy ready to give palm wine to the people his parents had shown him as being their friends, he would be pleased. If he saw his son going to these people he would like it. If the boy was obedient to his parents and pleased them, then the father, when he was sharing something among his family, would put a piece apart secretly and give it to him afterwards, as to his favourite. If he wanted to give him a present, whether he was old or young, he would give him a big one : but if he was disobedient and displeased his father he would only give him a small present however old the boy might be.

I asked what would be the sort of man that people here would respect. He said that if a big man like Nwa Ɛbodim[1] reincarnates, and if his reincarnation has sense and can go to market and trade and farm and cut palm nuts and has land and is able to marry a wife and gets children and money, people will respect him. If he just sits quiet and people see that he has little land and no wife, and that he does nothing to get money, people will not respect him. But if he helps his kinsfolk and has money so that when they are in trouble he can bring it out to help them, people will respect him and will give him a big portion when they are sharing anything. But if a big man reincarnates and his reincarnation has no sense, people will not respect him.

When I asked Nwa Onyɛ Okoro how a boy would learn

---

[1] A famous ancestor.

what things are against the laws or taboos of his place he
replied that in his son's presence he would say that he himself
does not steal : nor does he speak any word that would
" lose " his brother. If he feels such a word coming into
his mouth he will clap his hand over his mouth—he suited
the action to the word—to prevent its coming out. " Losing "
one's brother means things of this sort, he explained : if
one's brother owes money and one sees that he has plenty,
and if one goes to his creditor and tells him : " See, my
brother has money now—why don't you claim your debts ? "
and if in the meantime the brother has spent the money on
something else, he is lost by the word one has spoken.
Further, if one's brother is marrying a wife, one must not
go to the woman's family and tell them that one's brother
has no money.

A girl who is considered to make a good wife is one who
is not shy of work, who will go for water and firewood,
who will cook and go to market. C.M.'s wife, asked what
qualities a man would want in a wife, said that she should
have a good heart—*obi ɔma* [¯ _ ¯ ¯]—that she should not
steal, that she should help her husband well in work, go
to market, finish quickly whatever she is doing, be strong
and not picksome about what she will do and not do. One
of the younger men explained that a man would ask his future
mother-in-law whether the girl he has in view as a wife
steals, and would explain to her that it is a law of his place
that a married woman found stealing will be fined by the
other wives in the village. A woman must not be extravagant
with food. In Umuɛkɛ, where food is not plentiful and
yam particularly is a luxury, a woman must be sparing in
her use of the latter. My staff, from Owerri or near-by,
noted with interest points of difference in food habits when
we first arrived. They told me that in Umuɛkɛ a woman
who made fufu—*ɵtara* [¯ _ _]—of yam alone would be
thought bad because thus she would use up the yams too
quickly. She must mix cassava—*ji apɵ* [¯ ¯ ¯]—and coco-
yam—*ɛdɛ* [¯ _]—with it. This, said a woman from Ɛgbu,
Owerri, would only be done in their country in the famine
time before new yams are cut. In Owerri, said S., it is forbidden to pound cassava or coco-yam with yam. In these
parts food is, of course, more plentiful than in Agbaja,
there being less pressure on land ; but all the same a thrifty,

careful woman—*nwanye okε akpere* [⁻ _ _ ⁻ ⁻ ⁻ _ ⁻]—is admired in Owerri, according to S.

Women tend to be associated with a pacific rôle in this society. Speaking one day, for instance, of the kind of people he thought suitable to judge a case, Nwa Onyε Okoro said that among others it would be good to have one or two women who knew their own minds and who could help to make peace in the case. It was also said that in a case between two brothers, women born in the village and married elsewhere might be summoned to try the case and to put peace between the parties to it.

One was told, also, that if two villages fight, the women may try to stop the fighting, and one would hear incidental remarks such as those of the bystanders after the death of J.'s sister, a girl just growing up. Some of them were praising her and saying that she did not quarrel, that she always saluted people, and so on. One is struck also by the quietly resigned bearing of some of the women in situations of distress.

Any discussion of education or of ethics in this society would have to take account of the theories of moral cause and effect and of motivation that are current among the people. Here, where we are attempting only brief indications, it is enough to say that there are echoes from Erewhon in that sickness tends to be regarded as the result of neglected duties to ancestors or departed kinsmen, and therefore implicity if not explicity to have a moral aspect. On the other hand, bad temper or wicked behaviour may be regarded in that particular individual as a result of his reincarnation. If the man who has come back in him, for instance, killed many people in his former existence their blood may trouble him in his present existence if certain ceremonies were not done in the former one.

The son of N.ε. who fought with him was a case of this sort. The ancestor reincarnated in him had killed many people and when he died a fowl ought to have been killed for his eyes—*ewa anya* [⁻ ⁻ ⁻ ⁻]. Neglect of this ceremony is believed to make the man mad when he is reincarnated. In this case it was not done because the man died of elephantiasis of the scrotum. It is custom that when someone has died of this disease his fellow villagers should flee from the village every night until the corpse is buried, and indeed one saw it happen in the case of a man in the village next door. Nwa Okwɛ's ancestor was hastily buried by a few kinsmen and no cock was killed for his eyes. His reincarnation was consequently a turbulent and troublesome youth. It was said that it would be possible to get a *dibea* to make medicine for him and to put it in his eyes to cool his blood. But this, of course, involved spending money.

In various ways the deeds of a man and particularly his evil deeds are believed to affect his reincarnations. People will go to a *dibea* to know what is troubling a child and may be told that it is *ihɛ ewa* [¯ ¯ _ _]—a matter of a former existence.

Erratic behaviour may also be thought to be due to Agwe Nshi—the spirit associated with divining and magic— troubling a person. The remedy for this is to become a *dibea*, and thus a servitor of Agwe Nshi. But this involves considerable expense for training and initiation. N.Ɛ. told us of another of his sons that we must not heed him when he was tiresome as it was Agwe Nshi troubling him. If he had money, he said, he would do the Agwe custom.

These points are enough to indicate that the beliefs as to motivation and moral responsibility among these people need careful study. It would be particularly interesting to examine the part played by reincarnation beliefs in various aspects of their social life, but it cannot be attempted here.

THE AVOIDANCE OF TROUBLE

When one is seeking to discover how a society preserves itself from disruption and achieves a *modus vivendi* it is important to consider not only how it deals with situations which threaten its order or its existence but also how it prevents such situations from arising. Its survival depends on a balance between its institutions and the challenge they have to meet from the circumstances of daily life. It is therefore important to consider both sides of the equation.

An example of prevention may be seen in the Ibo convention that the knives of those engaged in verbal dispute or of the bystanders should be taken away from them. This may seem a small matter, but in a community where every man, woman or child is apt to walk about with a knife about two feet long, where tongues are voluble, tempers excitable and reactions quick, it is no small thing to have lethal weapons out of reach until matters have calmed down. With no organised police force and no strong public authority in indigenous society it is important that brawls should be kept within bounds as far as possible. An analogous attempt to forestall breaches of the peace may be seen in the branding of false accusation as a serious offence. Even a hinted slight upon a person's reputation may be penalised. A case is described later[1] where a woman missed one of her fowls and shortly afterwards smelt a fowl cooking in the pot of another woman in her house-group. She went, it was said, and sniffed the pot and said that she wondered where the fowl had come from, whereupon the other woman cried out that her good name had been tarnished and her accuser was tried and fined for false accusation.

The institutional device which meets this situation is the consulting of a *dibea* to find out who is guilty when an offence has been committed. A *dibea* cannot be formally charged with false accusation. Justice can thus go forward but the clash and bitterness of a direct accusation is to some extent mitigated. I was talking one day to a sophisticated Ibo from Onitsha, who held a high place in one of the missions, and he condemned this accusation through a *dibea* as a cowardly shelving of responsibility. Whether or not this is so one cannot I think doubt that it has its social function.

We have already referred to the fact that in some cases erratic or anti-social behaviour is held to be the result of some circumstance in a former existence rather than the direct fault of the individual concerned. Or it may be referred to the action of a supernatural being such as Agwe Nshi. This impersonal view of cause and effect in such matters may do something to mitigate the consequences of provocative behaviour. This would need detailed observation. My impression is that a tiresome individual is sometimes tolerated to a degree which would be unusual among many Europeans.

In the village sharing arrangements, which are considered a matter of great importance, self-knowledge has dictated a conscious avoidance of trouble. When certain things such as food and drink at a funeral ceremony are to be shared

---

1 See p. 199.

among all the males of taxable age, the things are divided into four and the men and boys are divided into four sharing groups—ɔtɵ okɛ [_ ⁻ _ _]—but it was explained that these sharing groups are not based on the division—nce—of the village, such, for instance, as Umuɛkɛ-ama. If they were there would be disputing about the shares, each division saying that its share was too small, but no Umuɛkɛ-ama man would want to quarrel for the sake of a man from Umuɛkɛ-owɛrɛ who might be his co-sharer. By mixing them, therefore, disputes are avoided.

Perhaps one of the most interesting ways in which social disruption is avoided is in the beliefs current in this society about the causes of death and disaster. Evans–Pritchard has described how, among the Azande of Central Africa, witchcraft is a common explanation of untoward happenings,[1] and accusations of witchcraft are a frequent occurrence. He also explains, and this is of interest in our present connection, that witchcraft is believed to operate more effectively at close range than at a distance, and that people therefore tend, for precautionary reasons, to live in scattered hamlets rather than in close settlements. This is presumably made possible by a relatively sparse population. A further point of interest is that in cases of death, accusations of witchcraft must be referred to the prince's oracle ;[2] in other words, a centre or centres of authority exist among these people and can be invoked when situations fraught with peril to the society arise.[3]

If one turns now to the Ibo situation one sees that the density of the population makes it impossible for people to live far away from each other. A belief, therefore, in the danger of living near witchcraft would be extraordinarily inconvenient ; but more inconvenient and more dangerous to social stability would be a general tendency to witch hunting in a community where the exercise of authority is, politically speaking, hardly yet institutionalised and in any case tends to be dispersed rather than concentrated. The fact that witchcraft beliefs appear to be absent in Agbaja and, so far as I saw, among a considerable number of the inland Ibo, whereas belief in black magic is widespread and strong,

[1] E. E. Evans–Pritchard : *Witchcraft, Oracles and Magic*. Clarendon Press, 1937, p. 63.   [2] Evans–Pritchard, *op. cit.,* p. 33.

[3] See also *re* Nupe—Nadel : *A Black Byzantium,* p. 142.

may possibly be due in some measure to psychological factors.[1] The point that is relevant here is that though people constantly talk of black magic being made and of their fear of it, the attribution of any particular case of death or sickness to this cause is, so far as I have seen, rare. A *dibea* must of course be consulted in every case of death, to learn the reason of it, and the cause of sickness can only be discovered in the same way. In one instance after another an offended ancestor or a deceased kinsman or the sufferer himself will be cited as the cause of the death or sickness in question. The consequent steps to be taken are of the nature of a ritual propitiation of the spirit involved. They do not entail vengeance against a living individual : in fact they are of a pacific nature and do not start up a feud which, among a densely populated, volatile people with little authoritative organisation, might quickly grow to deadly proportions. One has only to see how excitement flares up and spreads in the case even of a small incident to realise how vital it is that such occasions should be eliminated as far as possible. In pursuing a policy of ancestor propitiation instead of one of witch hunting these inland Ibo avoid a menace to their social stability and economise in the lives of their individual members. This same economy is seen in their method of appeal to the supernatural in the testing of innocence. Whereas some of the neighbouring tribes have recourse to a poison ordeal the Ibo people are content with taking an oath. No doubt they believe that to swear falsely is as dangerous as to swallow poison, but, objectively, the former is probably less likely to deplete the population even when the possibility of manipulating the poison ordeal is taken into account.

It would seem that in the Ibo situation this social factor, which one might perhaps call the factor of avoiding unnecessary trouble, is of considerable importance. The survival of a society depends largely upon a balance between its organisation and the stresses and strains that organisation has to contend with. Among these stresses it may be that beliefs as to the cause of death and disaster are more important than we have always realised, and the way in which they are correlated with the institutions and the temperament of a

1 See p. 250.

people may be an important element in the survival of that people. The nature of a people's beliefs as to the causes of its misfortunes will dictate the nature of its reactions to these untoward circumstances. Such beliefs are therefore one of the nodal points in the life of a community. It is of no small moment, for instance, that Nazi Germany selected the Jewish people as the source of its ills.

RECIPROCITY

Malinowski has stressed[1] the importance of reciprocity in the maintenance of law and custom, particularly in the sphere of civil law. Obligations, he says, tend to be mutual and therefore to be fulfilled for that reason rather than for fear of penalties for default. Certainly in Ibo society the element of reciprocity is ubiquitous. One might almost say that it is the network upon which society hangs and that the holes in the net are filled in with discussions about these reciprocal obligations.

When we discuss the question of exogamy we shall see[2] what a multiplicity of ties bind the villages together by reason of their enforced intermarriage. One or two examples will be enough to show the element of mutuality that is all the time exerting pressure towards the fulfilment of obligations as between members of different villages.

At the birth of a child certain gifts and payments must be exchanged between the husband's people and those of the wife. When N.Ɛ.'s daughter-in-law had a baby, he explained to us that shortly after the event her relatives from her native village came to him to demand money. He then plunged into a balancing of accounts over a period of years, explaining that when the first child, a daughter, was born the mother's relations ought to have brought a cock and a basket of yams and part of the fee for the *dibea* who has to be consulted about a newly-born baby's name and identity. They did not bring these things and he himself paid the *dibea*. At the same time he himself was supposed to make a customary payment of £1 to these relatives of the baby's mother : in fact he paid 15s. When the second child was born he paid 5s., and again had to pay the *dibea*. On the

---

1 Malinowski : *Crime and Custom in Savage Society.*
2 See Ch. XIII.

third occasion, the one in question, he once more had to pay the *dibea*. The woman's " father " went with him, but paid nothing. Her people were now clamouring for a further 5*s*. He had paid them 2*s*., but had said that he would give no more, as they had not done their part. Nothing could have been clearer than his recognition of the reciprocity of the whole situation.

In marriage, again, the same reciprocal element is strongly marked. The parents of the girls are supposed to give her a number of things, and particularly yam and coco-yam for planting, before she goes to her husband. The amount they give her will depend on how fully the fiancé pays the agreed bride price. In passing it may be stressed that in this as in other preliterate communities an important part is played by witnesses in the legalisation of such contracts as the payment of bride price, or the pledging of land. In the absence of written documents it is the living witness who in many cases provides evidence of a legal reciprocal situation.

It is perhaps at the death of a woman that one of the most dramatic examples of the lever of mutuality can be observed. Having to marry outside her own village and live in that of her husband a woman normally dies away from her own kinsfolk. It is they who have to come to fetch her for burial in or near her native place, but before this is done her children must give them certain customary payments of food and money. Until they are satisfied that they have received their due they will not remove the corpse. On one occasion people set out to fetch for burial a woman born in Umueke and returned empty handed because the requisite payments had not been made. Negotiations continued over a considerable number of days but were at last completed to the satisfaction of the woman's kinsfolk. The argument of a corpse, left day after day unburied in a tropical climate, is apt to be a convincing one.

Within the village, too, reciprocity is constantly operative in turning the wheel of economic and social life. In the basic occupation of farming a father portions out land to his sons for the season and they in return work for him. Even when they are married they should work for him on every Orie day, that is to say on one day in four.

As between husbands and wives, the husband must show his wives land for their crops, and they in return feed him.

One saw, in N. &'s case, how this balance worked. To some
of his wives he no longer gave land for their crops and they
therefore no longer fed him. On one occasion my girl S. saw
one of them cooking and asked if it was for her husband. In
reply she said would she give it to someone who did not
give to her? On another occasion, a woman complained
to me that her younger sons did not help her with her farm
work, to which one of them chaffingly retorted: " How
many wives have you married for me ? " Whether in joke
or in earnest this thinking and speaking in terms of mutual
obligations recurs again and again. It is not only a factor
of widespread implications in this community but it is
one of which people are constantly aware.

Chapter VIII. The Law in Breach (I)

We have seen that there are many reasons why, on the whole, the rules of the group are kept, but there are none the less occasions, as in any other society, when they are broken. When we enquire how such breaches are dealt with we find that there are certain rules the breaking of which will or may call forth action, ultimately backed by force, on the part of, or endorsed by, the community. These rules may therefore for practical purposes be regarded as laws, and may be distinguished as such from other customary rules.[1] Judicial methods may at times appear informal, but they follow recognised if diverse lines. This distinction between law and custom would certainly seem to correspond to a distinction of principle among the Ibo themselves. Talking one day of the return a man would make to a neighbour in whose yam barn he stored his yams, A. explained that at harvest time he might give some yams to the owner of the barn, and he added : " *ɔ wa omɛnala, ɔ weghe iwu* "—" it is custom, not law." On another occasion he explained that in his own village-group of Mbiɛri a man who has leased land, but not for money, will give the owner some yams at harvest time though it is not a legal obligation, and the more yams he gives the more kudos, apparently, he will get. People will say that he has " *aka ikɛ* " [⁻ ⁻ ⁻ ⁻]—" strong hand."

Offences which are *Nsɔ*

Legal rules are of two main classes and are recognised as such. There are those which might be called ordinary human laws and those whose breach is held to be not only illegal

---

[1] See Meek : *Law and Authority in a Nigerian Tribe,* Introduction, p. xiv, for a discussion of the distinction between law and other kinds of social rules and of the attitude of Malinowski, Radcliffe-Brown and others to this problem. I follow Meek in distinguishing law from other socially sanctioned rules and also in his qualifying statement that " legal " cannot always be fully equated with " authoritative " when applied to means of regulating social relations.

but also an offence against a supernatural power and particularly against Ala, the land. Of the perpetrator of such an offence it would be said : "*o mɛrɘrɘ ala*"—"he polluted the

land." Such offences are usually said to be *nsɔ* [⁻ ⁻]—taboo—and are distinguished from merely natural offences. In many cases they involve a propitiatory rite for Ala in addition to the punishment of the offender. The fact that they are penally sanctioned distinguishes them from offences which involve a purely automatic sanction such as the illness of a child in consequence of its mother conceiving again before the existing child is weaned. Of such penally sanctioned supernatural offences the one which seems to bulk perhaps largest in people's minds is incest. I asked James one day what were the things that offended Ala, and he at once began with the offence of a man and woman born in the same village—*otu nga* [⁻ ⁻ _ _]¹—having sexual intercourse. They would *mɛrɘ ala*—pollute the earth. Stealing is different : it is against the law, but it does not *mɛrɘ ala*. The offenders would in the old days be buried alive at Oriɛ Ekpa, the centre of Agbaja. No further propitiatory rite would in this case be necessary. As they are buried in the earth, it is as though Ala takes them to purify herself—*epɘ ala* [⁻ ⁻ _ _].

So strong is the feeling against incest that another man told me that nowadays when the old penalty cannot be carried out, if people knew of a case occurring they would go out at night and kill the man and put his body under a palm tree. The British authorities would then think he had fallen and killed himself while climbing for palm nuts. So far as actual occurrences of this offence are concerned, I only heard of one suspected case between a man born in the next door village of Abɔse and a woman born there and now married in Umuɛkɛ, but the man had sworn his innocence. In any case, the two came from different halves of the village which at one time had been allowed to intermarry. It would seem that in this rural community this offence is rare, and the feeling about it is strong. I gathered the impression that in more sophisticated Owerri it was not so rare, nor so strongly condemned. The strength of the feeling in Agbaja was interesting in view of the important

---

¹ Lit. : one place. This is an example of the impossibility of understanding the Ibo terminology of social groups except in its context.

part which the system of exogamy plays in the general cohesion of Ibo society.[1]

Among other offences against Ala given by James was the case of a man and woman having sexual intercourse after the birth of a child and before the woman has menstruated again. If the women were to conceive and bear a child she and her husband would be sent to bush alone to an ant-hill where she would deliver the child. Afterwards the child would, in the old days, be thrown away and the parents would be buried alive.

It would also have been an offence against Ala in the old days if an Agbaja man, in payment of a debt for instance, seized the son of another Agbaja man and sold him. He would be hanged in Orie Ekpa. In view of the fact that Agbaja and Umukabia are said to be one in the sense of having one *umune* and being therefore of common descent, I asked whether prohibition would apply between the two village-groups. James hesitated. Then he said that Agbaja and Umukabia are one and it would apply, and the Umukabia man would be hanged in his home market place. But he had not volunteered it, and on the whole one did not get the impression that the professed links between the village groups had very strong practical repercussions in matters of this kind.

Asked whether an offence against Ala would bring harm on the whole village, James said that people would die or fall ill in such a case, and that in such circumstances the elder women would take money and go to a *dibea* and ask what was causing the sickness. He would ask them if they knew whether anyone had offended Ala. If they did not know, he would tell them that Ala was angry and would tell them what sacrifices must be made. If the elder women did not go to consult a *dibea* the elder men would go, he said : but one notices here again the recurrent notion that the women are to some extent the watchdogs of the community, the people who try to restore equilibrium when anti-social behaviour is on the increase.[2]

I did not see any case of people consulting a *dibea* in the circumstances described above : but if James's account is correct the commission of an offence which is *nsɔ*—forbidden—would seem to involve the whole community and

---

1 See Part II.   2 See p. 230.

not merely the individuals concerned. The individuals who take action do so on the part of the community. If there is any point in trying to apply the categories of criminal and civil law to Ibo judicial matters, then presumably offences against Ala and probably other such *nsɔ* behaviour might be classified as criminal cases.

OFFENCES AGAINST HUMAN LAWS

If we turn now to offences such as theft or false accusation which are breaches of the law without having a supernatural reference, we find that it would be said of an offender of this kind : " *ɔ dara iwu* " [¯ _ _ _ ¯]—" he broke the law." Or one might say : *o mɛrɛ iwu ala* [¯ _ _ _ ¯ _ _]—he broke a law of the place—which is quite a different thing from saying : *o mɛrɘrɘ ala* [¯ _ _ _ _ _]—he polluted the land—One also hears : *onyɛ mɛrɛ ihɛ iwu* [¯ ¯ ¯ ¯ ¯ ¯ ¯ ¯]—one who broke the law. An offence against the law is distinguished from an action of which people may strongly disapprove but which is none the less within the bounds of legality. In the heat of the moment people will talk as though a breach of the law has occurred, but others, whose personal interests have not suffered, will point out that no such breach has in fact taken place.

Iwu [_ ¯] seems almost to have the meaning not only of law but of penalty. As an example of the first one may give a sentence which occurred in a description A. gave me of a woman of his own village-group who broke the law forbidding a wife to lurk outside the house where her husband is sleeping with a co-wife.

Iwu wɘ nwanye ɛcɛla di ya nɛɛ mgbɛ di ya na nwanye ibɛ ya labara nimɛ ihɛ—The law is that a woman must not await her husband when her husband and another wife are sleeping in the room.

An example of the second meaning is the expression *iri iwu* [¯ ¯ _ _]—to receive a fine from someone who has broken the law. *Ha ga-ɛri ya iwu* [¯ _ _ ¯ ¯ _ ¯]—they will receive a fine from him.

OFFENDER KNOWN OR SUSPECTED

We shall not try to give a complete account of Ibo judicial

methods, but we shall indicate some of the possible courses of action open to anyone against whom a breach of the law has been committed. This will be relevant to our enquiry into the location of authority in the village.

When the law has been broken and the culprit is known or suspected, the injured party or parties have a number of possible courses open to them. There is no specific judicial body to whom they must, of necessity, refer their case, and their method of initiating judicial proceedings will depend to some extent on the particular individuals or group they choose.

One must be prepared for what, to European eyes, may seem a high degree of informality, but to withhold from such informal or apparently informal methods the term judicial would be to fail to recognise an undeniably judicial function in an unfamiliar form. This indeed has happened in some cases where questions rather than observation have been employed. It is essential in this matter, as Dr. Wagner says,[1] to consider functions rather than institutions. Judicial work is certainly performed, but differentiated judicial institutions can hardly be said yet to have emerged. As Wilson shows, it is important in defining judicial or legal action to exclude none of its simpler forms. He says that " it may be defined as any customary action on the part of some member or members of a social group, one or more of whom are not themselves directly and personally concerned in this issue, to prevent breaches in the pattern of social conformity, to ensure the recurrence of human actions in the customary form which obtains in that particular social group."[2] This definition is broad enough to cover the many possibilities open to an injured party who seeks to obtain justice in an Ibo community. Nowadays, of course, in addition to these indigenous methods, he can, if he likes, avail himself of the local Native Court set up by the British authority. In this case the Court was about five miles away,[3] and administered justice for eight or nine village-groups in addition to Agbaja, each of whom sent representatives to act as judges. In the case of Agbaja the British authorities,

1 Wagner : " Bantu of Kavirondo " in *African Political Systems,* edited by Fortes and Evans-Pritchard, p. 201.

2 Wilson : " Introduction to Nyakyusa Law." *Africa,* x, p. 25.

3 Recently set up to replace former Warrant Chief's Court.

after trying to discover who were the " natural rulers," had decided that the holder of the big ɔfɔ from each village should be the Court Member. It will be remembered that in Umuɛkɛ the big ɔfɔ-holder had refused this honour and that another man had grasped it. The Native Court administers indigenous law and custom in so far as they are not repugnant to " natural justice," and has power within its own sphere of competence to enforce its decisions which, in certain circumstances, are subject to review by, or appeal to, a British official.

The Court was there : but in point of fact the people of Umuɛkɛ did not use it. In all the time that I was in the village I only heard of one case taken to it. Now and then people from neighbouring places would come with stories of their court cases, their grievances, the bribes they had to produce and so on, but Umuɛkɛ managed its cases at home and in its own way.

Shortly after I arrived in the village I fell in with the Court Member of the next door Agbaja village of Umuɔbea a forthright and friendly person whom I also knew in his capacity as local midwife. On this occasion he had just returned from court. In reply to my polite hope that things were going well with him he said, with some annoyance, that his fellow Court Members complained that the people of Agbaja did not go to court and that in consequence the Agbaja Court Members would only receive a small share of the total incoming bribes.

Much later in my stay I found that this abstention from the court was at least in part a conscious and, so to speak, official policy on the part of the village. When the case of the sacred spear[1] was at its height one of the youths of the side that was faring worst said to me that it would be better if people would take cases to court and get them settled peacefully, but the elders, he said, had told the young people they would kill anyone who took a case to court.

If the Native Court was not used it none the less had repercussions to some extent on village judicial matters. The very fact of its existence and that recourse to it was always a theoretical possibility must to some extent have modified the existing situation in ways not easy to assess.

---

[1] See infra p. 107-8.

In one definite point modification could be observed. Cases which looked as though they might ultimately go to court tended to be taken first to the Court Member of the village. The member for Umuɔbea, to whom reference has just been made, explained that both he and his colleague in Umuɛkɛ judged cases at home, that is to say in their villages, and he added that the District Officer had told them that if they could not keep peace between the parties they should take the case to Elɛndǝ of Umuɔfa Agbaja, " as he is the head of the Agbaja chiefs " (i.e. Court Members). It may be said that the attribution of headship in this sense to Elɛndǝ. the holder of the big ɔfɔ of Agbaja, was British rather than indigenous. The remark suggests that the British authorities were understood to favour the settling of cases out of court by the Court Member concerned. There had thus grown up a certain tendency, not universally followed, to take disputes in Umuɛkɛ to the Court Member in his own home, but it is difficult to be sure here how far new and how far indigenous factors were concerned. Early in my stay I heard that he would try cases for a fee of 5s., as would also Elɛndǝ of the senior village of Agbaja, to whom people would also very occasionally go, particularly if they had on a previous occasion found the village Court Member unable to keep peace between the litigants. If there was a chance that the case might ultimately have to go to court people would feel it necessary first to bring it to their own Court Member, otherwise, as it was pointed out, when the case came to the court he would say he knew nothing about it and thus block it.

A case of this kind, which I was told about but did not witness, happened shortly after our arrival in the village— a fight in which blood was drawn and a tooth knocked out and a court case seemed possible. It was therefore taken to the Court Member who, it was said, had other elders sitting with him. In such circumstances, the desire to avoid going to court will probably incline the litigants to abide by the decision of their arbitrators.

On two other occasions when I knew that cases were taken in their early stages to the Court Member it happened that one or both of the litigants were members of his extended family. They might thus have gone anyway, and it was difficult to tell whether an old or a new precedent was being followed. But in spite of this difficulty in analysing the facts with precision I am inclined to think that it was village custom that an injured party should in the first instance call in a few individuals who might serve either as go-betweens or, perhaps, as judges. Since it would be important to get effective individuals this custom might well be extended to include the Court Member when such a functionary came upon the scene. In the same way he had been co-opted by the elders—the *nde ama ala*—and took part, among other things, in the judicial doings which were a part of their activities. In quite other matters—the offering of a sacrifice, for instance—he was sometimes invited to be present though not immediately concerned. On one occasion when I asked why he was there I was told that he " held a piece of paper " —the British warrant for the Native Court—and it was therefore considered good policy to include him.

When therefore one is describing the possible courses open to an injured party it is probably correct to say that one of the normal methods is to call in a few individuals as arbitrators, in the first instance. One certainly found it happening, sometimes the Court Member being included and sometimes not. If the small group could settle things to the satisfaction of both parties to the dispute there was no need to take matters further. A penalty would be imposed on the guilty party and if he was prepared to abide by it the thing was settled. The group settling the matter was not in any sense a specific judicial institution but it had none the less exercised a judicial function.[1]

If the small body of chosen arbitrators could not find a solution acceptable to both parties, and they had of course no means of enforcing their decision, the litigant who felt that he could not abide by their verdict would take further steps. It was open to him to beat a drum through the village announcing that he had a grievance. The elders would then go in the course of the next few days and arrange for the whole village to come to judge the case. An example of this will be described later.[2] The dissentient party might, on the other hand, go to the elders and tell them that he had

_____
[1] This method might be employed not only by fellow villagers but by those who came from different villages or village-groups. See p. 141, where each side summoned arbitrators from his own place.
[2] See infra p. 117.

a case to be tried and they would then appoint a day for the judging. This was perhaps the method most generally talked about as a judicial expedient, and it was certainly employed. It would, however, be forcing the facts to represent the elders as the judicial authority of the village. They were one among other means of seeking justice, and even when they were invoked the actual trial would not necessarily see them all present nor would other people be excluded. " A case forbids no one," say the Ibo, and on the day of trial anyone turns up who is interested or whom the litigants have specially summoned, and anyone who can gain a hearing may participate in the proceedings.[1]

Another judicial possibility of considerable interest did not come to my notice until my second tour visit to the village. I did not witness it myself but was told about it on a number of occasions in considerable detail by James, my *dibea* friend, and by his wife. It was from him that I had learned about the organisation of *dibea* meetings by which members of the profession were in touch over a considerable area. One day his wife told me that he, together with the other *nde dibea* of Agbaja, had been summoned by one of their number in the next door Agbaja village to try a case. Later, James, her husband, told me about it. It was the brother of a *dibea* who had asked them to take proceedings against a runaway wife's family for the recovery of bride price and they had done so. He said that the man would have to pay them far less than he would have had to disburse in bribes to the Native Court. Shortly after this case James came to see me in a state of high excitement. He said that another man had asked the *dibea* people to judge a similar bride price case for them and that they had gone two days before to the village of the wife's people about the matter. There, the official Court Member had seized the *nde dibea* and taken them to his house and had objected angrily to their trying cases because, as he said, it prevented people from taking

---

[1] This universal right to take part in a trial was rumoured to have been something of an embarrassment to the British authorities when in some places they had appealed to the village-groups to send to the Native Court the people who by indigenous custom had a right to take part in judicial proceedings. It was said that they had found it necessary after a time to stipulate that for practical reasons not more than fifty per cent. of the population should come to court to take part in the trial of cases.

their cases to court and therefore he was cheated of bribes he would otherwise have had. He then sent people from his house to fetch Court Messengers—a kind of policemen authorised by the British—who would, he said, deal with the *nde dibea*. What steps they would in fact have taken one does not know, as the people sent to fetch them were overcome with fear lest the *nde dibea* should kill them by magical means, so they turned back half-way. Thereupon the irate Court Member set out himself, but also thought better of it and returned and released the prisoners, saying he would later send Court Messengers and police to seize them. The *nde dibea* had at once had two meetings and had planned a third for the day after on which they were going to choose sixteen of their number, one from each village-group, to go by night and put " medicine " in the Court Member's yard which would kill him. He would not see it and would not know they had been, said James, demonstrating with evident relish how the " medicine " would be placed.

When I enquired sometime after how things were going I was told that the Court Member had " begged " the *nde dibea* and they had had mercy on him—a good piece of bluff on each side in fact. The whole episode suggests, I think, that this trying of cases for terms which undercut the Native Court is probably a new feature. It shows what flexibility is possible in Ibo institutions and again is an example of judicial functions performed by people whose primary institutional purpose is different. One sees, too, how any permanent organisation like that of the *dibea* people tends to increase its power and extend its functions, particularly if it also possesses magico-religious prestige.

A further method of dealing with a dispute was employed not long before I left the village by an Umuɛkɛ man in a land dispute with the son of his eldest brother. After trying the mediation of various third parties and getting no satisfaction, he invoked the sacred spear of the important yam spirit, whose cult involved the whole of Agbaja but had its local habitation and its officiants in the Agbaja village of Abɔse, near to Umuɛkɛ. This meant that the second village, led by the *osu* of the yam cult, became involved in trying the case, with, eventually, interesting and dramatic consequences. In taking the drastic step of going outside his own village and of invoking a supernatural power the man of Umuɛkɛ,

A-ziɛ, was no doubt influenced by the fact that the dispute in question was the latest incident in a long standing state of friction. Moreover he was unpopular in his own village and had, shortly before this, been strongly ·condemned and fined by the village in another connection.[1] He therefore had his reasons for not wishing to submit his case to purely village jurisdiction.

Invoking the sacred spear of the yam cult meant that the spear was brought and placed outside the house of his opponent's mother, since the youth had as yet no house of his own. When these people found the spear outside the house they and the youth's father and his elder brother were roused to fear and anger and declared that a monstrous thing had been done, and that putting the spear was equivalent to putting *nshi*—black magic or poison—for them. The putting of *nshi* is, of course, highly illicit in an Ibo community and an Umuɛkɛ man of a different kindred explained that the spear was not *nshi* except in the sense that its presence was very dangerous. The putting of it was, he said, a correct judicial procedure and he quoted precedents for it. Later in the case precedents were in fact invoked and it was clear that the method was a regular, if not a very frequent one.

It may be noted, in passing, that there was a constant tendency in any dispute for the injured party to say that what had been done to him was illicit and for the aggressor to protest that he was acting according to good custom or law. This is one of the reasons why it is often difficult, not in principle but in any particular case, to draw the line between good and bad magic. The magic one makes oneself is practically always good : the magic made against one is almost invariably bad—in one's own opinion.

This is not the place to go into the details of the yam spear case, interesting as they were : but it was necessary to note this method of taking judicial action.

It must also be noted that as the yam cult, located in the village of Abɔse Agbaja, belonged to the whole village-group of Agbaja, there were repercussions from this case beyond the two villages concerned. The situation was complicated by the fact that the case occurred when the time for doing

---

[1] See p. 111.

the annual new yam ceremonies was nearly due, and these ceremonies had to be initiated by Abɔse and could not be done so long as the sacred spear was absent. When, therefore, the case dragged on between Abɔse and Umuɛkɛ, both of which were villages of the *owɛrɛ* half of Agbaja, the rest of Agbaja-owɛrɛ joined in the proceedings to urge a settlement. When this was still delayed the rumour went round that the *ama* half of Agbaja would intervene and would confiscate property from Umuɛkɛ. It was said that on a certain Oriɛ Ekpa day this would be decided. The day came and went without any apparent move and Abɔse then resorted to violence. As there chanced to be a white woman in the village her help was sought and there was no alternative but to put the matter in the hands of the British-controlled police in order to prevent a fight between Abɔse and Umuɛkɛ. The course of indigenous justice was thus fortuitously interrupted, but it was interesting that a case between two brothers potentially involved the whole village-group because of the judicial methods chosen.

Kinship gatherings, such, for instance, as those connected with a second burial, could be used as an opportunity for getting a case discussed or dealt with. On one occasion the men of the village had gone to the house of one of their number whose kinswoman, married in another place, had died. Her children had made the customary payments to the people of her native place, and they, the people of Umuɛkɛ, had met together to share five shillings which had been sent. I was not present but I was told that while they were there one of the men of Umuɛkɛ said that people had been breaking the law made earlier that year in the village, by which no one was to cut palm nuts except on his own land. The assembled people asked him if he could name the delinquents. He said he could. They then asked if anyone would come forward and admit to the crime. No one answered. The accuser therefore named a youth, P., of the family at whose house they were and said he had caught him cutting palm nuts on his land. The elders asked the youth if this was true and he did not deny it, but remained silent. Those present then mocked and hooted at him in the traditional manner of shaming a thief, and then demanded that he should pay a fine of 1*s*. 8*d*. He said he had not got the money, whereupon the crowd promptly seized two of his fowls.

This had the effect of making him produce the amount demanded, which was shared among those present. There was no doubt of his guilt. It was proclaimed to those present and the sentence was swiftly given and summarily executed. In this case, as we have seen, judicial work was done by a body of people not formally constituted for that purpose, but simply met together in the customary course of kinship obligations.

The various kinds of procedure we have been discussing are those open to an individual who has been injured by another person or persons. How far there is any idea of an offence against the community it is hard to say. But the fact that the village may be summoned by a drum and is given a goat to share before judging the case indicates that there is some notion of the community being concerned in these breaches of the law. None the less, in the cases of law-breaking we have discussed so far, the injured party is an individual. On one occasion, however, I saw a case in which a man was held to have perpetrated an offence against all and sundry. The culprit was the same A-ziɛ who was involved in the sacred spear case. He had put medicine which people described as *nshi*—bad medicine[1]—on a tree of the kind used in house-building, and therefore an economic asset not communally owned. Using *nshi* was in itself illegal, but what excited the village at large was that the tree was near the place in the stream where people drew water, and they complained that the medicine was harming them. There was, therefore, what appeared to be a general, rather than an individual, taking of action and a fine was levied on the offender. Whether it would be right to describe it as a reaction of the community or whether it was not rather the individuals of the community all feeling themselves menaced, it is difficult to say. The case

---

[1] I use the term " bad medicine " or " bad magic " for the kind of medicine or magic that this community holds to be illegal. I hope elsewhere to discuss what it is that constitutes " goodness " and " badness " in their eyes, but I believe that the essential element in bad magic is the fact that it is directed specifically, and by name, against an individual. Underlying this, I believe, is the notion that if the individual is known one should proceed against him by judicial means. Supernatural means should be used against the unknown only. The situation is complicated by the fact that people are apt to use the word *nshi*—bad medicine, poison—for any kind of medicine or magic that they think may harm them whether it is technically " bad " or not.

was, I think, different in degree rather than in kind from those in which an individual was the injured party. As to the procedure followed by the people of Umuɛkɛ in this case, I tried to find out to what extent there was any particular authority to whom they should appeal. I asked James whether anyone who found that an offence had been committed, such as putting bad medicine on a tree, would have to appeal to any particular elder first. He said, and I had already been told it in another connection, that anyone finding such a thing would go and tell the various family or extended family heads, and ask them if any of their people had done it, and that afterwards people would come together to judge the case. There was, however, no special person to whom recourse must first be had. There is in fact no special, judicial machinery, but things are done in a recognised and ordered way. In this case, after people had seen the medicine and talked together about it, they waited for Oriɛ Ekpa day, when the village was assembled for path clearing, to bring the matter up officially. There is no question of unpremeditated mob action.

I only saw one case judged in which the parties came from different villages, though I was told of a number of others. In the case I saw, between a woman of Umuɛkɛ and a woman of the neighbouring village-group of Umunumu, a few people from each village, kinsfolk of the parties, judged the case as they might have done between two people of the same village. It happened that the Umuɛkɛ woman was of the extended family of Umu Nwa Ɛbodim, to which the Native Court Member, also belonged. The woman whom she accused of stealing came to the Court Member with her supporters and put the case to him. Whether she would have gone to him in his official capacity even if her accuser had not been of his extended family I do not know, but the case was settled peacefully to the satisfaction of all parties without any recourse to the court. I stumbled in upon the proceedings by chance. The two litigants, with various women supporters, were sitting together, and explained that they had finished talking over the case—*anyi ɛkpɛcaana* [_ ¯ – – – ¯]—and that the men had withdrawn to consult and decide—*ibi ikpɛ* [¯ _ – ¯]. We joined them and found that they came quickly and quietly to agreement. The woman of Umuɛkɛ had admitted herself mistaken in her accusation and so was only being asked to pay the sum in dispute, 1½d., and to take palm wine and oil bean to the accused woman so that they might eat together and thus make peace. After this decision the men rejoined the women and both sides produced palm wine before the decision was announced. A. commented that he thought the women would have spoken little in the preliminary discussion, as men were there. He said that if the case had been between two women of the same village it would have been judged by women. Being between different villages it was judged by men.

Certainly this case was child's play compared with the inter-village strife which arose in connection with the case between two full brothers of Umuɛkɛ when one of them invoked the sacred spear of the yam spirit whose shrine was in a different village.[1]

I was told of a case where two villages of Agbaja fought during the path clearing for the annual religious rites and the case was judged by all Agbaja; but I doubt whether there is much territorial conception, so to speak, of judicial action. A case is normally regarded as between individuals and whether or not they are of the same village they have a variety of judicial possibilities open to them. It will be remembered that bride price cases, which always involve more than one village, were being taken for trial to the *nde dibea*.

OFFENDERS CAUGHT RED-HANDED

We have seen that where there is overwhelming evidence of guilt and the culprit does not deny it, as in the case of P.,[2] summary justice is executed, the verdict being carried out on the spot by those who have judged the case. Where an offender is caught red-handed, the procedure is even more swift and drastic.

There was a woman in the village who had the reputation of being an habitual thief and it was said that her husband did not allow her to go to market for fear of her stealing. His prohibition was evidently not very effective for it was at the nearby Umunumu market of Afɔ Ɛgbu that she was caught one day *in flagrante delicto*. It happened, we were told,

---

[1] See p. 108.   [2] See p. 111.

while a European's car was passing through the market place. People crowded to look at it, and the woman, seizing her chance, took a penny off another woman's basket and tucked it in her cloth. The owner did not see her, but a woman standing by did so and told the owner. Then the penny fell out of the thief's cloth and her guilt was manifest. So the women took her market basket away from her and tore her cloth and beat her. She came home with her arms folded in front of her, as A.'s sister witnessed. It still remained for her to be fined by the married women of Umuɛkɛ in accordance with legal usage; but in the meantime her patent offence had been dealt with by those on the spot. Again it was not, I think, mere mob violence but a recognised method of dealing with such a situation.

With the same promptitude the married women of Umuɛkɛ dealt with those of their number who defaulted on the day on which they did their annual religious ceremonies. In this case, too, the guilt of the offenders was apparent to all present and was drastically dealt with on the spot.[1]

OFFENDER UNKNOWN

We have discussed some of the various possible judicial methods of dealing with a breach of the law when the offender is known or suspected. When, however, the offender is unknown the situation is more difficult. In the absence of any efficient police or detective system there is, in such cases, an extension of that reliance on the supernatural which was seen to be a factor even in the cases we have described.

In the matter, for instance, of missing property people could go to a *dibea* to discover what had happened. One of the elders told me he did so several times when a goat that he and the other *nde ama ala* had given me got lost. He explained that he thought it might have wandered in the direction of Umunumu so he went to a *dibea* there. The *dibea* said that it had strayed in the opposite direction and that if they tried they would get it—which they ultimately did. There was evidently an idea that the *dibea* might be expected to have local knowledge, but whether by natural or supernatural means did not appear.

If theft is suspected the same method of consulting a

1 See p. 196.

dibea is available, after which the whole village may be made to swear, or threatened with it, in order to catch the criminal. So at least one is told : but on two occasions when property disappeared, the owners, women in ęach case, said that it was useless to take any steps at all.

A supernatural object called *ɔdɵ ɛʒɛ ɛlu*, associated with the spirit of thunder, Amade Ɔha, can be invoked against an unknown offender. Certain people " get " or possess *ɔdɵ ɛʒɛ ɛlu*, though no one in Umuɛkɛ had it as far as I know, and it is to them that application must be made if its services are required. One of them will sometimes turn up when a case is being tried in case he may be called upon. *Ɔdɵ ɛʒɛ ɛlu* is much feared as it strikes the innocent as well as the guilty. If it is invoked in a case of theft, it is held that it will harm not only the thief but those who have shared, even in innocence, the stolen goods with him. If a person is ill he or she may start wondering whether *ɔdɵ ɛʒɛ ɛlu* may not be striking them because they have, in ignorance, eaten stolen food or otherwise received stolen goods from someone under the curse of *ɔdɵ ɛʒɛ ɛlu*. At one time N.Ɛ. fell ill and this was one of the many fears that beset him and one of the possible explanations of an obdurate sickness.

The attitude of the Ibo to property is again emphasised by this elaborate means of discouraging all accessories to the act of stealing, and this incentive to buyers to remain inside the honest channels of trade.

Chapter IX. The Law in Breach (II)

We have looked at some of the various possibilities for dealing with a breach of the law : a description of one or two actual cases will supply certain details of technique and procedure without which any account of judicial methods in this society is an empty shell.

A case which occurred between a man and woman of Umuɛkɛ has a number of points of interest. In the course of a quarrel about the cutting of some palm nuts a man, K., of the kindred of Umu Nwa Ɛbodim, and the widow, G., of his dead father, fell to abusing one another. She said that he and the other sons of his father were talking against her to the family of the girl she was trying to marry to her son and were telling them that she had not enough money to pay the bride price. The man, K., retorted by asking if that was why she was trying to kill them by supernatural means, by magic that is to say, or by making sacrifices to a spirit to kill them. The widow then made the provocative remark : "*E daa anwɔ a kwa ge ?*" [_ ‾ _ ‾ ‾ ‾ -]—"Why don't you die and let us mourn for you ?" She then called in one of her kinsmen who was not a man of Umuɛkɛ since the village was exogamous. She reported to this kinsman what K. had said and he interviewed K., who said that he had indeed made the accusation attributed to him. G., the widow, thereupon charged him with the serious offence of false accusation. In the initial procedure followed by G. it is not easy to be sure how far village methods were influenced by recent British innovations. She took a fee of 1s. 6d. to the Court Member of Umuɛkɛ, but he was also the eldest surviving son of her dead husband by another wife, and was the elder of this branch of the kindred of Umu Nwa Ɛbodim. He was therefore an obvious person to whom to appeal. He, and according to one version G. too, chose several other Umuɛkɛ men to help him, not all of them from among the elders, and two kinsmen of G. were also of the party. The case was thus laid before a small selected group to see if they could find a solution acceptable to both sides before recourse was had to a larger or more authoritative body. The defendant, K., refused to produce his 1*s*. 6*d*., which, if he was acquitted, would have been refunded to him, or, if he were found guilty, would have been forfeit to the judges, the same rule applying equally to the plaintiff. A further sum of 6*d*. each was also involved as a kind of stake to be lost or won according to rules which depended on the outcome of the case.

It must be pointed out that normally K. and G., who both belonged to the same branch of the extended family of Umu Nwa Ɛbodim, would both have lived in the same house-group. But K. had not married and settled down in his own house-group. He had, on the contrary, become the lover of a widow of Umuɛkɛ owɛrɛ. She was older than he and had a skin disease, and a kinsman of K. told us that he could not think how K. could live with her. In any case a man of marriageable age who lives with a woman lover is regarded as foolish.

The litigants were therefore more closely matched than might have appeared at first sight. G. had no husband alive to help her, and her eldest son was only a youth : but K., though he might hope for and, indeed later received, some support from Umuɛkɛ-owɛrɛ, was not on a normal footing with his immediate kinsfolk. As for G.'s complaint that the sons of her dead husband were preventing her from marrying a wife for her son, she was evidently struggling with the difficulties of bride price payments that bulk so large in the life of these people. Her eldest daughter had married during her husband's life time and the bride price had gone to him. She was now left to marry a wife for her son and though she hoped to use for the purpose the bride price of her younger daughter, the girl's fiancé had, she said, produced no money yet. The relatives of her son's prospective wife were asking her for an instalment of two pounds, and she did not know how to pay them. The whole matter was, therefore, a sore subject just at this time.

In the case between her and K., the selected group of people tried it after several of the postponements which seem almost invariably to accompany such matters, and gave judgment in favour of the woman. The defendant, K., was told to refund to her the 1*s*. 6*d*. and 6*d*. she had spent. He refused to abide by their decision and fell back on the recognised expedient of taking a drum and beating

it through the village, saying that a bad thing had been
done to him and let the elders, the *nde ama ala,* come at
daybreak. The elders did so, and decided that the disputants,
G. and K., should each pay 2*s.* 6*d.*, which should be given
to the head of their branch of Umu Nwa Ɛbodim—in this
case, the Court Member, as we have seen—to buy a small
goat, which would be eaten by all Umuɛkɛ before the case
was tried. It was not easy to discover the exact reason for
this communal eating of a goat in this particular case. Three
different explanations were given : first that the accusation
was one of encompassing the death of a person by supernatural means : another was that the case involved a man
and his father's wife, but the third, which concerned the
procedure adopted and not the nature of the case, was that
a goat had to be provided because all the village had been
summoned by the beating of a drum. The informant, an
elderly man who gave me this reason, explained how careful
he would be, if he missed any property, for instance, to
ask people for information one by one and not collectively,
for fear he should be thought to have beaten a drum and
so be let in for the expense of providing a goat.

In the case under discussion the widow, G., came and
asked me to produce her 2*s.* 6*d.* I did so as payment for
some *uri* [_ _] paintings she did for me and also on condition
that she called me when the case was to be tried. The course
that events now followed gives some idea of the informality
and lack of haste that characterise Ibo litigation. When
G. borrowed the 2*s.* 6*d.* from me she said that the case would
be tried that day or the one after, and K. had already said
that it would be tried that day. In fact it was not, but a few
days later G. sent me a message that the case would be
tried that day. Instead of a trial, however, there was a
meeting of some of the elders to discuss the buying of the
goat, as the Court Member, though he had been given the
money, had not yet done so. Four days later it was announced
in the market place that the goat would be eaten the next
day, and that those who failed to come would not get a
share. In fact it was not eaten the next day. Meanwhile the
case was being discussed. N.Ɛ., the oldest man in the
village, told us that people had come and consulted him
about it. He added that when the goat had been killed the
case must be judged in peace.

Ten days later, during a discussion of other village matters, one of the elders of Umuɛkɛ-owɛrɛ announced that the goat would be eaten the next day, to which the Court Member, who was responsible for buying the goat, said didn't he know that it had been decided to postpone the matter till the day after, which would be Umuɛkɛ market day. On the market day in question the elders went up to his place, but the matter was postponed for eight days till the following market day, as G.'s money was not complete. It appeared that each party, in addition to bringing 2s. 6d. for buying the goat, had also to bring a further 2s. 6d. wherewith to refund the winner of the case. K. had produced his 5s. on the previous day, but G. had not completed hers.

Nine days later the goat—which in the end turned out to be a ram—was eaten. The morning had been spent by the males of the village in sharing a goat for the second burial of a dead brother of N.Ɛ. When this was finished great discussion arose as to whether the ram should or should not be eaten the same day. Finally, every one adjourned to the Court Member's place and killed and ate the ram. Having already on a hot morning witnessed the goat sharing at close quarters, I sent one of my staff to the ram eating.

Proceedings having got so far, a day was fixed for the case. On this day, about six weeks after the preliminary trial, the elders and as many of the younger people of the village as were interested met together about mid-day in the middle of the village in the open space of Umu Nwa Ɛbodim—the extended family to which the litigants belonged. When I arrived the men were sitting about round the big tree in the middle of the clearing, some of them making climbing ropes with characteristic industry. A gathering of people merely sitting and listening was a rare sight in the village. As an English woman might take her knitting, so an Ibo woman would take her cassava or oil bean to slice or a man his climbing rope to twist. In addition to the people of Umuɛkɛ there were two of G.'s male kinsmen and a leading elder from the next door village, who was also a supporter of hers. There was also a man I did not recognise who appeared to have some connection with K. There were no women present at first except the plaintiff G. herself, sitting by the tree with her daughter, but a number turned up later and sat under a mud wall near by.

In this informal-looking assembly, K., the defendant, got up and demanded that ɔfɔ be brought to be sworn on, that they might judge the case truly. This produced a search for ɔfɔ as hardly any elder had brought one. N.O., the senior man and holder of the big ɔfɔ of the village, was sent to fetch his, but before he had gone far, being by nature a slow mover, he was called back by the Court Member, whom G. had originally invoked to try the case, who said N.O.'s house was too far and they would get another ɔfɔ instead of his. The eldest man of the village, whose house was nearer, was sent to get his and three other elders produced theirs on the spot. Four with its multiples is, of course, the number usually associated with magico-religious ritual in this society.

No one would have questioned the fact that the ɔfɔ of N.O. took precedence of all others in the village. The stable framework of theory was there ; but the strong practical sense of these people, who are usually busy with something or other, was irked by delay, and they proceeded as speed and circumstances dictated.

When the four ɔfɔ were brought, they were put on the ground near a big stone at the foot of the tree. The two litigants were then told to bring palm wine for them. Each produced a gourd full, G. buying hers with 1d. provided by one of her kinsmen. Those present drank, so far as I remember. Then N.O., the senior man, took a cup of palm wine and poured it on the four ɔfɔ, saying as he did so : " Onyɛ ɔ wɵ, ya wɵrɵ ya. Onyɛ ɔ wɵhɵ ya awɵla ya." Lit. : " Who-ever it is, let it be him ; whoever it is not, let it not be him." That is : Whoever is guilty, let him be guilty ; whoever is not guilty, let him not be guilty.

The second most senior man of the village, Nwa Onyɛ Okoro, head of the big extended family of Umu Nwa Ɛbodim, took a small chick, brought by the defendant, and, holding it up, pulled its head off and let the blood drip on the ɔfɔ, and then threw it away. It would not be eaten by anyone. Having done this, the same man who had killed the chick spoke as follows :[1] " Onyɛ hɵrɵ ɛzhi okwu n'ɵka a, na-ɛkwuhɵ,

---

[1] These words were heard by my interpreter who gave them to me afterwards. They were spoken too quickly for me to pick them up at one hearing.

ɔfɔ gbuo ya, ha ! Onyɛ ga-agha ɵgham, ɔfɔ gbuo ya, ha ! Onyɛ

nɵrɵ okwu n'ɵka a, na-ɛkwuhɵ, ɔfɔ gbuo ya, ha ! Onyɛ na-agaghe

ɛkpɛ nkanne, ɔfɔ gbuo ya, ha !" That is: "Whoever sees the

truth in this case and does not say it, may ɔfɔ kill him, ha !
Whoever speaks a lie, may ɔfɔ kill him, ha! Whoever hears
a word in this case and does not speak it, may ɔfɔ kill him,
ha! Whoever does not judge aright, may ɔfɔ kill him, ha!"

All present joined, as is customary, in the Ha! at the end
of each phrase. As they did so the ɔfɔ holders who, with
other people, were crouching round their ɔfɔ, picked them
up and knocked them on the ground, and everyone else
present either knocked their hands on the ground, or, with
the same intention, on their sides. Any swearing by ɔfɔ
seems to be accompanied by this cry of Ha! which, on its
falling tone, sounds almost like a snarl, and certainly gives
the impression of a curse.

After this rite people sat down again and the defendant
began to state his case. In considering procedure it is worth
noticing that the ritual with ɔfɔ was of no small importance.
It had, of course, the effect of introducing a supernatural
sanction, a feature with which all who have any experience
of Ibo judicial methods are familiar in principle.[1] Beyond
its evident supernatural significance the ceremony, performed
in the setting of a village assembly, had a further effect.
The meeting had, so far as one could discern, no chairman,
and always in any large Ibo gathering it is a problem for
a would-be speaker to get a hearing above the excitement
and the roar of general conversation. In this case the well-
known ceremony had secured a pause which gave the defendant a chance to start a speech and to continue it if, by his
wits or oratory, he could hold the crowd's attention. The
defendant, moreover, launched on the speech in which he
stated his case, had hit on a plan which, whether or not it
was intentional, was certainly effective. He had a heavy,
pointed, wooden stick, and as he talked he stumped up and

---

[1] The fact that the Native Courts set up by British Government
warrant do not, so far as I have seen, follow this usage of ɔfɔ for all
present makes me wonder whether this particular ceremony is very
widely known.

down among the elders, accentuating his words by jabbing the stick into the ground so that one trembled for their bare feet. If any of them had felt disposed to doze or so much as to let their attention wander the stick allowed of no such relaxation.

The defendant spoke fluently but without shouting over-much. When he had finished, the widow G., the plaintiff, stated her case, speaking quietly most of the time. Two witnesses spoke next, first a man and then a woman. The speeches were apt to be punctuated by roars from the audience and were usually followed by them, individuals working themselves into frenzies of fury, their eyes starting out of their heads. One of the characteristics of these people was that individuals who were apparently mild and who had eyes and voices of velvet would suddenly be roused by circumstances to a paroxysm of rage the violence of which made one almost recoil. It may well be, however, that so long as the demonstration remained within the vocal sphere it was in the nature of a safety valve.

When the woman witness had finished there was a special outburst from the crowd. Some people said she had given a different version now from the one she had given when the case was originally judged by a small group. Others retorted that on that occasion she had been prevented from saying what she had said to-day.

Several other people then addressed the gathering, and one of them was interrupted by a fellow villager and told to keep to the point and to remember that they had brought ɔfɔ and that it would kill anyone who did not speak truly.

There was then much noisy general discussion, but a prominent part was played by the man who had interrupted with the reminder about ɔfɔ. He was a member of that branch of Umu Nwa Ɛbodim which now lived in Umuɛkɛ-owɛrɛ where K. also lived, or stayed, with the Umuɛkɛ-owɛrɛ woman, his lover. The man was not an elder but I had noticed on several occasions that he was ambitious and had a quick eye to the main chance and was always ready of speech. I was particularly struck, during this trial, by his technique for assuring himself of a hearing. His plan was to sit away outside the circle. When he wanted to say something he arrested attention by sweeping dramatically in, resplendent in unaccustomed shorts, a singlet and a great broad-brimmed hat, and said what he had to say bitingly and with no pause between his sentences in which anyone else might forestall him. If inspiration failed for a moment he took refuge in the bore's device of loudly prolonging a word while he sought for another to follow it. He produced a considerable effect on his audience, suggestible as they are and susceptible to oratory, in favour of K., the defendant.

Another man, an *osu,* spoke a good deal. He seemed to call people to order now and then to get silence for speakers. People who wanted to speak undoubtedly got a hearing, though it was hard to say quite how. Often everyone was talking at once, or people were running round addressing small groups. The plaintiff, G., was doing this at times. The second senior man of the village presided as much as anyone but there was no apparent chairman. An elder of some weight from a neighbouring village, who was on G.'s side, helped matters by remaining good-tempered and calling people to order at intervals. He also spoke once or twice, as did G.'s male kinsman. Several of those participating were from places other than the home village.

After about three hours of raging talk the man in the large brimmed hat suggested that, without any select band of people withdrawing to consult, it should be decided that G., the woman, should swear to her innocence for the defendant, and that if she did so he should pay her back her expenses in the case. He and most of the younger people were on the side of the defendant who had been improving his position by giving away food before the case came on. The people who had originally judged the case refused to accept this suggestion, but they said they were tired and other people must go out and consult. A number of people, elders and others, not including the parties to the dispute, then withdrew. The large-hatted man and the *osu* talked strongly in favour of the defendant. The final decision was something of a compromise. It decreed that not K. only, but his brothers by the same father, should swear by a supernatural power that they were not preventing G. from getting a wife for her son. If they refused to swear, K. was to pay G. her expenses and take action against the sons of his father to recover it.

When the people returned to the assembly from this consultation they demanded palm wine. They said that it

was the custom to demand that the litigants should give
them food before they announced the decision, but that
as they had provided a goat for this case they would only
ask one gourd of palm wine from each. The wine was
produced and after drinking it and after requests for food by
other people had been made in vain, they returned to the
big tree in the middle of the circle and embarked on a discussion as to who should announce the decision. People called
on N.O., the man who held the big ɔfɔ of Umuɛkɛ, saying
that he was their head. He tried to make an announcement
but it was too much for his feeble wits and he got it all wrong.
It was interesting to see that he was hooted and jeered at
for his incompetence, in spite of his position. People remarked
that he was all right at coming forward to take first share
when there was anything going but that he was unable
to announce a decision correctly. The eldest man in the
village, N.Ɛ., then came forward saying that N.O. had
made a mess of it, and gave the verdict himself. The incident
was an interesting commentary on the extent to which
hereditary position commands respect. In this case the
senior man was admitted to have rights, such as the right
to the first share, and the fact that this was not disputed
was, as we have seen, a definite factor making for order.
Where his personal attainments were too feeble to enable
him to fulfil the requirements of his position, as in this case,
he was simply pushed aside with scorn. Position without
ability was, in fact, accorded recognition but not respect.

As for the decision, its announcement was greeted by a
wild outcry. Both sides were outraged by it, or behaved as
though they were. G., the woman plaintiff, objected, so far
as I could gather, because the decision involved not only
the man with whom she had a case but all the sons of her
husband, who would thus, she thought, be turned against
her. The sons themselves refused to abide by the judgment
and demanded that the case should be retried. With everyone
shouting at everyone else the assembly broke up.

When I returned to the village a year later the case had
not been retried nor had the decision been carried out.
Also G's opponents had tried to make her refund the money
they had spent on the case but she had refused. It is easy
to point to this as an example of the often-quoted weakness
of Ibo execution of justice, but there is perhaps something

to be said on the other side. In a judicial system which still relies largely on the supernatural method of swearing and has therefore not yet developed an advanced technique of sifting evidence, miscarriage of justice may often be avoided if judgments are not too rigorously carried out. One gradually gained the impression that if public opinion were more or less unanimous, or if a culprit were caught red-handed or with no reasonable chance of denial, sentence was likely to be executed.

A case which raises a number of points of interest arose between two near kinsmen of the kindred of Umu Ebo Durake. I was told about the early stages of the dispute by a married woman of the family, and was present at the trial which eventually took place.

The elder of the two, a young man named J., accused the younger, a lad called E., of stealing 2d. from his house in circumstances which made it difficult to suspect anyone else. E. went out and called two other young men who were nearby, but of two different kindreds, and told them to witness that J. was accusing him. They laughed and went away. E. then went and fetched two elders of Umu Nwa Ebodim, and the osu living with Umu Nwacuku, and told them what had happened. They took J.'s side saying that he would not have accused his " brother " for nothing, and the fact that E. was rather a tiresome youth was probably not irrelevant. Talk of the matter got round and the members of the meetings to which E. belonged said that they would drive him out of the meetings. This was serious. He was said to belong to three meetings and this expulsion would mean that he would lose any payments he had already made and would not get his turn of scooping the pool.[1] He therefore went that evening to J. with a half-penny and asked J. to add a half-penny of his own so that they might send to a dibea—diviner—to ask who had stolen the money. A. and the mission teacher were present at this interview, and A. said that J. declared that he was not going to a dibea about two-pence and that as the money was lost, it was lost, and they must leave it at that. In passing one may note that both J. and E. were mission members. I asked A. whether anyone raised the question of consulting a diviner in relation to mission principles and he said that no one had done so.

The next morning, E. returned to J.'s house bringing with him the officiant of one of the guardian spirits of the adjacent village-group of Umunumu. He had taken twopence to this man and had got him to bring with him the ɔfɔ of his cult. E. also brought with him several elders of Umuɛkɛ, including N.Ɛ., the head of the kindred to which he and J. belonged. He explained that he wished to swear his innocence on this ɔfɔ and I was told that he kept trying to do so, goaded by the desire to establish his innocence in the eyes of his meeting members. But J. would not allow him to swear as he said that it would kill him, he, E., being guilty. The other people present said that in any case, if he wanted to swear, it would have to be on an *agbara* [⁻ _ _]— spirit—of J.'s choice. After this unsuccessful effort to clear himself E. went right away for about ten months doing farm work for other people.[1] On his return he took up the matter again. One Oriɛ Ekpa day, when the men and boys of the village were returning in the early morning from clearing their path to the central Agbaja market, A. saw E., who was of Umuɛkɛ-ama, go up to one of the chief elders of Umuɛkɛ-owɛrɛ, Nwa Onyɛ Ohu, and to some other people who were with him.[2] E. said that he had a case to be judged as he had been accused by J. of stealing. He was told that as most people had already gone home nothing could be done on the spot ; also, another case was pending, that of A-ziɛ's medicine put on a tree by the stream, which must be judged by all, both old and young, and that

---

[1] See *re* going away to farm, p. 40.

[2] A point of procedure may be noted here. A. said that he had not heard that E. took palm wine to the elders when he summoned them, and, he added, there is no need for palm wine in a case like this where the law has been broken because those called to judge know that there will be a fine which they will get. In a case like debt or of a wife leaving her husband without refunding the bride price, the injured party would take palm wine and money and go to the elders, perhaps 3*s.* for a big bride price case and double if people with ɔzɔ title are called in. This money, said A, is not a bribe ; a bribe would probably come later. The money and wine they take first is for the work they are asked to do. A. gave this account as of his own part of the country, but said he thought it would also apply to Umuɛkɛ. I did not systematically investigate the matter, but it points to a differentiation of procedure suggestive of a distinction between criminal and civil cases.

he must wait for that occasion to have his own case judged.

When the appointed day arrived I went with A. to the village market place, which was also the open space of Umuɛkɛ-ama, to which both litigants belonged. It turned out that only their case was judged and not that of A-ziɛ. Only a few elders were present, two from Umu Nwa Ɛbodim, one from Umuɛkɛ-owɛrɛ, and N. Ɛ. from Umuɛkɛ-ama, he being the head of the kindred to which both parties to the case belonged. The inevitable O.E. was there and some young men, including age mates of J. and E. and some of the members of the meetings from which E. had been excluded. Anyone interested in the matter had, in fact, turned up in answer to a general summons. They were sitting scattered about informally on the ground or on tree trunks with N.Ɛ. sitting apart at the foot of the market shrine of Ogbudi.

The gathering demanded money for palm wine from the litigants. E. produced twopence, but J., who seemed an unwilling participant in the proceedings, refused to give more than a penny, which he threw on the ground and which N.Ɛ., his elder, had to pick up. After an interlude for haggling which any money transaction tends to involve, the parties to the case were asked what they were prepared to "bet." E. said 5s., and J. said, though indirectly, that he would do likewise.

The procedure involved in this "betting," which is a frequent feature in Ibo cases, is that the two parties first produce tokens in lieu of their stakes and that these are given into the keeping of an elder. If, ultimately, either party fails to produce his money the elder is held responsible. The accused then swears his innocence on an *agbara* of the accuser's choice. If within the appointed time—a year, or whatever is fixed as the limit within which the *agbara* is to act—the accused dies, the accuser gets his 5s. back and the other 5s. is divided among the people judging the case. If the accused does not die he gets his money back together with half that of the accuser, the other half going to the people who judged.

In another case of this sort where a woman was concerned I was told that if she, the accused, were proved innocent this half share of the accused's money which she would

receive would be to " wash the shame " from her. This is
a recurrent motif in Ibo justice.

In the present case E. produced as his token a flute which
he was carrying, and J. a knife, both of which they gave
to N.Ɛ. to hold. He, however, objected, saying that he was
a near relative to both and therefore ought not to hold
them. He told J. to come and give them to Nwa Onyɛ
Okoro but, as A. translated, J. said he was tired of walking
about and let N.Ɛ. give them himself, which he did. Respect
for age could hardly be called a conspicuous feature of this
community.

The tokens were passed from hand to hand among the
older people, every one being unwilling to assume the
responsibility of holding them, and they finally returned to
N.Ɛ. who had no choice but to keep them.

E. then stated his case. He had adopted the technique
that we have noticed elsewhere of creating an effect by his
clothing. He had a short tunic and a bit of cloth flowing
behind him with an almost Greek effect as he stumped up
and down gesticulating. At intervals he clapped a deer-
stalker cap on his head which instantly, for the European
observer, changed the scene to Stepney or Limehouse but
was no doubt meant to impress those present as only
particular forms of head-gear can do. In his speech he claimed
that he had already sworn his innocence and wished the
elders to make J. go to his meetings to tell the members
that he was innocent and must not be driven out. After
him, N.D., who, in his large hat, had played a prominent
part in G's case, spoke. And then J., after putting the facts
of the case, explained that he had refused to allow E. to
swear. N.Ɛ. then spoke and said that E. had sworn the day
he brought the officiant of Egbu Mmiri. Other people denied
this. Some of them then pointed out that it is swearing
that kills people and let N.Ɛ., who is the " elder " for both
parties, find some way out of the impasse without anyone
having to swear. Then came the usual references to other
cases. Some told of people who had been killed by swearing,
others of those who had avoided going to such lengths.
N.D. told the story of a man who accused his " brother's "
wife of stealing a shilling from him, and he " bet " £1,
and because the woman had not got £1, she brought three
stocks of yams, and she was to swear for him. Then, according

to A's translation, the husband of the woman reflected
that if she swore and died the bride price he had paid on
her much exceeded the shilling in dispute. So he brought
£1 and gave it to the people judging the case instead of
" betting " it. The accuser took back his £1 and was given
the disputed shilling out of the £1 given to the judges.
So the case was settled and no one died, and, said N.D.,
he being an Umuɛkɛ-owɛrɛ man, he envies the places that
are full of people. It is the people of Umuɛkɛ-ama who
diminish the population of Umuɛkɛ by killing people like
this with swearing. However, N.Ɛ. said that if the litigants
chose to swear it was their business and he could not stop
them. The people present, therefore, feeling that unless E.
were allowed to swear the mud of accusation would stick
to him, particularly in his meetings, said that J. must bring
an *agbara* of his own choice for E. to swear on. He again
demurred, not wanting E. to kill himself thus, but he finally
agreed on condition, so far as I could understand, that at
the time of the swearing the elders should bring their
ɔfɔ and " knock " them for E. with the intention that if he
came back after death and killed anyone, ɔfɔ should kill him—
presumably if he reincarnated. The elders agreed to this and
the ceremony was fixed for sixteen days later.

Before the day arrived I left the village for several weeks
and did not hear what happened, but the case is of interest
from several points of view. It shows the strength of the
economic sanction in the matter of theft. Not only honesty
but an unblemished reputation is essential for meeting
members, and E. was prepared to take the risk of swearing
rather than forfeit his good name and his meeting dues.

A further point to be noted is the attempt made by those
present to urge moderation on the protagonists. They tried
to find some way of avoiding what was considered the
extreme course of swearing. There was, I think, very little
doubt in their minds that E. was guilty, and they did not
wish him to kill himself by swearing falsely. Among these
excitable people, quick to resent accusations and to take
dramatic steps, one sees how in a number of different ways
the community tries to exercise restraint.

The prominence given in this case to the question of
swearing is an example of the important part played in
Ibo judicial matters by the supernatural and particularly

by this form of appeal to it. The desirability of continuing officially the practice of swearing in the Native Courts is sometimes discussed. It is perhaps useful, therefore, to record something of the attitude to this practice which one observed in indigenous judicial situations.

In the case just described the position of E. is doubtful. He was inclined to cynicism at any time and had been away from the village working. He seemed ready to take a chance on swearing in a highly doubtful cause, but it is clear how seriously the village took the matter, including the shrewd and fairly sophisticated J.

On another occasion we had an opportunity of seeing J.'s reactions. He had married a wife some years previously, and after a time she had left him. He then heard that she was marrying another man without having refunded to him the bride price he had paid for her. He tried to get the money from her family but failed. As her new marriage was a Christian one, he went to the priest and got him to allow the woman's people to swear for him on the Bible about the bride price. On his return he came to tell me what had happened and was so jubilant that I asked if he had got his money back. He explained that he had not but that as his opponents had sworn, they would die and he would then be revenged. He spoke with great conviction.[1] Belief in the efficacy of swearing seems still to be a considerable factor in judicial matters.

One must also take into account the fact, to which we have already referred, that this method of discovering the guilty party, when guilt cannot otherwise be proved, must have retarded the development of a sound technique of evidence in trying a case, and until this technique has had opportunity to develop the supernatural method meets a real need. This is also true about the method, sometimes followed, of submitting a case for decision to an oracle.

A further point about this method of swearing or of appealing to an oracle is the part it plays in lessening social

---

[1] An Onitsha man, at present in England, who has had considerable Native Court experience, tells me that people who have undertaken to swear will be seized with qualms and go at night to the Court Clerk to ask him somehow to get them out of it. The practice evidently has some weight still even among people sufficiently " advanced " to use the Native Courts.

friction, a matter of importance among a closely packed, excitable people. If a human tribunal convicts a man and sentences him dire results may follow. It is not unknown for the defeated parties to ambush their judges on the way home. How much more prudent and peaceful to leave judgment and sentence to a non-human power against which revenge is impossible : how much less bad blood, in every sense, will result. This reliance on the supernatural as an alternative to human mechanisms for dealing with a social situation and all the complications of such reliance must be kept in mind in all spheres of Ibo social organisation. Of practical activity, technical knowledge and hard common sense there is no lack among this go-ahead intelligent folk, but an apparent lack or weakness in the social structure can often be explained by the use of a supernatural device where a practical one would normally be used by a European society.

It may be noted here that the procedure by which an individual who has sworn is, after the prescribed period, declared free of his oath is a further example of the informal yet recognised methods which characterise Ibo justice. The only case I saw was shortly after our arrival in Umuɛkɛ. It was the village market day and I saw one of the married women of Umuɛkɛ-owɛrɛ clothed as for a festive occasion, dancing and singing round the market, with a bunch of cassava leaves in one hand and a basket-work tray in the other. Some of the other women were giving cowries, and there were pennies in her tray. It was told that she was dancing on account of her brother, a man of the neighbouring village-group of Umunumu. He had been accused of being *onyɛ nshi* [¯ ¯ ¯], that is to say, of making black magic or poison against someone else. He had been made to swear by *ɔdǝ ɛʒɛ ɛlu* and Amadǝ Ɔha, and was to die in three years if he was guilty. The three years had passed on this day and his sister was therefore dancing. The cassava leaves she was holding were connected with the crime. The man had been accused of putting poison into a pot of cassava and water. When a person is thus finally cleared of accusation his people rejoice with him—*eŋǝ areshe* [¯ _ ¯ ¯].

Chapter X. Law Making

TURNING from the judging of cases to the making of laws or regulations one finds again that a variety of groups can take part and that a forceful individual can make himself felt. There seems to be no specialised institution for this function and one meets again the fact that a group of people met together for some economic purpose such as a market or some traditional purpose such as a second burial will use the occasion of meeting to discuss public matters. It is as though the *res publica* were only gradually emerging from the sphere of the kinship group, but if specialised institutions are hard to discover this is not to say that the Ibo do not make and proclaim laws—*iti iwu* [⁻ ⁻ _ ⁻]. Parliament in the Middle Ages in England may, according to some historians, have been a law-declaring rather than a law-making body, but an Ibo community, far from resting on immemorial custom, seems always ready for new departures even to the extent of discussing, as Owerri was doing, the alteration of such apparently fundamental conditions as the rules governing exogamy. In the same way, in the judicial sphere, case law as well as custom is invoked.

Again our best method will be to look at a number of actual examples of laws being made or public business transacted. We may start with the case of an assembly whose primary function was, as often happens, different. On one occasion all the men of the village had assembled for the second burial ceremonies of one of their number. As these proceeded with great leisureliness there was time for much talk and there was a good deal of discussion of matters, some of which though apparently informal, had a bearing on general village affairs. The case was discussed of a man of the village whose wives had left him, one after another, in such a way that it seemed clear that he must be the party at fault. People shook their heads and asked why in these circumstances other men should be blamed if they took these wives for themselves in spite of the general prohibition on marrying another man's wife. Other cases of undesirable conduct were also discussed, and though actual rulings were not made a number of questions of public interest were ventilated. One piece of public business was definitely brought forward. The Court Member exhorted people to remember that taxes were now due, whereupon a lively gossip ensued about those who had already paid tax and obtained their receipt tally and could now lend the tally to those who had not paid so that they could go to neighbouring markets safely without fear of seizure by the police for non-payment. Those present would not discuss the question definitively as they said the Court Member must give them due notice and they would come to his compound : but he had none the less used the occasion to notify the village of taxation dates.

Markets are, of course, the most frequent and regular occasions for the assembling of a large number of people. Local patriotism decrees that the majority of the village or village-group shall turn out for its own particular market and there is then clearly an opportunity for the discussion or transaction of public business, particularly by the men, as the main economic activity is carried on by the women. In the Umuɛkɛ village market the men sat together in their age groups, drinking and chatting, while the women did the lion's share of the buying and selling.

The important question of the right to cut palm nuts was regulated one market day in Umuɛkɛ. The prevailing system, which had already replaced another before I arrived, was that people might only cut from palms on the land belonging to their own small land-owning group. This favoured the older men whose strength would not have allowed them to profit fully from a right to cut over a wider area, but it did not suit the younger men. It was from one of these, J., that I heard about the change in the law. He was my next-door neighbour and a strong-minded and independent young man. On the evening of one Umuɛkɛ market day he came to my house looking very cock-a-hoop and said that he and his age group—ɛbiri [⌐ _ _]—had gone that afternoon in the market to the age group of the elders of the village and had made them alter the " law " about cutting palm nuts. The young men, he said, had insisted that henceforward palm nuts should be cut in general, each man cutting where he liked, and, the younger men being numerous, they had borne down the opposition of the elders. If the latter had refused to concede what they wanted they would have seized their cows and sheep, he said, and sold them, since they must live somehow. It was all very well, he said, for the old men : they all had got wives, but the young men still had to get together bride price to marry theirs, and they needed palm oil to sell.

As time went on one noticed that a compromise had apparently been reached in this question of cutting palm nuts and that the right to cut, though not entirely communal, was less restricted than before.

From time to time " laws " would be made or attempted which concerned the whole village-group of Agbaja, and therefore the village, as part of it. Those which came to my notice concerned the central Agbaja market of Oriɛ Ekpa, and in the making of them the *nde dibea* apparently had a hand. This was not surprising. A body of intelligent men with something of a professional organisation was likely to step into this sphere as they had stepped into the judicial, in a society whose legislative institutions were embryonic.

One Oriɛ Ekpa market day a number of people told me that a law had been made that all men and women of Agbaja must go regularly to Oriɛ Ekpa market or be fined, because the people of Agbaja wanted their market to be big.[1] Also, they must not do palm oil work on market days as it would delay their starting. When I asked who had made this law I was told it was the ɔfɔ-holders of Agbaja—the senior man from each village—and that they had talked with the *nde dibea*. I did not know what this meant, but on the previous day, Ɛkɛ Nzɛrɛm, I had seen my *dibea* friend, James, setting off to what he said was a meeting of the Agbaja *nde dibea* in the central Agbaja market place on the day before market day. When I heard, therefore, of the new law and of the *nde dibea* as associated with it, I asked him what it all meant. He told me that some time previously the *nde dibea* of the sixteen village-groups had held one of their meetings at Oriɛ Ekpa, the Agbaja market, and the *nde dibea* of Agbaja had entertained them. Each *dibea* of Agbaja had brought twenty yams and three gourds of palm wine. After the

---

[1] Oriɛ Ekpa, the central Agbaja market, was rather insignificant compared with others in the neighbourhood, and there had already been competition and the boycotting of a rival.

assembly had re-enacted a professional law, the Agbaja
members, a little swollen one suspects with pride at being
the hosts, had said that as they were the head of the sixteen
village-groups, let them make Oriɛ Ekpa a big market.
The others demurred, and indeed the claim to headship
was on other evidence probably unfounded : but the Agbaja
members, undeterred, decided on the market regulations
already described, and on the following Ɛkɛ Nzɛrɛm day[1]
they summoned the eleven Court Members of Agbaja—in
theory they should have been the holders of the big ɔfɔ
of the villages and in most cases, though not in that of
Umuɛkɛ village, they were—and asked them if they agreed
to these laws. They did agree. On yet another Ɛkɛ Nzɛrɛm
day the *nde dibea* summoned a woman from each of the
eleven villages of Agbaja—the Umuɛkɛ woman was specified
to me—and told them about this law. Young men were also
chosen to enforce the law, on the dual division principle
which will be described later. I was given the names of
the two Umuɛkɛ men, and I noticed that one was an *osu*,
though no comment was made about this. James told me,
with what degree of accuracy I do not know, that where
fines up to about five shillings had been collected from
offenders against the regulations, these would be given to
the *nde dibea*, who would give the finers three shillings for
their trouble, and keep two shillings for themselves. When
I asked if the *ɔfɔ*-holders of Agbaja would get a share James
said that they would be given something for palm wine.
He was my only informant in this matter and I give his
account for what it is worth. I asked A. if he thought it
was true that the *nde dibea* made laws concerning the market,
and he was inclined to believe it as he said he did not think
the *nde ama ala* of Agbaja were in the habit of all meeting
together, and as the *nde dibea* did have meetings it seemed
likely that they would discuss market matters and then get
the assent of the *nde ama ala*. Later he heard from other
sources that the *nde dibea* did play a part in these matters,
and we also asked James later if the elders of Agbaja had
any regular meeting at Oriɛ Ekpa. He said that they had not
but that the *nde dibea* had told them that they ought to build
a house there and have meetings, but that they had not

---

[1] Ɛkɛ Nzɛrɛm means the market of Nzɛrɛm held on Ɛkɛ.

yet done so. I regret that I did not obtain more conclusive evidence on this point.

To return to the market regulations : they were later extended, but how far the *nde dibea* as a body took part I do not know. I had gone one afternoon to the house of an old woman of the village and had found her getting ready to go to the market of a neighbouring village-group which was much patronised by Agbaja people. She had had a bad foot for a long time and had been unable to walk and this expedition was a great occasion, even to the extent of inducing her to put on a festive headcloth. She had got a basket of palm kernels ready cracked and was preparing to start when a woman from the same house-group came to the door and said that the men had put a new law forbidding the women of Agbaja—and the men, too, so far as I understood—to take oil or kernels to sell at this market, Afɔ Ɛgbu, under pain of a fine of one shilling, to be levied at Oriɛ Ekpa. Instead of selling at Afɔ Ɛgbu, the market of a neighbouring town, they were to sell at the home Agbaja market of Oriɛ Ekpa. I asked when and how the men had announced this law and was told they had done it two days before at Ɛkɛ Nzɛrɛm market, and the preceding day at Oriɛ Ekpa market. They had told the women who were there and had told them to tell the other women at home.

The old lady with the bad foot said that a few months earlier the men of Agbaja had decreed that Agbaja people should take their oil and kernels to Oriɛ Ekpa, but that what remained unsold might be taken to the rival market of Afɔ Ɛgbu, which was always held on the next day. Now they had changed this ruling. " The people of Agbaja must always be doing something new " was her comment.

What is difficult is to assess the extent to which new laws are obeyed. On this occasion the old lady put away her kernels resignedly and deplored the fact that she could not warn her daughter, married in another village, of the law in time to save her being fined a shilling. On the other hand, I had that morning seen two women of Umuɛkɛ making palm oil to take to market. I pointed this out to Salome and asked her what she thought. She said that some people would not take the law seriously at first ; also she gathered that the women were displeased about the law. I learned from another woman that on this day some women took their oil and kernels to the forbidden market and others, having started out with them, deposited them *en route* for fear of being fined. A week or two later I asked a woman of Umuɛkɛ how the law was going and she said that since it was made she had not seen Agbaja women selling oil at Afɔ Ɛgbu market. This did not agree with the observations of my staff, but it showed that lip service was being paid to the new law. As for the prohibition about making palm oil on market day, one woman informed me that if the people appointed to catch and fine defaulters came upon anyone making palm oil they would smash the mortar in which the nuts were being pounded and throw away the contents. None the less, a few weeks later I saw two women in the same morning making palm oil on the forbidden day, one of them in an exposed position by the side of the path leading to the market. I had also asked previously whether anyone had yet been fined for not going to the Agbaja market, and was told that they had not been : but certainly as time went on they did not all go.[1]

One had the impression again that laws only establish themselves by degrees and then only in so far as they gain general acceptance. A law does not either exist or not exist : rather it goes through a process of establishing itself by common consent or of being shelved by a series of quiet evasions. The law *in posse* may or may not become the law *in esse*.

Nor is there any one recognised body with legislative functions to the exclusion of any group. A group such as the *nde dibea* or an age group can take the initiative and win the day if they secure enough public support. Here, as on the judicial side, institutions are still to a certain degree undifferentiated. This does not mean that political activities are absent, but they are carried on within the framework of a small-scale society where the primary needs of kinship organisation, of dealings with the supernatural, of the fundamental crises of birth, marriage, illness, death, have received a socialised response through institutions which can also be used for other purposes. Taxation can be discussed at a second burial, theft can be punished at a funeral gathering : far from implying that indigenous methods in the sphere

---

[1] See Part III, p. 210, for example of one village-group trying to impose a law on another and the consequent fighting.

of law and order can be brushed aside, this all means that they must be studied with the utmost care and in their own setting.[1]

As to the delimitation of spheres between village and village-group, the facts suggest that matters which are felt to be of common concern to the whole group, such as the market, fall within its sphere; but most matters are dealt with on a village scale by the village in, its own right and not by any delegation of authority from the group. Only if things take a turn which affects the whole group or one of its halves does the larger unit become involved.

In this whole discussion as to the location of authority in the Ibo community two things emerge clearly; we see that in each separate side of life, whether economic, military, supernatural or legal, there is no concentration of power in any one centre; in intimate relation with this fact we also see that there is in the whole village or village-group community, no one centre of power based, as is the power of the chief among some other peoples, on authority in all these spheres of life. We see, too, that the individual of ability or force of character can make himself felt; so also to some extent can the head of a large family, or a man of wealth. In this case, however, we have been dealing with a village where wealth is rare.

---

[1] See Nadel: *A Black Byzantium,* pp. 63-65, for a discussion as to whether the absence in Nupe village organisation of the " more conspicuously political instruments of control " can be explained by the " multiple control " kinship and religious system of the village. The question, he says, cannot be answered without comparative data since the Nupe State removes from the village sphere military matters and the graver legal cases. In the Ibo situation no such State organisation exists. As an Ibo village is both a kinship and a religious unit, there would seem to be a possible basis of comparison. A significant point of difference.lies in the fact that whereas a Nupe village intermarries for choice, an Ibo village is exogamous.

Nadel also raises the " question of the resistance of this delicately balanced system of multiple control to outside influence and generally the influence of change." A further instance of delicate balance in Ibo organisation is the factor of dual division discussed in the next chapter.

Chapter XI. DUAL DIVISION

A CERTAIN amount has been written on diffusionist lines about the possible origins of the dual division which characterises Ibo social organisation over a wide area, but there has been little attempt, so far as I am aware, to discuss the significance of this feature in the present day working of Ibo society. Its meaning begins, however, to emerge if one studies the day to day life of an Ibo community. One sees how yet another device exists for securing that essential minimum of social achievement which in many societies is assured by the exercise of a central authority. In the absence of such authority other forces are brought into play to achieve the desired end. It may be that this will throw light on the significance of this dual system in other societies. Linton[1] points out how little is known about it at present. In this community rivalry is institutionalised to promote common ends. Instead of the principle " divide and rule," one finds what is almost a principle of dividing instead of ruling. There is a balance rather than a concentration of forces.

When first confronted by Ibo dual division one tends to seek its connection with their system of exogamy. It may happen, as in Ɛgbu Owerri, that the two halves of the town or village group are exogamous. In near-by Owerri, on the other hand, the whole town is an exogamous unit though it has its two halves for other purposes. In Agbaja, as we have seen, the *ama* and *owɛrɛ* halves are not exogamous units : inter-marriage takes place within each half. As for Umuɛkɛ, which is also divided into *ama* and *owɛrɛ,* the whole village, together with the next-door village of Umuɛcɛlɛ is an exogamous unit. Thus, in this society there is no connection in fact between the halving system and exogamy, and for this reason the term " dual organisation " has been avoided. As for any connection in people's minds, I only once heard it suggested. An elder of Umuɛkɛ had been talking about the two halves of Agbaja. In answer to a question of

---

[1] Linton : *Study of Man,* p. 229.

mine he said that all people are divided into *ama* and *owɛrɛ,* and that *ibɛ ama* [⁻ ⁻ ⁻ ⁻]—*ama* half—can marry *ibɛ owɛrɛ* [⁻ ⁻ _ _]—*owɛrɛ* half. This was true as far as Agbaja was concerned, but it was incomplete since each half could also marry within itself. Other explanations that were given of the dual division principle have ·been recorded elsewhere. Here we have to examine the part played by this division in the working of the community.

The division of Agbaja into Agbaja-ama and Agbaja-owɛrɛ and of Umuɛkɛ into Umuɛkɛ-ama and Umuɛkɛ-owɛrɛ has already been described. We have seen that Umuɛkɛ had modified the facts though not the principle of this division. It had happened with the passage of time that Umuɛkɛ-owɛrɛ had greatly outgrown Umuɛkɛ-ama in numbers. It had, therefore, been decided to take the large extended family of Umu Nwa Ɛbodim out of Umuɛkɛ-owɛrɛ and include it in Umuɛkɛ-ama so that numbers should balance in the doing of communal work. This in itself plainly showed the practical part played by this dual division principle. It also showed that the village recognised it and would take steps to keep the balance. This was perhaps the chief move so far towards the differentiation of political from kinship organisation. The needs of the village as a whole had over-ridden the kinship principle of division into two *umunnɛ.* One noticed, however, that though Umu Nwa Ɛbodim now belonged for practical purposes to Umuɛkɛ-ama, its heart was still with Umuɛkɛ-owɛrɛ, its co-children of the same original mother. It became evident early in my stay in the village that there was considerable community of feeling within each division and marked rivalries and jealousies between the two ; but it was not till the time came, at the end of the rains, for the annual path clearing to the central Agbaja market, at the time of the annual religious rites, that I had a clear demonstration of the positive aspect of this dual arrangement.

Each year, towards the end of the farming season, the religious festival of the guardian deity of the whole village-group of Agbaja is celebrated, and in preparation for this, we have already seen, the paths leading from the villages to the market place are cleared, each village being responsible for its own path which, by the end of the rainy season, is usually heavily overgrown. I was told beforehand that this

festival was approaching and that it was a great occasion
for all Agbaja. The path clearing in preparation for the final
day would not be done all at once but on several occasions,
and all the village would be summoned for the work by the
blowing of a horn. The owner of the horn in question was
a man of no particular authority or standing, so far as I
could see, but the right day was a matter of common
knowledge.

When the time came, Umuɛkɛ-ama, including Umu Nwa
Ɛbodim, cleared the right-hand side of the path, and Umuɛkɛ-
owɛrɛ the left. So swift were they on the first day that when,
about twenty minutes after I heard the shouts of those going
to work, I went to see how they were getting on I found
that most people had already finished for that day. Practically the whole male population had turned out, from the
oldest elder to small boys of about six.

On the next occasion I saw how it was that the work got
done so quickly. As before, Umuɛkɛ-ama cleared the right
side of the path towards the stream, and Umuɛkɛ-owɛrɛ the
left. Great bustle and excitement prevailed, the work being
enlivened by song, dance, stamping and shouts. Umuɛkɛ-
owɛrɛ happened to possess one of the best singers in the
village. He told us that Umuɛkɛ-ama was more numerous
than Umuɛkɛ-owɛrɛ but that Umuɛkɛ-owɛrɛ would finish
first all the same. He then sang to his workers on the left
side of the path and they sang back as they worked. Others
were giving the shout of *ti ho !* [_ ‾], which accompanies
dramatic activities. Rivalry between the two sides was such
that both worked till the sweat streamed down their bodies.
It was noon on a hot day and the work went on for an hour
or more. When a group of Umuɛkɛ-owɛrɛ youths on the left
finished their piece before their opposite numbers of the
right, they gave vent to their feelings by tramping up the
path between the lines of workers and then swinging back
down it, singing and dancing, to wash and cool themselves
in the stream. There was no doubt of the efficacy of a spirit
of rivalry in getting quickly through the communal work.
It was the principle of the port and starboard watch.

When I returned to the village in 1937 after a year in
England I found that the path to the market had been greatly
broadened and that it was now the habit for the village to
sweep it every eight days, on the morning of the Agbaja

market day. Umuɛkɛ-ama had to sweep one part and
Umuɛkɛ-owɛrɛ another, and if any man failed to turn up he
was liable to have some of his possessions seized by the
rest as a fine.[1]

In Agbaja the device of dual division does not only
promote the quick doing of communal work, it contributes
towards a solution of that vexed primitive problem, the
policing of society for the enforcing of laws and regulations.
It is one thing—and a comparatively easy one—to pass laws :
it is another to see that they are carried out. Even an acknowledged central authority may find itself weak on the executive
side, and where central authority hardly exists one looks
with interest to see how decisions will be enforced.

One of the preoccupations of Agbaja during my stay in
it was, as we have seen, to increase the size and importance,
and thus the profit, of its central market. It was therefore
decreed, as we have already seen, that everyone, man and
woman, should attend Oriɛ Ekpa, the central Agbaja market,
held every eight days. To facilitate this and to prevent people
from going late it was decided that no one should make
palm oil on market days, a drastic rule when one realises
the feverish oil-making activity of the busy season and the
fact that the proceeds from the sale of oil seemed often
to be used to buy food. Failure to comply with these rules

---

[1] In Owerri I was told that dual division for communal work implied
the same division in matters of sharing. *Kpa ɛ jiri rɔɔ ɔhɔ kpa ɛ ji ɛri*
[‾ ‾ _ _ ‾ ‾ ‾ _ ‾ ‾ _ _ ‾]—as one did that work, so does one eat.
In Umuɛkɛ I was also sometimes told that anything to be shared by the
whole village would be divided in two between the two halves. That
seemed to be the theory, but the shifting of Umu Nwa Ɛbodim from
the *owɛrɛ* to the *ama* half of the village had evidently upset things. Isaac
explained that after this shifting, which he said took place in his father's
father's time, anything shared by all Umuɛkɛ would be divided into
three equal parts, one for Umuɛkɛ-ama proper, one for Umu Nwa
Ɛbodim, and one for Umuɛkɛ-owɛrɛ. I gathered that Umuɛkɛ-ama
proper would not have consented to get only a quarter share, the other
quarter going to Umu Nwa Ɛbodim, but, said Isaac, when " meetings "
came into fashion, the system of sharing by individuals was adopted.

The current and admitted practice of the men of the village, when
I was there, was a division of tax-paying males into four groups, not
on a kinship basis. It was said that thus quarrelling would be avoided.
A group would not contend for a larger share if it were not united by
kinship sentiment.

The women were said sometimes to share according to the two
halves of the village, and on one occasion I saw them do so. On another
occasion they divided themselves into nine groups of twelve each.

involved the payment of a fine. The enforcement of such
regulations presents perhaps special difficulties in a society
where kinship bonds strengthen those of common locality.
The delicacy of the English village policeman about the
doings of his neighbours is increased here by ties of relationship. Who is going to give away his neighbour and kinsman
for a lapse from strict legality, apart even from the possibility
that the kinsman, living next door, has every opportunity for
counter observation ?

In this dilemma the principle of dual division is invoked.
When Agbaja decided thus to improve its market it arranged
that members of Agbaja-owere should detect and penalise
defaulters in Agbaja-ama and *vice versa*. The enforcers of
the law would thus not merely be exempt from neighbourly
and family scruples, but would tend to be urged on by a
feeling of inter-group rivalry.

In a further way the principle of dual division enters into
the sphere of the execution of justice. On one occasion
I saw the married women of Umuɛkɛ village descend at
midnight on the house of one of their number to demand
payment of a fine which they had previously imposed upon
her for the offence of making a false accusation against
another woman. I tried afterwards to find out whether there
were any head women whose duty it would be to initiate
proceedings in such a case as this collection of a fine. I was
told, however, that in theory anyone could take the initiative
but that Umuɛkɛ-owere would turn out first if an Umuɛkɛ-
ama fine were involved and *vice versa*. This was borne out
by what I had seen. The culprit was from Umuɛkɛ-ama,
and it was the women of the far, *owere* end of the village
who came down and roused those of Umu Nwa Ɛbodim,
originally an *owere* group, and went in company with them
to call out the women of Umuɛkɛ-ama.

I noticed, too, during the very lively proceedings of
the midnight session that a prominent part was played by
an Umuɛkɛ-owere woman of forceful character, named Lɔlɔ.
She was not, so far as I could see, formally acclaimed as
president or official leader of the proceedings, but in the
discussion that followed the swift raid on the offender's
house, and punctuated the wild outbursts of dance and song,
Lɔlɔ took a leading part. When the women of the offender's
house-group pleaded for a postponement of the fine, it was

she who withdrew, followed by the other women. Lest this should give a misleading picture of authority quietly accepted it is well to add that the women discussed warmly whether or not Lɔlɔ had been bribed into this easy retreat. With that inability to rest on a decision which makes impressive final-seeming withdrawals and immediate returns a recurrent feature of Ibo discussions, she and the rest of the women returned to the fray, only to withdraw again later on the understanding that they should return next night for the fine. In point of fact, when they returned, the women of the culprit's house-group had had time to think—a process which would certainly have been difficult during the noise and excitement of the raid, of which the technique was evidently an attempt to carry the case by storm. They therefore pointed out that certain offences in Umuɛkɛ-owɛrɛ were still awaiting final settlement and that what was sauce for the goose was sauce for the gander, and they intended to wait till others also met their obligations. Dual division is evidently a double-edged tool, but that it is a mechanism for getting things going in the absence of a central authority seems clear from one case after another.

It may also, apparently, be used by an individual who has a grievance against his own family. A dispute to which reference has already been made arose in Umuɛkɛ-ama about a piece of land. A youth cleared for farming a plot of land that had belonged to his father's dead brother. A widow of the dead brother, now living with his younger brother, contested the lad's right to plant in the land, and planted her own crop of coco-yam, which he tore up. The brother, A-ziɛ, with whom she was living, now intervened. He wished to approach the lad's father, his own elder brother, but instead of calling on members of Umuɛkɛ-ama to undertake the mission he summoned several people from the Umu Nwa Ɛbodim family group of Umuɛkɛ-owɛrɛ proper. As they got no satisfactory answer, he invoked the aid of the *osu* of the powerful yam spirit, who took the alarming step of planting the sacred spear of the spirit as a threat of doom in the yard of the offending youth's house-group. When the youth's elder wanted to approach A-ziɛ, he took with him several elders not of his own side of the village but of Umuɛkɛ-owɛrɛ, to ask why such a drastic step had been taken. One can, I think, conclude that strangers are invoked as being more likely than relatives to pursue zealously the cause in hand.

Seen as a factor in the working of an Ibo community, this dual division is of evident practical importance, but its theoretical interest lies in the pluralistic principle that it embodies. It reinforces what has already emerged, namely, that a pluralistic spirit informs the methods by which an Ibo community manages its affairs. Not only is there no chief with anything approaching autocratic powers but there is no one hierarchy of powers rising from a broad democratic basis through ascending levels to one central peak. Democratic the system is, and allowing considerable play to the individual. " Ɔ deghe onyɛ nwɛ anye " [_ ‾ ‾ ‾ ‾ ‾ _ _ _], as the people of Owerri say : " there is no one who owns us." We have no rulers, that is to say. Ibo democracy, unlike English, works through a number of juxtaposed groups and a system of checks and balances rather than on a unitary or hierarchical principle.

Side by side with this pluralism is the fact that the Ibo community is organised on a very small village or village-group scale, but it is important to distinguish between these two facts. The smallness of scale can be correlated to some extent with a simple stage of development, but a pluralistic principle of organisation can be found in a society or state of any stage or size, as the jump from Ibo organisation to the constitution of the United States will show.

PART II

Exogamy

Chapter XII. THE SYSTEM OF EXOGAMY

ON the political level, as we have seen, the Ibo present a spectacle of large numbers of small, more or less independent units of which the village, or in some cases the village-group, may be the largest from the point of view of effective government. But it would be far from the facts if these small units were pictured as a collection of isolated cells. Such an impression could only arise from undue concentration on the political side of life among a people where this aspect operates on a very small scale and is still incompletely differentiated.

The very fact that the cells have survived calls for some consideration. No doubt it is true that before the establishment of British government at the beginning of this century there was little security in the land. There is not over much now except for the white man.[1] But just as the present degree of safety should not be exaggerated so, it seems, one should not over-stress the perils of the old days.

Certainly the accounts of informants do not depict a peaceful scene. A man in early middle age said, for instance, that when he was a child his parents kept him in so strictly for fear of danger that he did not realise the existence of any village other than his own though the next one was only a few hundred yards away. And people to-day describe how in the not far distant old days men would go to work on their farms heavily armed against possible enemies and how the food supply would fail because disturbed conditions prevented the planting or harvesting of crops. Even now, after more than thirty years of British administration, a man is apt to look on everyone beyond a radius of a few miles from his own home as an enemy. Quite sophisticated individuals, as we have said, refer to people living beyond

[1] Those who look on the great main roads running straight for miles through the Ibo bush as factors of progress—as no doubt they are—would none the less have listened with interest to the views of my sophisticated cook. He would explain with appropriate gestures how the nefarious character would hide in the bush at the roadside, peering out at intervals till he spied a traveller alone upon a stretch of road, upon whom he could thus fall without fear of witnesses.

a radius of six or seven miles as " very wicked." And even
near their own homes they hesitate about going out alone
on a dark night, particularly if an important man had just
died and heads for a funeral are likely to be wanted. As
one stays on in the country it becomes increasingly clear
that fear is a marked element of every-day existence.

Certainly in the old days much sporadic fighting must
have gone on, but it is not easy to assess the scale of it.
The Aro people were hiring mercenaries and raiding for
slaves in a large way. But for the most part the scale of
actual warfare, as distinguished from general insecurity
must probably be accepted as modest by modern European
standards. One man described a fight which his people had
with some people of a neighbouring village group when he
was a child. Hostilities lasted for two years and it was, he
said, an outstandingly great war. Asked how many people
were killed, he replied twelve.

In addition to actual fighting, anyone straying injudic-
iously far from his own place would run the risk of being
killed or enslaved. In spite, however, of scrapping and
ambushing, the Ibo survived to the number of about four
million. What, if any, were the mitigating factors in this
situation of innumerable small and potentially hostile units ?
We have already seen that they share a culture which, with
local variations, has none the less considerable common
features, at least so far as the central Ibo are concerned.
They speak dialectal varieties of the same language, and
have a certain if limited sense of common identity. What
we must now emphasise is that, although these small cells
lack any pyramidal form of grouping under a centralised
authority, they are none the less linked horizontally one with
another in all directions like a well-articulated sheet of chain
mail. Certain of these interconnections are well recognised.
Powerful oracles, of which the notorious Long Juju of Aro
Cuku was only one though an outstanding example, had
and still have tentacles which, combined with a trading
interest, spread far and wide through Ibo country. Doctor—
magicians too—*nde dibea*—of a particular locality would
sometimes be visiting specialists with a range of a hundred
miles and more.[1] And over and above these sporadic contacts

---

[1] In Umueke there were certain purposes for which a *dibea* from
Umudiaka, about eighty miles away, was called in.

are the markets where regularly, week after week, people from considerable distances over a wide area meet together primarily for economic reasons but also for a number of secondary activities. So much is generally recognised. But the implications of Ibo exogamy are less widely known. From the fact that a man must seek his wife outside his own village there flows a host of consequences. It is of the greatest importance for Ibo society that the exogamous unit is also a local group.

This fact means, in the first place, that every man has contacts not only with his own village but with the birth place of his mother, with that of his wife and with the various places into which his sisters have married. But because of the customary and legal regulations governing the behaviour of relatives by marriage it also means that there are incessant comings and goings, year in and year out, between these villages and that the conduct of these groups towards one another is modified by the fact of inter-marriage.

Of great importance still, these links were vital in the old precarious days. The system of exogamy must have been one of the things that made inter-village or inter-village-group trading a practical possibility. I have asked women how in the old days they would dare to go to the market of a village-group other than the one in which they were married and living. They have said that they would get one of the wives of their husband's village-group, who had been born in the place holding the market and was therefore safe in it, to take them under her wing and accompany them.

Nwa Ori Ego, of Umuɛkɛ, recounted that when her husband was alive people of other places who wanted to go to Umukabia market would come to him with food and palm wine and cowries and his mother would lead them to Umukabia because her own mother, who had left her first husband, had then married an Umukabia man. Nwa Ori Ego's husband would tell his clients that if anyone molested them they were to come and fetch him.

Powerful individuals could act as protectors to people travelling to market. But here again it would sometimes be through relatives-in-law that an introduction to such an individual could be gained.

An Owerri man explained that formerly a man would arrange to marry a wife in a place with which he wanted to trade and he would try to manage so that the path from his group to hers passed through no other, and possibly hostile, group. He might even marry a series of wives along a trade route. To say, in fact, that trade followed the wife would hardly in such cases be an exaggeration. And this geographical factor still operates in the choice of a wife.

In addition to its economic effects exogamy was also a factor in softening inter-village disputes even though it may at times have provoked them. As Nwa Ori Ego pointed out, if an Umuɛkɛ man gave his daughter to be married in Abɔse and subsequently withdrew her and gave her to some one else the people of Umuɛkɛ would not dare to pass Abɔse for fear of being seized and sold. And the tale of quarrels concerning wives could be multiplied. None the less it seems certain that inter-marriage acted as a mitigation of inter-village strife.

A man of Owerri said that if his place were at war with another his people would try to hide behind such of their members as had married wives from the hostile group because they, as in-laws, would be safe from attack. If two village-groups fought, the *nde nwanwa,* the sons of women born in those groups but married elsewhere, would come to stop them. They would take young palm fronds and put them between the combatants and make them cease fighting till the case could be judged.

James, of Umuɛkɛ, too, described a fight he had witnessed in pre-British days. Four Agbaja villages of the *ama* side fought with three others of the *owɛrɛ* side in Oriɛ Ekpa market on market day. Eventually the women either born or married in Agbaja came and beat drums and stopped the fight, and the case was judged by the elders of all Agbaja.

On the judicial side, too, in Agbaja, exogamy played a part. Side by side with their peace-making functions was the fact that the women born in a village but married else-where were concerned with crimes committed by one of their classificatory brothers against another. If one of these killed a kinsman, his classificatory sisters might return to the village and seize his property. Such a case is discussed later.[1]

---

[1] An Mbieri man at present in London has recently stressed this point to me.

This fact of intermarriage between different and potentially hostile groups must have contributed in no small degree to the survival of the Ibo people.[1]

Clearly, then, it is important to grasp both the outlines of the Ibo system of exogamy and its implications. Here the situation will be described chiefly with reference to the village of Umuɛkɛ Agbaja. But in the main it seems to hold good over much of Ibo country.

The local and kinship principles of grouping underlying the village-group of Agbaja have already been described.[2] The whole group of eleven villages, forming a continuous territorial unit, claimed descent from one mythical ancestor and his wife whose eleven sons were the ancestors of the eleven villages. Each village is thus a collection of people claiming descent from a common ancestor and living on a certain area of land. Each village is an exogamous unit. That is to say that no man can marry a woman born in the same village as himself.[3] In addition, certain Agbaja villages may not intermarry with each other. Umuɛkɛ, for instance, could not intermarry with the adjacent village of Umuɛcɛlɛ, with whom it considered itself closely related. The two villages had a common ancestral symbol known as *umunɛ*. But Umuɛkɛ could and did intermarry with the villages of

---

1 Wagner suggests for the Bantu of Kavirondo, that groups of similar culture and with such links as intermarriage, be termed a political unit in spite of the lack of a common political authority. (See *African Political Systems,* ed. Fortes and Evans-Pritchard, p. 200.) But this would seem to hinder rather than help a true appreciation of the facts : it obscures what Malinowski stresses as of great importance in his introduction to Hogbin : *Law and Order in Polynesia,* namely, that a considerable degree of social integration and stability is possible with little in the way of political organisation, particularly of the State type. On the distinction between the State and other forms of political organisation see Nadel : *A Black Byzantium,* p. 69.

2 See Ch. II.

3 It was said that in the old days a man of the village of Abɔse could marry a woman of Abɔse though not of his immediate kinship group.

One man also said that in the old days the villages of Umuɛkɛ and Umuɛcɛlɛ could intermarry, but that the elders had forbidden it before he was born, in the time of his father's father. In other parts of the country one would sometimes find a tendency to a splitting up of the exogamous unit.

Owerri village-group or town was discussing the advisability of allowing intermarriage within its boundaries, hitherto not permitted except with a small group of strangers who had come from elsewhere and settled there.

Umuamɛkɛ and Umuɔbea which were as near, territorially, as Umuɛcɛlɛ, and it intermarried with all the other villages of Agbaja.

The table on this page shows which Agbaja villages do not intermarry with one another. Apart from this they can marry where they like inside or outside Agbaja with one important further restriction. No man or woman can intermarry with the native village of his or her mother. Thus not only can a village not be self-contained but it has to multiply its connections. The significance of this is particularly evident in a village-group of the type of Ɛgbu,

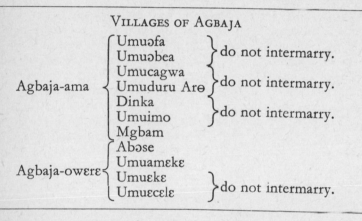

VILLAGES OF AGBAJA

Agbaja-ama
- Umuɔfa } do not intermarry.
- Umuɔbea
- Umucagwa } do not intermarry.
- Umuduru Arθ
- Dinka } do not intermarry.
- Umuimo
- Mgbam

Agbaja-owɛrɛ
- Abɔse
- Umuamɛkɛ
- Umuɛkɛ } do not intermarry.
- Umuɛcɛlɛ

near Owerri. Here the five villages of Ɛgbu form a compact group typical of this part of the country and quite unlike the scattered villages of the Agbaja region. Ɛgbu has the usual dual division principle and has two villages in one division and three in the other. Each of these divisions is an exogamous group but can inter-marry with the other. If that were all it is easy to see that Ɛgbu might be a self-contained unit from the marriage point of view with all the consequent loss of contacts of other sorts with neighbouring village-groups. But as a man cannot marry a woman either in his own exogamous group nor in that of his mother it is clear that though in one generation an Ɛgbu man of one division may marry an Ɛgbu woman of the other his son will be forced to go outside the village group for his wife and outside contacts will at once be established.

In Agbaja dual division and exogamy run along different

lines except for the fact that the villages which do not inter-marry are both members of the same division. But they have other villages within the same division with which they can and do inter-marry.

In all this it is primarily kinship that determines the fact of exogamy. It is not because two villages are near together that marriage between them is forbidden. The houses of Umuɛkɛ and of Umuamɛkɛ were at some points almost continuous yet inter-marriage was allowed. But Umuɛkɛ and Umuɛcɛlɛ had the same *umunɛ,* the same ancestral symbol, therefore they could not inter-marry.

This is not to say that the factor of common locality does not count. Slaves and, so far as I know, strangers observe the rules of the exogamous unit within which they live though they may have no blood relationship with it. But it is blood, not territory, that is the decisive factor in the general system of exogamy.

This being so, it is of no small importance that the kinship and the local groups coincide. People, that is to say, who are descended from a common ancestor inhabit a common territory. The village is both a kinship and a local unit. Since marriage is patrilocal, the wife coming to live in the village of her husband, the result is that the villages are everywhere linked together by their women, the daughters of one village being the wives in a large number of others.[1]

The taboo on sexual intercourse between men and women born in the same village ranks perhaps higher than any other for importance and gravity in local feeling. It may be considered as standing in the sphere both of incest and of exogamy since it refers to a man's immediate sisters by the same parents and also to his " classificatory " sisters who are all the women born in the same village. Any breach of this taboo is a contamination of the earth—*mmɛrɛ ala* [¯ ¯ ¯ _ _]. And in the old days the offenders would have been buried alive in the central Agbaja market place, Oriɛ Ekpa. This burying of them would purify and appease *Ala.*

---

[1] Of a sample of forty wives in Umuɛkɛ (Umuɛkɛ-ama and Umu Nwa Ɛbodim), sixteen were from other Agbaja villages and twenty-four were from outside Agbaja.

Of a sample of twenty-six women born in Umuɛkɛ (Umuɛkɛ-ama and Umu Nwa Ɛbodim), sixteen were married to other Agbaja villages and ten to places outside Agbaja.

It was maintained that even now if such an offence were
known to have taken place people would go secretly at
night and cut a hole through the mud wall into the man's
house and kill him. He would then be placed at the foot
of a palm tree, from which passers-by would imagine him
to have fallen to his death.

I only heard of one case of a suspected breach of this
taboo and that was between a man and a woman born in
opposite halves of the neighbouring Agbaja village of
Umuamɛkɛ. The woman was married in Umuɛkɛ. But guilt
was not proved since the man had sworn to his innocence
on a supernatural symbol.

The taboo certainly seemed to be respected and observed
in Umuɛkɛ, so far as one could judge. In Owerri town, on
the other hand, which is far more exposed to external influences of all kinds than Agbaja, I was told that it was
breaking down.

It is relevant to the question of this taboo to point out
that it does not, of course, apply to the relations between
a man and the women married into his village. And with
them he does, in fact, quite often have relations. It is not
in theory socially approved for a married woman to take a
secret lover, though there does not seem to be much strength
of feeling about this practice, which certainly occurs.
Whereas pre-marital chastity is socially required, though
not by any means always achieved, post-marital conduct is
another matter. And a woman, usually an only wife, who
finds that she has too much work to do, may, by arrangement
with her husband, take a lover to help her with her farm
work. This is socially allowed in theory and in practice.
A man without a wife may for his part get a woman lover
to weed his farm for him.

There are also cases in which the parents of a young boy
marry a mature woman to him and get one of his fellow
villagers to impregnate the woman. The sociological father
of the children she bears will be her husband, the immature
boy.

A consideration of all these facts would seem to show
that, for the area we are discussing, the view of exogamy
put forward by Malinowski needs some modification.
" Exogamy," he says, " eliminates sex from a whole order
of social relations, those between clansmen and clanswomen.

Since the clan forms the typical co-operative group, the members of which are united by a number of legal, cere- monial and economic interests and activities, exogamy, by dissociating the disruptive and competitive element from workaday co-operation, fulfils once more an important cultural function."[1]

As we have seen, in this area it is the village or groups within it, consisting of the men born in it and of their wives, which is a co-operative unit or collection of units of the kind described by Malinowski. Yet there is no taboo com- parable to that of exogamy on the sex relations between the men and their fellow villagers' wives. It would seem, in fact, that the social function of exogamy is not so much the preservation of " clan " or " village " unity as the ensuring that each village shall be linked to the surrounding ones by the bond of intermarriage. The importance of this linkage in breaking down local self-sufficiency and in facilitating inter-group economic exchange can hardly be exaggerated. It is the great factor mitigating the centrifugal force of Ibo separatism.

In addition to the taboo on marriage and intercourse there are certain other taboos and customs between men and women born in the same village. For instance, a woman will feel great shame if she sees her classificatory brother urinating. Nor will she be free and easy in her talk if they are in the same room. As one woman explained : " If there is talk of buttocks—akɔkɔ otulɛ [‾ ‾ ‾ _ _]—and my ' brother ' comes to that place I shall keep silent." And if he comes and sits beside her on the same bench or bed she will get up and sit on the floor. Brothers and sisters by the same father or mother sleep together when they are small. But in Agbaja this is taboo when they reach maturity though customs vary in other places. In fact a boy of about eight will no longer sleep with his sisters. As between father and daughter they will not see each other washing, nor will they talk of sexual matters. And if the daughter is mature she will not sleep in her mother's house on the nights her father sleeps there. In Owerri it is forbidden for classificatory brothers and sisters to wash in the stream at the same place. The formula of reassurance by which a man may tell a

---

[1] Malinowski Art : " Culture " Encyclopædia of Social Sciences.

woman who does not see him clearly that he is not her
" brother " is " *A ma a ge ri'ara anǝ* "—" We can eat each
other, *i.e.* we are not so closely related that it is taboo for
us to eat each other."

There is one other important marriage prohibition which
has quite a different principle from that of kinship as its
basis. Something has already been said of the *osu* people
who form an element apart in Ibo society. They are people
who, themselves or their ancestors, have been bought and
sacrificed as slaves to a deity of some kind whom they
thereafter serve. From that time onward it is strictly taboo—
nsǝ [¯ ¯]—for them or their descendants to marry or have
sexual intercourse with any free-born Ibo.

These *osu* people can only inter-marry with each other,
but, endogamous as a class, they also observe the same
inter-village rules of exogamy as the free-born. That is to
say that an *osu* in Umuεkε could not marry another *osu* of
this village nor of the village of Umuεcεlε. To this extent,
therefore, the *osu* fall within the general plan of Ibo exogamy.

Intermarriage and sexual intercourse with an *osu* is not
only *nsǝ* for a free-born, but the idea of it fills him with
horror. And this is true, though unofficially, of Christians
as well as of pagans. I discussed the matter often with a
middle-aged man in Owerri who was an earnest and educated
Christian of many years standing. He admitted that *osu*
status was incompatible with Christian principles and was
not recognised by the Church. But he was emphatic that he
would not contemplate a daughter of his marrying an *osu*.
He was quite frank. He said that officially he preached in
Church against any discrimination in the matter, but that
none the less when it came to putting his principles into
practice his heart said no.[1]

---

[1] The *osu* element in Ibo society is an exceedingly interesting
phenomenon. It is also a considerable social problem. Slavery has of
course been abolished as a legal status since the coming of British
government. But the stigma attaching to the fact of being *osu* remains
and is a matter of great distress to those *osu* who are being Christianised
and given Europeanised education. We cannot here discuss either the
phenomenon itself nor the practical problem it creates. But in this account
of marriage regulations it will perhaps not be out of place to raise
tentatively a point which has not, I think, hitherto been discussed. My
own observations suggested that there was a fair amount of marked

In an account of Ibo exogamy it was necessary to speak of the *osu* situation. But it is a side issue in our present attempt to explore the links created by the rules of exogamy between the village units of Ibo society. The rules have now been described. But it remains to consider the innumerable comings and goings between the villages that result from this network of intermarriage.

---

physical or mental defect among the *osu* members of the population. This was certainly not always the case. Some of them were fine specimens. But, among the relatively small number that I knew personally, two were epileptics, one was in an advanced stage of leprosy, another had a lump on one shoulder, another had some form of retarded physical and mental development. The evidence, in fact, was such as to raise the question whether the taboo on intermarriage or sexual intercourse with an *osu* was not, incidentally, an unconscious social device for segregating the less healthy strains in the population. The fact that an *osu* is someone who has been sold and who is thus probably regarded as an undesirable would help to account for a degree of inferiority either mental or physical. This point is, however, merely raised to suggest a possible line of enquiry. My own evidence was quite insufficient either to prove or disprove it.

I have lately been told by an Ibo man in London that a considerable proportion of the prostitutes in the big towns are *osu*.

Chapter XIII. THE IMPLICATIONS OF EXOGAMY

IN considering the implications of exogamy one must first look at the position of a man in his own village and village-group. His relations with the village of his mother will then be considered.

As between the individuals born in any one village-group or possibly in two or more village-groups if they claim a common ancestor, and more particularly between the individuals born in one village there are certain taboos. It is taboo to kill or eat a fellow villager or to make black magic against him. This is not to say that such things do not occur, but the prohibition is there and applies increasingly with the decreasing size of the unit involved. A man should thus, in theory anyway, be able to feel himself fairly safe in his own birthplace and in fact he does so. But it is in the native village of his mother that he really feels himself to be *persona grata*. "I can climb up and pick their cocoa-nuts and they will not mind," said one man to me as we walked through his mother's village, and his bearing was that of one who knows that he is welcome. And he took me into some wedding celebrations that were in progress because he had the right of entry. A man is greatly respected in his mother's village, said another of my informants. Talking with a third man one noticed how his voice changed when he came to the congenial subject of his mother's native village. He spoke as though it were with her people that he really felt safe—an unusual feeling for an Ibo. He said that his own native place might harm him—one of the many discrepancies between social theory and hard fact—but that he would not fear in his mother's place. He would eat without being afraid. If he goes to his mother's village and steals the people will not hold him, they will let him go. If one of them tries to make bad medicine—practice sorcery—against him it will not harm him and the maker himself will die. And the same thing will happen if he tries to make bad medicine against his mother's people. If, as he expressed it, people do any bad thing to him the people of his mother's village will ask them to stop. And if people, even of his own native village, fight him his mother's folk will come to his assistance. If he should commit any crime so serious that it involved his being taken to the central Agbaja market place to be killed in the presence of all Agbaja, the people of his mother's village—in this case it was one of the Agbaja villages and of the same group as his own—would run away that they might not see him killed.

Clearly matriliny plays a considerable part in Ibo society. Descent and succession are patrilineal, marriage is patrilocal and a man inherits from his father. But the matrilineal principle is there asserting itself both legally and emotionally.

As for the comings and goings between a man and his wife's village they are incessant. From the time that a man starts marrying a wife—for the term, *ɵlɵ nwunye* [‾ ‾ ‾ _ _], to marry a woman, covers a long and complex process—to the time of her death there is a constant exchange of visits, of gifts and of payments between the husband and his kinsmen and the wife and hers.

Courtship starts formally by the prospective husband, accompanied by a friend, carrying palm wine to the girl's family, who in return entertain him with food. After further gifts of palm wine from the man the girl comes for a succession of visits, each lasting a few days, to the husband's home and gifts specified by custom are exchanged between the wife's family and the husband and his kinsfolk. After this, when the amount of the bride price is to be settled, the man takes with him a number of elders of his own village and goes to the girl's home and the matter is decided between the elders of the two villages. Thereafter till the bride price is paid the girl will pay frequent visits of several days duration to the husband's home. When the bride price is paid, both the girl's parents getting a share, the latter give her yams and coco-yams, domestic animals and so forth and she goes to live permanently with her husband in his village.

Her mother must then come to " put her hearth "—*iʒhi akwɵkwa*. This is an important affair and it is essential that it be done before the woman bears a child or the child, it is thought, will die. If, as frequently happens, the girl goes to live permanently with her husband before the bride price is fully paid there will be perpetual negotiations and bickerings between her parents and the husband until the matter is settled.

At the birth of a child the patrilineal principle is emphasised by the fact that the wife bears the child in her husband's place and is looked after by women of his housegroup during her confinement. After the child is born the mother stays either in her own house or sometimes in that of a senior wife of her husband for four days without going out and is usually cooked for and she and the baby looked after by the senior wife of her husband or his mother for at least four days and often longer. Her own mother would only be allowed to cook for her if invited to do so by the husband's people. In one case I saw, the daughter of the woman's eldest sister cooked for her after the first few days.

But custom ordains the exchange of presents and visits between the relatives of the husband and those of the wife when a child is born, and the nature and extent of them is laid down in detail. Immediately after the event the husband's family gives the wife's family a gourd of palm wine, four yams, some leaves of *okase,* some palm oil in a cocoanut shell, four cakes of salt, four pieces of firewood, one or two oil beans, and cowries to the value of several pence in the case of the first child and to the value of about three farthings for the others. In one case that I witnessed these things were carried over to the wife's village by the husband's mother and an elderly woman of the husband's village on the day after the child was born. In return the wife's people come another day to the husband's place bringing a cock and four big yams, and on a succeeding day they bring eight yams more. The cock and the eight yams are then cooked and eaten by the husband's and wife's people together. On that day the custom is that for the first child the husband, or, if he has no money, his father, should give the wife's father £1. If he has not got so much he must produce something, whether 10*s.* or 5*s.* The wife's father or, if he is dead, her brother, must not be allowed to go away empty handed.

On the fourth day after the birth the wife's people come to her husband's place for the naming of the child. The father of the husband and sometimes the father of the wife, too, go to a diviner, *dibea,* to learn what ancestor or spirit is reincarnated in the child and what its name is in consequence. The fee to the diviner should, as far as I could make out, be paid jointly by the grandfathers. But any exchange of gifts or payments among the Ibo involves much bickering and mutual adjustment and in one case to which we have already referred,[1] the husband's father admitted that at the birth of the first child he had only produced 15s. instead of £1 but he complained that the wife's father had brought no money for the *dibea* and no cock or basket of yams. The argument was running on through the years, the birth of each successive child provoking it afresh. The contacts, in fact, occasioned by intermarriage, important though they are as social links, are none the less accompanied in many cases by considerable friction.

Patriliny is again emphasised in the fact that a woman is not supposed to take her child to visit her own family until it is old enough to walk.[2] When it is eventually taken its mother's people will give it yams which its mother will plant for it in her husband's land. As the child gets older it pays periodical visits to its maternal grandmother, staying for several days at a time or for longer. One will see a small boy helping his old grandmother to pound her palm nuts, and he will of course be in the privileged position of *nwanwa*—the son in his mother's village. If a woman's baby should die, she will return to her own mother for a time.

When a woman has borne several children she may, on the occasion of some illness, be told by a *dibea* to make a shrine for her *Ci,* the personal spirit which everyone has and which is in the nature both of a creating and a guardian spirit. If her parents are alive they will come to take part in the ceremony.

Thus the birth and rearing of children involve much exchanging of visits and gifts, many laid down by custom, between the husband's place and that of the wife. In addition, a woman will pay constant informal visits to her parents. If her mother is ill she will go to her and her mother may even depend considerably on her daughter's care. One elderly woman of Umu Nwa Ɛbodim, who was often ailing, had a daughter married to a man in European employment. He was moved to a distant place and the old woman tried to prevent her daughter from going to him because she said she could not get on without her.

---

[1] See p. 96.   [2] This custom was said to be breaking down.

In 1937, Nwa Ori Ɛgo, an old widow in Umuɛkɛ-ama, who had no sons and who was consequently rather a lonely figure in her house-group, was for some time immobilised by a bad foot, and was later seriously ill from an abscess in the ear. She had two daughters married in neighbouring villages who were greatly concerned about her and paid her frequent visits or sent their children to help her. But for them, she said, she would not have survived. In the same way a mother will go off to see a married daughter who is ill.

If a woman's husband neglects her or treats her badly she may return to her parent's home. There were at least four women in Umuɛkɛ-ama and Umu Nwa Ɛbodim living thus with their parents. This may also happen if a woman's husband does not finish paying the agreed price for her. My garden boy's wife had returned to her people for this reason. A woman may also, if she is annoyed or offended, sweep out of her husband's home and back to her native place for a day or two.[1]

One has the impression that a woman in her birthplace has a feeling of superiority that she lacks in her husband's village. There she has been acquired by payment : in her own place she is native of the soil. *"Anye nwɛ ala"*—" we own the soil," as two women remarked one day during a visit to the village of their birth.

There are certain social occasions when there is a general movement of visits between in-laws. At the end of the wet season, when the whole of Agbaja village-group clears the paths to the central market place on the same day, there is much visiting and entertaining between relations by marriage : and shortly after, just when yams are beginning to be dug and when the religious festival of the local deity is held, married daughters, taking presents of food, return to their parents' place accompanied by their children and sometimes by their husbands. They may be present at the family sacrifice and will be given return presents of food when they go home. At the time of the new yam festivals, too, when yams are not dug but cut, a man's small unmarried daughter may go to stay for several weeks with his married sister who will of course be living in some other village.

---

[1] See p. 85.

There will be many informal comings and goings between the villages of husband and wife. The wife's unmarried sister may come to visit her for the day, or she may fetch a small girl from her native place to stay with her for a few days : or I have seen an old woman going off at the request of her son-in-law to fetch him a *dibea* as he was worried about one of the medicines he kept in his house and which he said had got out of order.

But if in life there is much inter-communication between the families of husband and wife there is, on the death of the woman, a rallying of her whole native village, both men and their wives, to fetch her back for burial either in or on the road to her birthplace, according as a *dibea* may direct. Many regulations are decreed by law and custom for this occasion. In the same way I was told in Owerri that when a man dies his sisters will come from their husbands' villages, accompanied by their husbands and possibly some of their husbands' relatives. The dead man's daughters will come from where they are married, the eldest daughter contributing more or less equally with the eldest son to the funeral expenses.

In Agbaja, after a man has died, his classificatory sisters, the women, that is to say, born in his village, may be called in to deal with offences committeed against him by his wives during his lifetime. Death is, in fact, the occasion for much movement among the living. One was constantly meeting people going off to visit some village because a relative had died there.

It would be possible to multiply almost indefinitely the account of inter-village contacts occasioned by marriage ; but enough has been said to show how ceaselessly and in how many directions a village is linked with its neighbours by the workings of exogamy. Without a realisation of this factor no understanding of the Ibo situation is possible.

PART III

Women's Organisation

Chapter XIV. WOMEN'S WORK

THE rules of Ibo exogamy mean, as we now see, that whereas a man lives and dies an inhabitant of his native village a woman spends her childhood in the village where she was born and her adult life in the village of her husband. This double charter of residence, the having of a foot in two camps, is reflected clearly in the organisation of the women, which is both of an intra-village and an inter-village character with important results for Ibo social life.

This is not a discussion of the whole place of women in village life. It deals rather with their public than with their domestic life. It is specifically an account of the nature and activities of the various kinds of women's groups. But a few words of introduction are needed to give substance to the picture.

An Ibo woman, if questioned, will say that she stays at home and obeys her husband—who is she to be a public figure? But, in fact, not only does she take a part with the men, though overtly a lesser one, in the management of village matters—" a case forbids no one," say the Ibo—but she has her own quite separate and distinct organisations for the managing of women's affairs.

One hears Europeans talking of "these matriarchies of West Africa " where, in popular imagination, fierce Amazons or wise and powerful grandmothers hold sway over tribes of apparently unprotesting males. And the Aba women's riots of 1929-31 did nothing to counteract this view. On the other hand we have the dutiful and obedient wife story put forward, as we have seen, by the women themselves. The observer on the spot finds elements of both accounts in the actual situation. To all appearance there is much truth in the women's contention of quiet wifeliness. In general village affairs the men take the predominant part. For one thing, they have time. Certainly they take a more vocal part. Women, except where they are directly concerned, talk far less in public than men. There is, I think, a sense of seemliness in women's behaviour which in normal circumstances demands a certain reserve on public occasions. Such occasions are for the men.

On the other hand the part women play in the economic and family life of the society means that without public position they have much quiet power. In Umuɛkɛ and its neighbourhood the women are the chief breadwinners. Among this agricultural people who live almost entirely on the products of the soil, it is the crops grown by the women that provide the staple diet. For the purpose of food the economic unit is basically the individual family, which grows or buys its own food and is responsible for its own members. Husbands and wives both have crops, the men having chiefly yam and the women having coco-yam and cassava and often a certain amount of yam.[1] The women also have the lesser, hunger season corn crop and the leaves and vegetables that are the indispensable ingredients and relishes, together with a very little dried fish and some palm oil, of the soup with which the main food is eaten. It is the women who provide the lion's share of the normal family food, buying such extras as salt out of their own money. The men provide the palm wine, that important vitamin-bearing element of Ibo diet of which the women and children get a share but a far smaller one than that of the men. The men also bring out their yams for visitors and buy a little meat on special occasions and may now and then put some yams into the common pot. But they admit that it is normally the women who feed them. This they do so far as possible out of the crops they grow. But if these are not adequate, as in Umuɛkɛ, with its poor soil, they often are not, the women must supplement by buying food in the market. The money for this they get chiefly by selling the kernels from the palm nuts their husbands cut and from which they help them make oil.

A woman may also earn money by petty trading in tobacco or may occasionally sell a fowl or any surplus farm produce she happens to have. It is not easy, as we have said, to see how the balance of the sale and purchase of crops works out. But constant observation in Umuɛkɛ suggested that many people were not self-supporting in the matter of home-grown crops like yam, coco-yam, cassava and unripe bananas, but had to buy from more fertile or less heavily populated areas.

---

[1] For the ownership of crops and the production of food as between men and women, see M. M. Green : *Land Tenure in an Ibo Village*.

The men help with the heavier parts of the farm work such as bush clearing and hoeing. But there are months when they have little if anything to do in the farms whereas all the year round, though particularly in the wet season, the women are occupied in weeding, planting, tending the crops. They it is, also, who fetch food from the farm and who do the hard and tedious work of pounding and cooking it. Several women, not necessarily wives of the same extended family, will sometimes help each other in turn with farm work and men may also help each other in this way.

In addition, most women, particularly those with a large family to feed, go frequently to one or other of the local markets or to their own. As each is usually held only once in eight days it means that at times it may be necessary to walk several miles to the market of the day, carrying a head load that personally I could sometimes barely raise from the ground, far less carry.

Clearly, then, Agbaja women are not idle. I never saw a fat one among them. Most were extremely thin and often undersized. But it was interesting to notice that the Ibo women, fond as they and the men are of small children, did not go about their constant walks either to market or to farm with their babies on their backs[1] as do the Yoruba women. The babies were left at home and looked after, if very small, by another woman of the house-group. But from a very early age they would be left in the care of other children, often quite small ones. The fathers of the small children would often be found left in charge while the mother was at the market. Time and again, if one were paying late afternoon calls, one would find the father of the family in charge of the domestic scene, singing to the baby or, on a wet evening, holding a small and probably protesting child under the dripping roof eaves as the quickest way of washing it in the absence of its mother, the water drawer.

But it is the women who for the most part supply the food and who cook it. And from first to last this gives them a lever both individually and collectively by which they can,

---

[1] An Ibo baby is carried on the hip, not on the back, and care is taken to protect its head from the sun. In this and in the fact of not being carried on long journeys it would seem to have a better start than the babies in some other parts of Nigeria.

if need be, quietly bring pressure to bear on the men. This used to happen with my next-door neighbours. The man had only one wife. But he had a lover, a widow, to whom his wife took strong exception. She protested vehemently but without result, the lover being an attractive creature. She therefore fell back on stronger measures and her husband would find, on returning from the other lady's house, that no supper had been left for him and that no breakfast appeared next morning.

The women as food producers and crop owners con-stituted a motif that was heard time and again. Not only was it a pretext that could be used individually or as we shall see later, in organised fashion, against the men, but it was part of a situation of recurrent strain. For if the women owned the chief crops the men were, on the whole, the owners of the livestock, such as goats, pigs and cattle, which were a perennial menace to the crops. In this tsetse area there are only the small, immune, native cattle used as symbols of wealth rather than for food, and owned in such a poor neighbourhood as Agbaja in very small numbers. In Umuɛkɛ village the average number probably did not reach a dozen. But the men owned them and these cows, together with an also very limited number of goats and pigs and an occasional sheep, were a constant source of grievance to the women. One difficulty lay in the customary regulations about the tying of animals. As in so much of Ibo country, yam was the traditional food crop and around it had grown up a system of rules and of magico-religious ritual that regulated both its production and its eating. An important rule was that livestock should be tied up during the months that yam was in the ground, to prevent damage to the crop. But in many parts of Ibo country cassava had been introduced, in some cases quite recently, in very considerable quantity. In Umuɛkɛ some of the old people were still afraid of it and refused to eat the new fangled foodstuff with its potentially toxic properties. But it was none the less becoming more and more a staple element of diet. It had particular attractions in a poor and densely populated region like Agbaja. Whereas seed yams, if one has none, have to be bought, cassava is grown by planting, not the edible root, but sticks of the plant, and these can be got for the asking. Thus the whole root crop may be

eaten, whereas with yam a considerable proportion has
to be set aside for seed. In a bad year this may even amount
to the whole crop. Moreover cassava can be left in the
ground until required and once it is established it needs
no weeding. In fact the bush can be allowed to come up
with it and the land carrying it can be counted as fallow.
Small wonder that cassava, the lazy farmer's crop, is increasing yearly, regardless of its poor dietary value, its
bad effects on eyesight and its poisonous properties if inade-
quately washed and cooked.[1] These drawbacks are not
recognised. But what is crystal clear to the women, the
chief cassava growers, is that no traditional regulations for
the tying of livestock exist for cassava, which can thus be
decimated as soon as the yams are harvested and the animals
released. There are not many animals. But dwellings and
farms are so closely packed and pasture is so inadequate
that even a few hungry beasts can do considerable damage.

A number of ways round the difficulty were tried. A
neighbouring village on one side and a village-group on
the other had more land than Umuɛkɛ and more chance
therefore of farms being far from animals. Many people
therefore got land on " lease " or pledge[2] and planted their
cassava there grumbling a good deal and understandably at
the extra distance involved.

On the other hand a particular type of animal might be
proscribed by a village. I was sitting in my house talking
to an Umuɛkɛ man one day when we heard the unusual
noise of pigs squealing outside. My companion explained
that they were being driven back from market by people
who had taken them there earlier in the day to try to sell
them. And he added that, on the previous day, the women
of the next door village to our own had made an onslaught
on the pigs in their village, which were, they said, eating
their cassava, and had killed two of them. These two belonged
to a man of Umuɛkɛ who, my informant said, was keeping

---

1 Land which is lying fallow is now often made to carry cassava
which grows up with the bush. It has been contended that cassava is
an exhausting crop for the soil, in which case this practice would have
serious consequences in over-populated country. But " experiments
in Nigeria have proved that it is not so if the stems and leaves are not
removed from the ground." See Hailey : *African Survey*, p. 896.

2 For these methods of acquiring temporary rights over land, see
my *Land Tenure in an Ibo Village*.

them in this adjacent village because the guardian spirit of Umuɛkɛ kills all pigs kept in his own village. I did not enquire into the apparently feminist leanings of Ogbudi [_ ̄ ̄], the guardian spirit, but I asked whether the man would not take any steps against the women for killing his animals. My informant, a man, shrugged his shoulders and laughed and said what could the men do ? They would not take action in court. " It is the women who own us," he said laughing, and went on to say that it is the women who give the men food and cook it for them. What the men bring is palm wine. The owner of the dead pigs would not go to court, because the women would defend them-selves by saying " Do we not feed the men morning, after-noon and evening ? " Implying : " And then the men's pigs come and eat our cassava ! " The question of food happened to bulk large to the speaker since at that time his wife had gone off to her parent's place and he was left to fend for himself and had to go to another village and eat with a " sister " when he could not be bothered to cook for himself—which in any case is an undignified job for a married man. But though his personal feelings added point to his remarks they none the less described the general situation as between the men and the women.

I enquired what would happen after the pig killing, and he said that unless the owner removed the carcases at once they would be eaten by the women. A man who wanted to take action could not remove them. But I gathered that anyone who hung about making a fuss of this kind would lose his meat. Certainly in the present case the pig owner took no chances but removed the dead animals at once. He had already, the evening before, asked if I would buy some pork from him.

This was a particular episode in a more or less permanent state of affairs—the friction between the men and the women in the matter of crops and livestock. Later we shall discuss organised manœuvres of various kinds in the same campaign.

In other spheres there is a further division of labour between men and women. In farm work the actual planting should normally be done by women, possibly from some fertility association though I did not myself hear this ex-pressed. And in a poor community such as Agbaja, where there is the minimum of specialisation, almost all principles of the division of labour may at times give way before considerations of convenience or common sense. Unmarried men, lacking, as was often the case, means to marry a wife until comparatively late, might often be forced to do work such as planting or cooking that is really considered a woman's province. Women, on the other hand, would often help with the work of bush cutting and hoeing. They would, I think, practically exclusively do the work of weeding. Where, in a wealthier society such as that of Owerri town, men would scorn to carry oil to market in pots, to sell in small quantities, in Agbaja they could be seen doing so particularly if they were unmarried and young.

On the other hand, certain provinces were, so far as I observed or learned, exclusively male. Only men climbed palm trees, whether to cut nuts or to tap for wine. The idea of a woman climbing was unthinkable. In some parts of Ibo country it is taboo as an offence against *Ala*, the ground. But in Agbaja it was simply unheard of. So, too, was the notion that a woman, even in a sacrifice on her own behalf, should do the actual killing of the sacrificial animal. " Have all the men finished that women should have to do this thing ? " said one of the men in amused indignation, when I made the preposterous suggestion. And, in fact, one noticed that even a widow with no sons and no near surviving kinsman of her husband would get the eldest man of her house-group to sacrifice for her if need arose. With one exception, to be mentioned later, this rule seemed to hold.

A further distinction in the religious sphere, whereby the women of the village perform distinctive rites for the female aspect of the male-female guardian deity of the village, will be made clear when the organisation of the married women of the village is described.

In this patrilineal society the symbol of family authority, the sacred club or *ofo* is of course held only by men and not by women. Women, particularly quick-tempered ones, will none the less sometimes be heard cursing by *ofo*, but using some other thing in its place. The usual substitute is the wooden pestle used by a woman for pounding food. And this curse is said to be more feared than that of a man's true *ofo*. It is thought that any one under the curse who eats food pounded by this pestle will fall ill.

In a number of ways it would, I think, be true to say that the men and women of a village felt themselves to be separate entities. Partly it was due, perhaps, to the fact that the women, being married in the village but born elsewhere were, to that extent, an alien element. Partly, no doubt, there was the characteristic Ibo feeling for separation rather than for merging, but the lines of the picture should not be overdrawn. When all was running smoothly things were much as they might be in any village. One side would get a good humoured dig at the other when occasion offered. The men would tell the women that they took unfair advantage of them when a male child was born by holding it upside down so that its head touched the ground or by putting a foot on its face to show their dominance. The women would reply in good part and the talk would flow on to other subjects. But in time of crisis one became aware of a male-female undercurrent of antagonism or suspicion. A woman in difficult labour would complain of the medicine made by men against women saying that that was what was troubling her. Or the women collectively might, as we shall see later, hold the men and their magic responsible for, sickness or death in child-birth among their ranks.

The theme must not be over stressed. But its social recognition appeared clearly in the accounts given of the boy's initiation ceremonies. These were not held every year and I did not see them. They have also gone underground very much since the increase of British influence. And the fact that at first it was not easy to get information about them confirms the story given me by a number of informants that they were largely concerned with the acquiring by the boys of strong " medicine " or magic which could be used against any one who had not done the rites and particularly against women.

In the whole magical sphere, women, as so often in Africa, are sharply differentiated from men. What has been called the belief in the physico-magical property of women, rising largely from the phenomenon of menstrual blood, is clearly felt in this society. In addition to taboos about menstruating women cooking for men or eating with them there is the fear that such a woman may go near her husband's " medicines " and so injure both them and herself. Men are the chief owners of magic, and a man will keep his medicines in a place apart in his own house or at least with *ɔmɵ* [_ ⁻]—knotted palm frond—in front of them, to prevent their being contaminated by the presence of a woman in a taboo condition. Even of the big protective medicines placed in the yard of the household to ward off enemies and evil from the whole family it is sometimes said that they " forbid " quarrelling women.

Within the making of magic itself it is interesting that medicines are divided into male and female not with reference to their ownership, but as to their inherent nature and properties. Every medicine has its antidote, the antidote being called either *nwunye ya* [⁻ _ ⁻]—its female—or *ajɵ ya* [⁻ ⁻ ⁻]; its cooler. *Okɛ ɔgwɵ* [⁻ ⁻ ⁻ _]—male medicine—can be neutralised or overcome by the appropriate female or cooling medicine. Side by side with this magical situation may be set the fact that in war it is the function of the women to override the fighting of the men and to make peace. Heat is, in Ibo imagery, associated with anger, and the female principle seems to be, in general, associated with a cooling, pacifying influence.

Chapter XV. GROUPS BASED ON PLACE OF MARRIAGE

EXTENDED FAMILY AND VILLAGE HALF

WOMEN, as a result of the Ibo rules of exogamy, have, as we have seen, affiliations of two kinds. They belong, as married women, to the village of their husband and, as daughters, to the village where they were born. In Agbaja they were grouped according to both these principles. As wives they formed a group within the village of their husbands. But all the women born in a village and scattered by marriage came together at intervals on the basis of a common birth-place.[1]

Taking first the situation of wives within their husbands' village there are some purposes for which all the married women of the village come together as a group. Within this group they take precedence according to the status of their husbands. In sharing—that all-important Ibo consideration—after a preliminary halving of the food or other article to be shared between the two halves of the village, the first share would be taken by the wife of the senior man of the village, of the man, that is to say, who held the big *ɔfɔ* and took first share among the men. In the case of Umuɛkɛ the big *ɔfɔ* holder had no wife so the senior woman of the village was the head woman of his extended family. She was one of the widows of his father, but not his own mother, who was dead.

This little widow named Mgbɛci was admittedly the senior member of the married women of the village with the right to the first share. But she was old and ailing and feeble and in any practical matters was quite eclipsed in influence by younger or more forceful women even though her seniority was acknowledged. As among the men, position was by no means necessarily associated with power.

In the *owɛrɛ* half of the village to which Mgbɛci belonged there was another widow, Lɔlɔ, with several sons, who often

---

[1] On the subject of women's organisation I am indebted to Dr. Jack Harris for sending me a reprint of his interesting and suggestive paper, " The Position of Women in a Nigerian Society," *Transactions of the New York Academy of Sciences*, Series II, Vol. 2, No. 5.

seemed to play a conspicuous part in the doings of the women. In ordinary life she was hard-working even above the average of those strenuous workers and her energy and ready tongue and a certain independence of character seemed to mark her out as something of a leader when communal activities were toward.

The woman, Ɛkutara Nene, who took second share was the senior surviving wife—not the first one, who had died—of Nwa Onyɛ Okoro, the senior man of Umu Nwa Ɛbodim, who took second share among the men. Ɛkutara Nene was, on the whole, a peace maker. Where others would try to take a position by storm she would try good humour. Among the women of her own large extended family this tended to be effective. And in the smaller group of her husband's wives and children one noticed greater concord than, for instance, in that of N.Ɛ. and his wives. Among all the married women of Umuɛkɛ, Ɛkutara Nene seemed to have a respected place, but she did not strike me as being an active force among them.

The taker of the third share among the women was M.A., of Umuɛkɛ-ama. The wife of Okoro Afɔ, the man who took third share among the men and who was also priest of the village guardian deity, was dead, and he had no other wife and no children. But his younger brother had a wife, M.A., and she therefore took third share among all the married women of Umuɛkɛ. Among the women of Umuɛkɛ-ama she took first share, as did Okoro Afɔ among the men. This was undisputed. She was their senior woman though quite young. But though she was not a nonentity in character, she was indolent and bad tempered and aloof. She seemed, as will appear later, to take little active part in the communal doings of the women whether of the whole village or of the *ama* half.

Before considering the activities of the whole group of wives of the village their smaller groupings in village halves —*owɛrɛ* and *ama*—and in extended families, must be described. Some account of actual gatherings will be given since it is only by watching the details of what happens that one gains some idea of how business gets transacted.

The married women of a house-group, which is the dwelling of an extended family, are expected to have a certain *esprit de corps* which may or may not be realised in fact. The first wife—the *lɔlɔ* [‾ _] of the senior man of the extended family, or his mother if she is still alive, is looked on as the head woman of the compound. But her influence will depend on her personality and on the attitude of her husband towards her. This varied greatly from one house-group to another but in no case, in this equalitarian society, did any great importance seem to attach to the head wife.

In the same way the amount of cohesion between the wives of a house-group varied in different cases. If relations were strained among the women and between the chief man and his wives, as in the case of the family on whose land I lived, there was bickering rather than unity in the house-group. But in theory the women were supposed to hold together. It was held to be unseemly that squabbles within the house-group should be discussed with those outside it. And women going to market with produce of their own to sell were supposed to give the fellow women of the house-group a chance beforehand to buy anything they might fancy. And at the market they would tend to sit together so that if one of them wanted to leave her wares and go off to buy in a different part of the market the others would look after her basket.

In the case of the exceptionally large extended family of Umu Nwa Ɛbodim the wives each year collected money for a fowl to sacrifice at the *Ci* shrine of the wife of the original founder of the family. This shrine was a large *ɔha* tree whose leaves are much used for soup and in this case the leaves of this particular tree were owned in common by the wives of the extended family. Shortly before the women's annual religious rites at the beginning of the dry season this group of wives gathered together in the open space outside their house-group to share the leaves and bring their contribution for the fowl. On the occasion that I witnessed, the leaves were divided up into bundles corresponding to the number of women. The contributions were small sums of cowries each equivalent to a penny or less. And the women had also collected a pot of oil between them and had given it to one of their number to sell at a neighbouring market. She had got twopence halfpenny for it and at this gathering the women were shouting to each other that this was not enough and were discussing how full the pot was and saying that she must have got more money for it and have embezzled some of it.

The senior woman of the group, Ɛkutara Nene, the head wife of Nwa Onye Okoro, the man who held the *ɔfɔ* of this extended family, had not been present during most of this scene. But eventually she appeared, slim and erect, and pleasant to look at, and went up to the bickering women and stood quite still among them for a minute or two while they seemed like waves breaking against her. Then she said " *Cokwa !* "—" Wait, wait ! "—in a quiet voice until she got a hearing. She then explained quietly—though she flared up once—that she had told the woman, who was in fact the wife of her husband's son by a dead wife, to sell the oil for twopence halfpenny. She handled the quarrelling women skilfully and with smiling good temper and got a hearing though there was more shouting and disagreement after she stopped, until a diversion was created by the sharing of the leaves.

It was interesting to notice that in the case of Ɛkutara Nene the combination of position and personality seemed to give her some measure of authority. She was not only the senior woman of this extended family, but as had been said, it was she who took the second share among all the women of the village, in virtue of her husband taking second share among the men. She was also the mother of several children, some of them sons.

At this gathering of the wives of Umu Nwa Ɛbodim one saw how sensitive people were about the question of sharing and how important was any convention regulating it. When the bundles of leaves were divided things started quietly by Ɛkutara Nene taking the first share. They proceeded in orderly fashion until an elderly widow took her bundle and also another for a wife of one of her husband's sons who had not turned up. At this a youngish and rather pert wife of a different man burst into loud protests, saying that she herself was higher in the sharing order than the absent woman. Another youngish woman, the wife of yet another son of the widow's dead husband, sprang to the defence of the widow and she and the injured party joined battle, one with her baby on her hip. The baby was snatched away by a bystander and the women then wrestled and wrangled. Relative peace was eventually restored, some of the elder women intervening, but the actual argument dragged on and on as Ibo arguments do. One has the impression that it is a matter of prestige to have the last word, which tends to prolong any contest. In this case last words were being exchanged up to the time the women all dispersed. Protagonists of each party joined in, arguing with that characteristic action as of a bull charging, their heads down and then suddenly raised aggressively at their adversary, their whole bodies backing up the verbal dispute with vehement gesticulations. In this case a number of women with babies on their hips were taking part in the argument, the babies swaying in and out to the contest apparently undismayed.

During the wrangle the man who was Court Member for the village passed by, but he made no attempt to interfere. Certainly there was noise and some apparent confusion, but things got done. And in with it all one would see a woman go up to a baby carried by another woman and talk affectionately to it. Or an argument would be dissolved by someone thrusting good humouredly into it and laughing it off.

The fowl for which these women had subscribed was sacrificed six days later by Nwa Onyɛ Okoro on the *Ci* shrine of the ancestress on the day of the women's annual religious rites. It had been bought, I was told, with the common money, by Ɛkutara Nene and kept by her till the day of the sacrifice.

On one occasion the women of the *ama* half of the village met together for what was ostensibly an arrangement about visiting their married daughters in other villages. These daughters would, as is customary, bring presents for their mothers at the time of the annual religious rites of the wives of Umuɛkɛ-ama.

I was told about the gathering beforehand by the widow, Nwa Ori Ɛgo. She was one of the oldest of the women of Umuɛkɛ-ama and poor, having no sons. She was shrewd and a most useful informant, not minding what she said, and she had a certain place in the counsels of the women of Umuɛkɛ-ama. I understood from her that such meetings of the women of the village took place periodically, but this was the only one I heard of or witnessed.

The date of the meeting was changed several times, one

of the channels of communications on the subject being the market. But on the appointed day Nwa Ori Ɛgo came to fetch me about six o'clock in the morning and we went down in the grey dawn light to a secluded spot where a man and his wife—or rather the widow of his elder brother— lived at some distance from the main house-group of their extended family and had a one-roomed house of a good size separate from their real dwelling. I had seen this house used before, though by members of its own extended family, for other purposes when privacy was desired. It was just, I think, a matter of chance convenience.

When we arrived there were about sixteen women[1] sitting huddled round a fire in the cool air of the morning, still looking rather sleepy. M.A., the young woman who was the senior with a right to take first share, had not yet turned up. She was sent for and eventually arrived, an elegant and supercilious creature with a light skin, who sat away out on the edge of the circle and said little. She was bad tempered and her husband had the reputation of making bad magic and she seemed often to remain somewhat on the outer edge of the women's doings.

Proceedings opened by the handing round of peppercorns, the equivalent, in a lesser way, of the kola nut of hospitality. The women then took the opportunity of my being there to explain certain questions of etiquette to me and to point out where I had offended against them. Three of the elder women were the chief speakers and though they spoke quietly and with moderation their remarks about my dealings with the women in the owɛrɛ half of the village were shot through with the local patriotism and jealousy that were so characteristic between the two halves—ama and owɛrɛ— of the village.

Just as the discussion of my affairs came to a close the husband of the woman in whose house we were meeting came in with a gourd of palm wine, the male contribution to any gathering, and we all drank. The women then settled down to a discussion of their own affairs as we all sat round the fire on small stools. The young senior woman remained aloof on the outskirts of the circle. For quite a time the

---

[1] It will be remembered that Umuɛkɛ-ama was considerably smaller than Umuɛkɛ-owɛrɛ. It contained perhaps a quarter of the inhabitants of Umuɛkɛ. On this occasion not all its women were present.

women talked pretty quietly, one speaking and then another chiming in. There was no apparent chairman, but if interruptions were too insistent there were the usual cries of "*Cokwa!*"—"Wait!" If two speakers agreed with each other they would knock hands in the Ibo manner of clenching the fist and knocking it lightly against the fist of the protagonist as a friendly gesture. There was a certain amount of good-natured laughter interspersed with the speeches. And once or twice a woman got up and danced to work off her excitement or, still sitting, made attractive dance movements with her arms.

The elder women spoke first and definitely took a high moral tone. Let the women, they said, do things quietly and in peace. If there are things to be shared let no one put herself forward, but let all sit quietly to see what will happen. And, said the eldest woman present, if there are quarrels between two women of the same house-group, let them keep it within the group and not let it appear outside. Even if two co-wives are in disagreement let them none the less co-operate with each other in marketing matters, such as one giving the other money with which to buy things for her if she does not wish to go to market herself. Let them not call on an outside woman for this.

At this the younger women chipped in and said that all this talk was good, but let the elder women see that they observed this good advice themselves. The elder women, in return, became reminiscent with obvious practical import. How different, said they, were things in their young days from the present fashion. In those days, if a woman delivered a child she would afterwards entertain the other women with food. But people nowadays do not care to do this. The younger women were nettled by these aspersions, and one of them who had recently borne a child said, with some heat, that she had cooked cassava afterwards for the women at her own expense and no one gave her any money in return. She was backed up by the young senior woman who said that the same thing had happened in her own case. One saw clearly enunciated the reciprocity principle that is so marked in Ibo entertainment or the giving of presents.

The elder women then retorted that when they were young a woman going to market for the first time after the birth of a child would cook food for the other women, who would give her presents in return. They also said that in that golden age a junior wife, if her husband gave her meat or anything else, would take it to the head wife who would decide what to do about it. But nowadays the young wives just eat what they are given on the spot, in their husband's house. This thrust the young wives countered by denying that their husbands gave them things. But to underline the principle and sound a warning one of the elder women described how she, as a youngster, had been given a leg of meat by a man and when she showed it to her head wife the latter had decided that it was poisoned and unfit to eat.

After this discussion the meeting passed to what had been given as its *raison d'etrê*—the proposed visits of those present to their married daughters. This again raised the question of reciprocity in gifts and entertainment. It was also urged that those who only made small presents should not be excluded when a return feast was arranged. One woman recounted, as is the habit in such circumstances, how once she and her husband had been done out of a feast though they had presented their gifts. At this someone suggested that they should call in some old man to swear on *areshe* [¯ ¯ ¯]—a supernatural symbol of any kind—in order, so far as I could make out, to bind them to observe fair play. But the rest refused, saying let them not allow the men to know what they were doing.

The discussion was brought to a close by the formality of all present touching with their hands first the ground and then their breasts.

They were then invited to a party at my house in a few days time and asked to pass on the invitation to the rest of the married women of the village. They said, using the usual channel of communication, that they would tell the others at their village market, held every eight days and due that afternoon. It could be assumed that practically every Umueke woman would be there and it was thus an excellent rallying point for information.

Before the meeting broke up I dashed some tobacco to those present, partly because the sharing of a common object was always instructive to watch. In spite of the homily delivered earlier in the proceedings the sharing caused a certain amount of noise and was not without incident. A whole leaf was first presented to the woman in whose house we were meeting to mark our recognition of her position as hostess. The cutting up of the rest of the leaves was then done by one of the elderly widows who had played a considerable part in the discussion. She had intelligence and force of character of the kind to make her something of a leader in this non-hierarchical society where individuality is one of the factors which confers authority. The tobacco was then divided into equal shares to the number of those present, this job being done, in accordance with custom, by two of the younger of the women. All then inspected it and the young senior woman, M.A., took the first share. My friend, Nwa Ori Ɛgo, the oldest of those present, took second share, but not before she had fingered several other portions and called forth from the other women a reminder of the principle of touch and take. Whereupon she sprang to her feet, seized a long oil bean pod which happened to be lying near and knocked it on the ground as though it were ɔfɔ, saying that if ever she came to any more of their meetings might she die. The words were followed by the traditional snarling sound—Ha ! Having relieved her feelings by this outburst, she then said that she would not refuse to take the white woman's tobacco, and removed her share. She was, in fact, poor and a great user of tobacco and was not going to let offended dignity defraud her of her rightful portion. After that the sharing proceeded quietly and the meeting broke up.

Incidentally, of the seventeen women who met together, nine were widows. And a tenth looked in at our proceedings but did not stay. The whole village contained, in fact, a considerable percentage of widows.

The ostensible cause of the gathering had been to discuss visits to married daughters. But the occasion had been used to stress, in conversation, the traditional norms of conduct. As with the men, any kind of gathering could be used as a platform for discussing and restating the ethical standards of the community. The men, however, would, as we have noticed, use the opportunity of some traditional kinship assembly such as a second burial for the discussions either of common business or of rules of conduct. Their wives, on the other hand, being separated by marriage from the kinship organisation of the village into which they were born, tended to organise themselves into groups and to come together for the transaction of specific practical business. This made the outlines of their organisation rather clearer and more easily definable than that of the men.

This meeting of the women displayed that balance between young and old, rather than any great respect for age, which seems to characterise Ibo society. This must not be pushed too far in the case of the women. The very young wives remained in the background of the women's doings. And among the rest age gave added status to strength of character. But age alone did not appear to involve any particular respect.

VILLAGE AND VILLAGE-GROUP

The whole body of married women of the village of Umuɛkɛ formed a group for common action in a number of different spheres. In religious and judicial matters and also for dancing which was part religious part aesthetic, and again in any matter affecting the interests of them all, the wives of the village formed a well-defined group more homogeneous and closely woven, or so it seemed, than any grouping one found among the men.

The most impressive of the occasions on which all the wives of the village came together as a unit was the performance of their annual religious rites for the feminine aspect of the male-female guardian spirit of the village. No one could be present without being struck both by the depth of religious feeling shown by some of the women and by the distinctively feminist tone of the whole proceedings. The way, also, in which defaulters from the rites were handled was a revelation in direct action and executive speed. Judicial doings in general village affairs might drag on without conclusion month after month. But the united will of the women gathered together for common action went straight to its goal in the summary chastisement of offenders.

The women's rites, which included the clearing of the paths to the shrines of the deity, were performed shortly after the annual Agbaja religious ceremonies of the men in the seventh month by Ibo reckoning. All the married women of the village of Umuɛkɛ performed their rites together on the same day, but on a different day from most of the other

Agbaja villages. The date on this occasion was 20th November and therefore at a relatively slack point in the farming season. The wet season was at an end and the main yam harvest would be dug in the following month.

For weeks before this ceremony took place the women talked to me about it at intervals. The exact date was known and talked about. It was the Afɔ Ɛgbu Day following the Oriɛ Ekpa Day after the Oriɛ Ekpa on which the men were to do their main annual customs. Any woman who failed to come would have one of her fowls seized. The women would clear the paths to the shrines of the female aspect, Lɔlɔ Ogbudi, of the guardian spirit of the village. They would also, unless they were menstruating at the time, rub their bodies with medicine from pots in front of the shrines and a fowl would be sacrificed. The medicine was to give life and health, said one of them, to them and their husbands and children.

It was always interesting to hear beforehand descriptions of customary events that one was able to witness when they took place. It was frequently difficult to gain any clear idea of what was supposed to be going to happen. The account was also apt considerably to exceed the facts in magnificence and scale. In this case, however, the anti-climax was markedly less than usual. In fact, apart from the failure of certain sections of the women to produce the required fowls, the day's proceedings surpassed in feeling and performance what the preliminary accounts had led one to expect. As for the fowls, one of the women of Umuɛkɛ-ama told me four days before the ceremonies that this division of the village had not yet bought its fowl. The right person to initiate the matter, she said, was M.A., the senior, though young, woman of this half of the village. She ought to approach the elder women who would then call the rest of them. If, however, the fowl was not bought in time it would be sacrificed later. This deferring of the killing of a sacrifice was a frequent event among these people, whether men or women. The expenditure of money on buying an animal was not an affair to be lightly under-taken, for whatever purpose. And in this particular case the senior woman was lazy and dilatory by nature.

When the day came, however, things went ahead briskly the absence of certain fowls notwithstanding. From about

8-30 in the morning one could hear the women in the village shouting one to another to remind each other what day it was. There was no mystery in this case about the technique employed in achieving co-operative action in the absence of centralised authority. About 9 a.m. the leader of the women's dances could be heard beating her *igbugbo* as a summons. Half an hour later old Nwa Ori Ɛgo came to fetch me and S., saying that the women were starting to clear their paths. We went down to the clearing at our end of the village and found some of the Umuɛkɛ-ama women there. A number of them had their bodies painted with beautiful *uri* [_ _] patterns as was the custom for any gala occasion. There was a great deal of calling of those women who had not yet turned up. A holiday mood was abroad, people laughing and playing and dancing little impromptu steps as we waited. With the ever-present spirit of rivalry, wives born in the same village were challenging those born in different ones. By degrees we moved up to the clearing of the Umu Nwa Ɛbodim section of the village. It will be remembered that this extended family belonged by right to the Umuɛkɛ owɛrɛ half of the village. But as this half was numerically much greater than the *ama* half, Umu Nwa Ɛbodim was, for practical purposes such as communal work and sharing, counted as part of Umuɛkɛ-ama. It was a very large extended family with its big house-group lying geographically just between those of Umuɛkɛ-ama and the others of Umuɛkɛ-owɛrɛ but much nearer to the former. From its size and structure it seemed to be on the way to splitting up into a number of lesser extended families. In any case, on this occasion its women produced a fowl of their own and cleared paths to its shrine for the village deity just as, in their turn, did the women of Umuɛkɛ-owɛrɛ and then those of Umuɛkɛ-ama.

In the clearing we found some of the Umu Nwa Ɛbodim wives collected and others were called for and came by degrees. A few brought their babies. The prevailing mood was still gay as we waited for further developments. At last one of the elder women, a widow, of Umu Nwa Ɛbodim led the women with a cry down the path they were to clear through the bush to the shrine of Ɔpara Iyi, the son of the village guardian deity.

All had knives with them and fell upon the grass and

weeds blocking up the path after the rainy season, the work being accompanied by a good deal of light-hearted chatter. Girls who were betrothed, though not yet finally married, to Umuɛkɛ men were among the workers. One woman was greeted by others with cries of " E yɔɔla " [_ ⁻ ⁻ ⁻]—" Have you come back? " and it appeared that she was a widow who had stolen and then run away. It was to some extent a recognised technique that those, whether men or women, who had committed an offence grave enough to warrant absconding might, when a long enough lapse of time had blurred people's memories and softened their feelings, be allowed to return. In this way the community was safeguarded by the absence of a criminal, but not permanently deprived of enterprising, if troublesome, individuals.

The ground immediately in front of the shrine was cleared by a large *osu* woman. She was the senior woman of a big family of *osu*[1] who belonged to the extended family of Umu Nwa Ɛbodim and who were the slaves of this deity. The ancestor of these *osu* had originally been bought for this deity several generations back, by the Nwa Ɛbodim from whom the present free-born family had its name.

The shrine is a group of small, thin-stemmed trees with two pots in front of them, one of the pots being buried up to the neck in the ground. The whole stands on the edge of a thick grove of bush sacred to the spirit.

After the clearing of the actual path some of the older women came up to the shrine and knelt near the trees clearing away leaves and grass, saying to each other as they did so that nothing must be rooted up, only cut or brushed away. Although the shrine was always spoken of as belonging to Ɔpara Iyi, the son of the male-female guardian spirit of the village, it was none the less to the mother spirit, Lɔlɔ Ogbudi, that the women were talking as they worked. It is this Lɔlɔ, they were saying, who upholds them and who gives them power to do anything, and it is because of her that they are proud. And anyone who has any sickness, whether of head or of belly, or anyone who has leg ache, she will speak of it when she rubs the pot medicine on her body and she will be healed from to-day. And next year they will come again. And anyone who has malicious feelings

1 See p. 23-24.

against them or takes anything wherewith to poison them, let Lɔlɔ kill them on Ɛkɛ [_ ⁻], on Oriɛ [_ _], on Afɔ [_ _], and on Nkwɔ [_ ⁻] [1] As they were speaking they touched the ground with their hands from time to time.

After this the head man of the *osu* family came up carrying the fowl which the women of Umu Nwa Ɛbodim had bought. He was to perform the actual sacrifice, this being man's and not woman's work. He stood in front of the shrine and swung the fowl round the heads of the assembled body of women and then bumped it on each of their heads in turn. As he did so he called on Lɔlɔ to look at the fowl, explaining that all the women had subscribed money and bought it. He begged for long life and health for them and said that if they were alive next year and other years they would come again to bring fowls and to clear the path and dance and sing. He kept repeating the word *nde* [⁻ _]—life—which is one of the key words in Ibo sacrifices.

He then pulled some feathers out of the fowl's neck and cut its throat, letting the blood drip on the pots of the shrine. He pulled the wing feathers out and threw them down and then went away, taking the fowl with him. It would later be roasted whole and the women would take it to market and sell it and keep the money for buying the next year's fowl.

The large *osu* woman of his extended family who had previously been clearing in front of the shrine now put her fingers into the pot buried up to its neck in the ground in front of the shrine and stirred up the medicine. She then smeared the medicine with her hands over the eyes, chest and back and sometimes the legs of each of the women present. Another *osu* woman joined her and after a time non-*osu* women began to help with the smearing process. As the liquid was rubbed on her each woman named the diseases of which she wanted to be cured or said if she wanted to bear a child. While the proceedings were beginning all the women sang in chorus very rhythmically and moving to the beat—" *Ame ɛji* " [_ ⁻ _ ⁻]—" to give birth and to keep "—repeating the phrase over and over again as they moved.

Before the medicine rubbing was finished the senior

---

[1] These are the four days of the Ibo week and are often mentioned thus in prayers or spells.

woman of Umu Nwa Ɛbodim, Ɛkutara Nene, told me that
her husband, the senior man of this extended family, was
just going to sacrifice a fowl to their ancestral grandmother
on the *ɔha* tree which had been her *Ci* shrine. We went
and witnessed this event, the fowl being the one bought
by Ɛkutara Nene with money we had seen subscribed some
time before by all the women of Umu Nwa Ɛbodim.[1] This
was an annual sacrifice, concerning this group of the village
alone, but done on the same day as the main women's rites
and as a women's ceremony to commemorate a famous
ancestress.

It was, however, something of a side issue and after it
we rejoined the women at their shrine and found some of
them now clearing the path to the stream. But all shortly
went back to the clearing in the centre of Umu Nwa Ɛbodim
and rested after the excitements of this first series of rites.
This also gave a chance to the younger women with small
babies to go off home to feed them.

So far only the women of Umuɛkɛ-ama and of Umu Nwa
Ɛbodim had collected together. But now all set off for
Umuɛkɛ-owɛrɛ to another shrine of Lɔlɔ Ogbudi in the
bush there. The women of that half of the village had already
cleared the path to it. The other women, when they got near,
began running up to it and rubbing each other with medicine
from a pot at the shrine. This liquid was of the same white
chalky appearance as the first one and the women, with only
their short cloths from hip to knee, were beginning to look
like ghosts, with the white mixture smeared over their brown
skins.

Some of them protested at being rubbed ; others caught
them and soused them, forcibly dragging them up to the
shrine.

Women who were menstruating were not rubbed with
the medicine. But at one point my girl assistant, S., heard
the other women demanding that they should show their
blood, to prove that they could justly claim exemption. A
good deal of singing and talking was going on most of the
time. There was an atmosphere of excitement and of good
cheer hardly interrupted by the struggles about the medicine
rubbing.

---

[1] See p. 180 ff.

The group was now joined by the Umuɛkɛ-owɛrɛ women and the whole party fraternised amicably. I saw one elderly woman putting her arms affectionately round another from a different, though nearly-related extended family.

The entire assembly then started dancing near the shrine, making a circle of dancers with some women in the middle singing and beating knives and with the usual little woman beating the *igbugbo*. There was great excitement and leaping and brandishing of knives in this dance.

At the end the women trailed off to the house-group of the extended family whose senior man was in charge of the shrine. Money was being collected here from the women of Umuɛkɛ-owɛrɛ for the sacrificial fowl which should have been produced for this occasion. As so often in this Ibo community the sacrifice was being tardily bought and was lagging behind the march of events. It was explained to me next day that it had been possible to smear with medicine from this shrine because, although there was no fowl, money was actually being collected.

The whole band of women then passed on to the clearing in the Umuɛkɛ-owɛrɛ half of the village where they again danced the circular dance, with soloists in the middle, with the clashing of knives and with the whitened dancers giving spread-eagle leaps into the air.

This was followed by a welcome proferring of pots of sliced oil bean and several gourds of palm wine by the Umuɛkɛ-owɛrɛ women. We drank and ate snacks thankfully for it was a hot day, but soon the party was on the move again back to Umu Nwa Ɛbodim, the women singing as they went.

Snatches of their songs—Is it any shame if we do not marry ?—Is it any shame if we will not lie with a man ?—Is it any shame if we wish to marry a young man ?—gave one the impression of a definitely feminist flavour, which was enhanced by the fact that during the whole day hardly a man was to be seen. The women were left in undisputed possession of the village.

In the clearing of Umu Nwa Ɛbodim we again paused and rested while the Umuɛkɛ-owɛrɛ women went to the shrine and rubbed themselves with medicine as the rest of the women had done earlier in the day. When they had finished it was the turn of the Umu Nwa Ɛbodim women to bring

out oil bean and palm wine and distribute it, after which
there was more dancing.

We then proceeded to the clearing of Umuɛkɛ-ama, which
was also the village market place, and sat about discussing
the hitch which had arisen because the women of this half
of the village had not only failed to produce a fowl for
their shrine but had not even collected money for it. The
young senior woman, M.A., was blamed, but she retorted
that as no one had subscribed any money there was nothing
to buy a fowl with. Could she take her own money, she said ?

Eventually, in Ibo fashion, some kind of a compromise
was reached and the women started clearing the path which
lead down to the stream Ogbudi, and to the shrine of this
part of the village. No medicine rubbing took place, however,
and I gathered that this was because of the failure to collect
money. But this did not prevent the carrying out of the
rest of the ritual and there seemed to be a greater earnestness
here in the prayers than at any other point.

The big *osu* woman again cleared the ground near the
shrine, which consisted of trees and pots on the edge of
thick bush on the way to the stream. Another *osu* belonging
to Ogbudi was there. The rest of the women came up to the
shrine and crouched before it sweeping away leaves from
the ground almost as though their hands were caressing
the earth. The *igbugbo* player came up and beat her instrument
and once again the women all sang with rhythmic movements.

There were also individual performances. One not yet
middle aged woman, who was outstanding as a good singer,
did a series of almost Greek postures in front of the shrine,
after which she knelt and prostrated herself with her forehead on the ground. Another woman did a *pas de seul* down
the path. One woman put both hands on the tree of the
shrine and then on her face. Old Nwa Ori Ɛgo went up with
outstretched arms murmuring what sounded like *nne*—
mother.

As the women came up to the shrine they were saying :
" Lɔlɔ, nnɛ di anye, anye beara n'udo, ihɛ anye na ge wθ n'udo.

Amθɔ ɛkuru ka mma."—" Lɔlɔ, mother of our husbands, we

come in peace, our thing and yours is in peace. To bear
child and nurse it is best." Some said : " Amθɔ ɛji ka mma "

[_ ‾ ‾ _ ‾ - - -]—"To bear child and keep is best." Each repeated : " Dɛbɛ m ndǝ [_ ‾ - - _] Ji ruɛ nnɛ [‾ _ ‾ ‾ -] Ɔmǝmǝ bea" [_ ‾ ‾ _ ‾]—" Keep me alive, let yam increase let births come ! "

Individual women, particularly the older ones, bowed themselves before the shrine in prayer and entreaty so earnest that no onlooker could have been unmoved. One old widow talked and besought for a long time, as did another oldish woman who also looked very ill. And I saw one of the wives of the old man on whose land I lived on her knees pouring forth a torrent of words. She had seemed ill for some time and she was now protesting her innocence to the spirit. This protesting, known as etǝ ogu [‾ - - _], and frequently accompanied by holding in the hand a piece of knotted palm frond, is an Ibo habit on any occasion of threatened ill or accusation. This woman was particularly given to it. She was now insisting that she had not killed another woman's child, she had not stolen another man's things, she had not got ill-feeling against any one, and let Lɔlɔ kill anyone who should try to do any of these things to her. She had looked wretchedly ill at the beginning of the day. But it seemed to me that after the ceremonies and her prayers she looked better. And several days later I was again struck by her improved health and morale.

By the time the ritual at the shrine was finished it was about two o'clock. On the way back into the village we passed the house of an Umuɛkɛ-ama woman married in the next door village whose boundary ran close here. She entertained us with some food and palm wine, I think because it was now the turn of Umuɛkɛ-ama to show some hospitality and although she was a daughter and not a wife of Umuɛkɛ-ama her house was conveniently near to the shrine.

Eventually we got back to the market place of Umuɛkɛ where a new phase opened in the day's events. Having cleared paths and offered sacrifices and prayers, it now remained to penalise, in the customary manner, any woman who had failed to take her part in the ceremonies. Here in the market place we found a number of Umuɛkɛ wives collecting mud to put in the house of the fiancée, born in the next-door village, of an Umuɛkɛ-ama young man. While we were waiting Okoro Afɔ, of Umuɛkɛ-ama, the priest of the spirit Ogbudi whom we had been honouring, came up with some palm wine for our refreshment.

At this point, and partly, no doubt, because most people were getting rather tired and hot, one of those sudden squalls that one came almost to expect in this society broke clamorously upon the assembly. A woman was set upon with fierce demands as to why she had come and shared oil bean with them seeing that she had now gone away from Umuɛkɛ to live with another husband. There was much wrangling, and one of the loudest in dispute was a woman who was well known as a habitual thief. It seemed that one did not miss the chance of shouting with the innocent if one had ever been among the guilty. In any case there was a crescendo of noise when suddenly a distraction broke upon the crowd. A file of women came tearing down the path from the neighbouring village of Umuamɛkɛ. They were the wives of that village coming to execute summary justice upon one of their number, a daughter of Umuɛkɛ, who had left her husband and returned to live with her mother in Umuɛkɛ-ama. She had failed to turn out to help the Umuamɛkɛ women with their path clearing and they had come to plaster her house with mud in customary retribution.

They sped on to their destination. Their quarry had gone inside her mother's house and shut the door. But the Umuɛkɛ women who defended the house were set upon by those of Umuamɛkɛ and were smeared from head to foot with mud. It was a real rough and tumble and the noise was deafening. But the victims, though indignant, eventually gave way to laughter.

It was interesting to notice the aloofness of the men. There were a few at the house-group during this incident, but they stood aside, including the husband of one of the women attacked, and did not attempt to interfere. The women did the job in the swift and effective manner that was reserved for cases where the culprit was found *in flagrante delicto*.

Returning after this interlude to the market place, I found that the Umuɛkɛ women who had been gathered there had themselves gone off on a like punitive expedition to the next-door village, to the house of the defaulting fiancée of whom they had already spoken. She was apparently not quick enough in shutting her door for the women said later that they had smeared mud over everything in it.

They had announced their intention early of dancing in the market place. But by 3-30 p.m. they decided that they were too late and tired and that they would call it a day. The men of the village were supposed to be cooking food for them in return for the food cooked for them by the women on the day they did their own annual path clearing. But whatever the theory, it seemed in fact to be the women who did the cooking though the actual food may have been provided by the men.

Looking back on the day one realised that one of its key notes was the prevailing air of excitement. Its religious activities also, whose scope was too broad to be adequately described as a fertility rite, had at certain points been deeply impressive in their sincerity and fervour, and it had been apparent how earnestly individuals reacted over and above the communal manifestations. The day was also markedly feminine ; more consciously and exclusively so than comparable doings by the men were masculine.

Most of the village public activities were predominantly male in character. But there were nearly always a certain number of women about. On this day, however, the men had obliterated themselves and left the village to the women, who conducted their affairs with a directness and sureness of touch that one came to associate with their methods of communal action. It may have been this that gave a feeling of completeness and homogeneity to the proceedings. No doubt there were the inevitable discrepancies between theory and practice, as in the failure to produce a fowl at two shrines out of three. But there was none the less a feeling of whole-heartedness in the actual carrying through of the day's events that was rare in the life of the village. It may have been that the men, being the natives of the place, had many kinship occasions of communal meeting which were lacking to the women and therefore made less of them.

It is possible, too, that the religious situation had something to do with this side of things. Although in the village as a whole it was the younger people of both sexes who were becoming Christianised, the married women were almost completely pagan still. Mission influence had gone less far with them than among the men and only quite young girls, practically all unmarried, took any active part in Church matters. This may have helped to give homogeneity to the group of the wives of the village.

One of the important points about this day was clearly the stress it laid on the loyalty of the women to the deity of their husband's village. Though on many other occasions the pull might be back to their native villages, this festival was one of the counterbalancing forces which kept them poised between the two social groups to which they belonged. Whereas the men had always their fixed centre of gravity in the village where they were born and where they lived, their wives were always members both of the village of their birth and that of their marriage, with complementary obligations keeping a certain equilibrium between the two. And this occasion not only underlined for each woman the fact that as a wife she acknowledged the deity of her husband's village, but it emphasised the solidarity of the wives of the village as a group. They were not bound as were the men, by ties of kinship. On the contrary they were largely a fortuitous collection of strangers. But as the wives of the village they were united in this great annual ceremony.

But there were other occasions beside this yearly festival when the women of the village acted as a group. In certain judicial matters it was customary that they should take common action.

In the first place their solidarity was symbolised by the fact that if any of their number committed a theft, even against an outsider, her fellow wives would fine her and leave her out of their doings. The fine would be a considerable one—about £1. If she was unable to pay it the other women would confine themselves to ignoring her in their common activities. But if she was able to pay and refused they would seize some of her property. If, for instance, it was the season of ripe maize they might seize her maize. She might steal at market from a woman of another village and the case might be judged by certain men and women of the two villages. But in addition the whole body of women of her own village would fine her. At the inter-village judging of such a case, if the accused woman were acquitted, one would probably hear one of her partisans insist that her fellow wives be notified of her innocence, lest they extract a fine from her. Moreover, when a man goes to marry a wife he will, as we have seen, ask the girl's mother if she steals, and will explain that if she does so she will have to pay money to the women of her husband's village.

The wives of the village as a body might also come together to judge or fine a woman who had stolen from one of their own number. We have already seen how varied both in method and personnel was the judging of cases,[1] and it must be added that, as a further possibility, a case between two women of the village might be judged by all the married women. I did not happen to witness this procedure, but I saw the aftermath in the shape of the exaction of a fine for an offence which had been judged by the women several months previously while I was away in England. This execution of a sentence already pronounced was a spirited and exclusively feminine happening. How often such mass action took place I do not know. I only saw this one occasion. But there was talk of others.

Old Nwa Ori Ɛgo, of Umu Duru Igwɛ house-group in Umuɛkɛ-ama, recounted the beginnings of the affair. A woman of her own house-group, a widow named Ng., had accused another widow, Nw., of the same house-group, but not a co-wife, of stealing a fowl from her. Nw., a soured old lady with a habitual sense of grievance, retorted by charging Ng. with false accusation. She had then taken a drum or its equivalent and beaten it as a notice to all the women of Umuɛkɛ. All the women, including those of Umuɛkɛ-owɛrɛ, had come to try the case. Men had not come, said Nwa Ori Ɛgo. Women judge their own cases, said she, and men theirs—a generalisation not altogether borne out by the facts. One saw that in some instances men would be included in the people judging a case between two women and the reverse would also be true. It usually seemed that the parties to a case could summon whom they pleased as judges. But in the particular instance which Nwa Ori Ɛgo was describing it was the women of the village who had judged. They had decided that the accusation was false and had fined Ng. a fowl which they all ate. They had also said she must pay *ɔla iri na atɔ,* a sum of cowries

---

amounting, she said, to five shillings, but this was an over-estimate. The money had not yet been paid, and the women would have to come back to collect it. But, said Nwa Ori Ɛgo, when they come the women. of the house-group will not allow them to take the money because other fines are outstanding in other parts of the village—in Umu Nwa Ɛbodim for one—and they will say let these also be paid. One saw here the dual division motif coming in again and the rivalry between the village halves acting as an incentive to each to exact justice from the other.

In explaining why stronger measures had not been carried out against Ng., she explained that the latter had not really out and out accused Nw. She missed one of her fowls and then saw the other woman, whose house was only a few yards from her own, cooking a fowl in a pot. She therefore went and took the lid off and said she wondered what was cooking inside. Whereupon Nw. who was, we knew, ill-tempered and at all times liable to give way to loud complaining, put her head in her hands—the speaker gave a dramatic representation of it—and cried to people to hear what had been spoken. And she accused Ng., whom we equally knew to be quiet and inoffensive, of accusing her falsely, and the case was subsequently judged.

The judging had taken place about three months before this account. One night about three weeks later, after an Afɔ day on which there had been no important local market to occupy the women, sounds of singing were suddenly heard coming through the village. My night watchman announced that the women were singing the song that indicates the execution of justice on someone. He and my interpreter, A., were eager companions in going out into the moonlight to meet the singers. Incidentally a band of children greeted us as we passed through Umu Nwa Ɛbodim. " Going to bed " was lightly treated by the children. If there was anything toward, particularly in the moonlight, they just tumbled out of their houses as if it had been day.

In the open space of Umu Nwa Ɛbodim squatted a band of women singing and looking spectral in the moonlight. They were on their way to Ng.'s place to collect the fine for false accusation which had previously been levied. It amounted to a pound, they said, in characteristic exaggeration. It turned out to be five shillings.

The women already there were mostly, so far as could be seen in the dim light, from the *owɛrɛ* half of the village. But they were engaged in calling out the women of Umu Nwa Ɛbodim who soon assembled. Among them was a comparatively young wife playing an active part and seeming much excited. It transpired that on another occasion justice had been meted out to her after she had stolen yams from her husband and put the blame on another woman.

The women moved down to Umuɛkɛ-ama singing and shouting and calling out the wives of this part of the village. In a high state of excitement and noise they went in single file down the path to Ng.'s house, saying that they would sleep there till morning if she did not pay them. In the darkness it was not easy to assess numbers, but a considerable proportion of the hundred and eight women of the village was there.

Some surged up to the house dancing and singing and others, also singing, sat down nearby. Everyone was keyed up. It was discovered that one of the Umuɛkɛ-ama women was not there. Her husband was, in fact, ill, but this did not prevent her being fetched. Several women flew off to summon her, moving with quite exceptional speed. As they came back they were singing a refrain of which the chorus, repeated over and over again, was: "*Ana m acɔ onye ga-ara m*"—"I am seeking someone to have sexual connection with me." Some of the songs were ordinary ones such as would be used at other times. But a number were of this sexual character and would only be used on such an occasion as this. For instance, in order to summon all the women to come there was a song which ran: "*Nwanye na-agaghe apɔta na ngala, arere gba ya n'imɛ ɔtɔ, idide gba ya n'imɛ ɔtɔ*"—"Woman who will not come out in this place, let millipede go into her sex organs, let earthworm go into her sex organs."

Such things would be said on no ordinary occasion to a woman, but were used here to induce the women strongly to turn out in force.

Another song, with its hint of condescension towards

sex affairs, recalled the note struck by some of the songs
during the annual rites. " A woman who allows her husband
to go and tap his palm tree[1] will have much pubic hair.
A woman who does not allow her husband to go and tap
his palm tree will not have much pubic hair." Much pubic
hair is considered a matter of pride and it is thought that a
man will love more a woman who has much than a woman
who has little. It is also thought that the pubic hair will
not grow if a woman frequently has sex connection. It is a
very serious abuse for a woman to taunt another with lack
of this hair and she is liable to be fined. Her fellow women
will deal severely with her.

There was another song about the sex organs being
bright—ca—during connection, and there was one in which
the name of the woman to be fined was mentioned : " N.O.,
ɔtɵ de mma iji n'aka de ka ɔja. Ɔ wɵ se ɔ dee nga a na-ɛji ya n'aka."—
" N.O., sex organ is good to hold in hand like flute. Only
there is no place one is holding it with hand."

A. explained next day that a man would feel shame to
go and listen to these songs because he is one and the women
are many. The women do not feel shame because they
are many, but they would do so if many men were present.
Far from being there in numbers, this was another occasion
on which men were conspicuously absent. Only A. and
my night watchman were there and next day people told
the former that he was strong to be able to go. In point of
fact they both showed every sign of enjoying their illicit
entertainment and giggled so unrestrainedly at the songs
that I had to tell them not to make their unwarranted presence
so conspicuous. Even so, all that A. could do was to clap
his hand over his mouth and then nearly explode.

As for the women, I never saw them so spirited. They
were having a night out and they were heartily enjoying it
and there was a speed and energy about everything they
did that gave a distinctive quality to the episode. It was
also the only occasion in the village that struck one as
obscene in the intention of the people themselves. Mixed
with what seemed genuine amusement there was much
uncontrolled, abandoned laughter. There was a suggestion

---

[1] The first tapping is done early in the morning.

of consciously kicking over the traces about the whole affair.

Dancing started as soon as the party arrived at Ng.'s house and was of an apparently impromptu nature. Anyone seemed to be able to start a dance and as she started those around would clap and others would join in. Then there would be a lull with much loud talk and discussion, after which someone would spring up again with a new dance. After one pause I saw a woman dart across the yard to join the dancers in a succession of wild leaps, her arms outstretched and the long, hanging breasts that so many of these women have adding to the grotesque effect. There was a kaleidoscope of swiftly-moving, slim, brown bodies in the moonlight, wild snatches of song and dance, and peals of spasmodic laughter.

Part of the time the women " danced at " Ng.'s door ; finally she opened it from within and came and sat in it. So far as one could see the women did not attack her in any way, but there was a menace in their dancing that must have been highly unpleasant for the object of it. They pranced aggressively, sometimes holding their buttocks with their hands, sometimes sticking them out and shaking them ; or they advanced making sexually suggestive gestures, and the quality of their laughter again conveyed their feeling of obscenity.

The women abused the senior co-widow of Ng. for not being present. It was explained that she was away and that as the women had sent no notice of their coming—as one of the elder women told me afterwards they should have done—she could not be expected to know of their plans.

Old Nwa Ori Ego, also a widow of this house-group but with a different husband from Ng., eventually came out to her assistance. She was the only other elderly woman of this house-group with the exception of the plaintiff, Nw., who was also in the offing.

As discussion seemed likely to be prolonged the visiting women made a fire to sit by. Lɔlɔ, the strong-minded, hard-working and sharp-tongued widow of Umuɛkɛ-owɛrɛ, took a prominent part in the proceedings, acting rather as a leader to the band. After a time Nwa Ori Ego spoke, explaining that nothing could be settled as Nwa Ume, the senior co-widow of the defendant, was not there, but let them appoint a day and the money should be paid to them. She took the side of Ng. in pressing for delay. Her suggestion was hotly discussed, both sides in the usual Ibo fashion quoting many other cases as precedents in support of their own points. But it was ultimately decided that the women should go away and come back the next night to receive the money. There was much talk about other cases in which the money had been paid at once. Those who had been made to pay on former occasions were, of course, among the talkers. On the other side, Nwa Ori Ɛgo, speaking for Ng.'s house-group, pointed out that other cases were still outstanding where no money had yet been paid.

At last Lɔlɔ moved off and the rest of the women slowly followed her and it seemed as though the party had broken up. But talk went on and the women hung about in the path leading back to the market place, reiterating that on other occasions the money had been paid at once. And some said that Lɔlɔ must have received a bribe from Ng.

Eventually the tide surged back to Ng.'s house, Lɔlɔ with it, but explosive talk about her conjectural bribe still going on. Singing and dancing started again, and again there was the same quick tempo and tense quality about the whole thing.

Ng. had, after the first stage, retired into her house and shut her door. The women outside now started banging on her door and lifting the palm leaf mats of her roof up and down in time to the dance rhythm. But one of their number, a youngish woman of the same Umuɛkɛ-ama half of the village as the victim but of a different house-group, said that they must not do this. The lengths to which they might go were, it seemed from this, recognised by custom, and anyone could point out where the limits had been surpassed.

After a time Ng. came out and announced that when she had paid her fine she would then have something to say to those who had beaten on her door. At last it was decided that as her elder co-widow was away the women would return the next night to collect the money. In the meantime we all withdrew and the women streamed off through the village singing and shouting. It was said next day that some of them sat up nearly all night discussing the case and talking.

Going over things the following morning with a youngish woman of Umu Nwa Ɛbodim, I asked whether there were head women of any kind who would call the rest out for such gatherings as these fine collectings. She gave the kind of answer that this sort of question usually evoked. Some of the older women would call them out, she said, adding later that the younger women could also do it. As for the little woman who summoned them to dance with her *igbugbo,* she was only a leader for dancing. Then, having got past the irrelevant question, she came to the crux of the matter and explained that if the fine were to be collected in Umuɛkɛ-owɛrɛ the initiative would be taken by Umuɛkɛ-ama, who would come out first and go and summon the latter. The reverse would also be true, and indeed we had seen it happen the night before when the *owɛrɛ* half had set the ball rolling against the *ama* division.

Talking later in the same day with old Nwa Ori Ɛgo, she confirmed this absence of " head women." Anyone could take the initiative, she said. But she also pointed out, as did another woman, that the two halves of the village would take action against each other.

The night after the orgy some of the women did in fact go again to Ng.'s house. But old Nwa Ori Ɛgo said that Ng. did not produce the money. She and the women of her house-group pointed out that several women had beaten drums because they had got a case—some of them in Umuɛkɛ-owɛrɛ—and the women had not yet answered these summonses. This being so, Ng. refused to pay. I asked Nwa Ori Ɛgo how long ago these drums were beaten and she said it was last year and that this is how things go on—delays and dawdling. She added that when the women, in due course, answer a drum summons, they give no notice of their coming to the accused. If she has not got money for a fine they demand at least a fowl, as they did of Ng. But when they come again to collect the money they ought to give notice and this time she protested, they had not done so. In point of fact she herself had been perfectly aware of the women's intention of coming. . . .

From this whole episode one sees again how the dual division principle supplies driving power for common action in the absence of formally recognised leaders or of centralised authority. And within this framework forceful individuals

like Lɔlɔ can exercise a certain amount of influence or at
least constitute themselves a mouthpiece for others less
articulate. And again one sees how, in judicial activites of
this kind, however informal they may appear, there are,
none the less, institutionalised rules of behaviour which
are generally known and which can be invoked by anyone
if they are in danger of infringement. One saw the small
instance where dancing and singing overflowed into tam-
pering with the house of the accused and at once a woman
of her side of the village proclaimed this as illegal.

The spur of rivalry between the two village halves and
the check of known and detailed rules fits into the general
picture of village organisation with which we began.

But in addition one saw that this, like the annual rites,
was exclusively a woman's occasion. Not a man appeared
except my somewhat nervous but infinitely intrigued night
watchman and interpreter. And again one was impressed by
the slick, wholehearted way in which operations were
conducted.

A further bond between the wives of the village was the
fact that they met together at intervals in the market place
to dance. They did not dance on the village market day.
They would have been far too busy. The younger men of
the village danced then, if their energy had not already
been exhausted by house building or some other such
strenuous activity. But the women, if they danced, did so
towards evening on Oriε Ajala day. This was the day of
an unimportant market at the other end of Agbaja and not
likely to compete for the women's time and energy. When
I first went to Umuεkε at the beginning of the wet season,
farm work was heavy and whether or not for this reason
the women were not dancing. But a few months later they
began and danced first at my house and then occasionally
in the market place till the death of one of the unmarried
girls of the village again made them stop for a time. During
my second stay of six months in Umuεkε between January
and September, 1937, I noticed little dancing on the part of
the women. They performed again at my house but little
otherwise and one realised that their meetings,[1] which
included dancing, were taking up an increasing amount of

---

[1] See p. 217.

their time. These meetings, as will be explained later, were formed, not by the wives of a village, but by the women born in the village and married elsewhere, and therefore concerned a quite different grouping of the women.

But the communal dancing of the wives of the village was none the less a formal bond between them. There was a leader of the dancing who would summon the women by beating an *igbugbo*, a hollow iron instrument rather like a large candle extinguisher. She would also lead the singing. She was small and old and gentle, with a weak voice, but she was said to have been chosen by Ogbudi, the guardian spirit of the village, in honour of whom the women danced, near the market shrine. Ogbudi came in a dream to her and to another woman who was also a leader of the singing. They had, in accordance with custom, gone to a diviner to consult him as to the meaning of the dream and he had confirmed the fact of their election by the spirit as leaders of the dancing and singing.

But this did not give them any further position of authority among the wives. When I enquired whether the *igbugbo* beater was in any sense a " head " woman the women I was talking to rejected the idea firmly, and clinched the matter by adding " Did not we all subscribe to buy the *igbugbo* ? " And even for her position of dance leader the little old lady was conscious of her shortcomings. She was a wife in Umu Nwa Ebodim, and on one occasion when the wives of this extended family had gathered together to share *ɔha* leaves[1] she came and addressed them. She explained that she was the woman chosen to sing for them when they danced, but if they could find a better woman let them do so. She was chosen by Ogbudi. But they do not, she said, answer strongly when she sings and she feels ashamed. They make her small. Let them find a better woman if they can. The women present, who had been sharing the leaves with a great deal of noise and some fierce disputing, listened remarkably quietly to this speech. But at the end they all burst into the cry that implies dissociating oneself from a risky situation. In this case it meant that none of them, for fear of offending the village deity, was willing to replace the speaker.

---

[1] See p. 180.

In the women's dances the *igbugbo* player would stand in the middle, with her singing colleague, while about thirty or forty women danced in a circle round them to the accompaniment of the alternate solo singing of the two women. Other wives would watch but there would be no audience as for the men's dances on market days. The women always had with them two or three of the men of the village as masters of ceremonies. These would stand with switches and sometimes flick at a woman who came late or threaten others who were moving lazily. On one occasion, too, they belaboured some other men who interrupted the dancing and of whose disturbance the women complained.

The dancing was much more varied and attractive than that of the men. The dancers revolved in a large circle, quite elderly women among them and some of these remarkable for their grace of movement. Some had anklets that rattled as they were shaken. In many of the dances the women growled like dogs. At these times a woman noted for her proficiency in making this noise would go into the middle to " lead " them. One would sometimes hear the girls in the village practising this growl, which was quite absent from the men's dancing.

There was no orchestral accompaniment to the dancing, as in the case of the men. This was replaced by the singing. The two women in the middle sang alternately and also called out the praise names of the dancers in turn and sang in flattering phrases, saying, for instance, that their husbands were moneymakers. The dancers would reply as they were called. Any one who had a special announcement to make would go into the middle. A woman might go in and explain that she had been prevented from joining them last time they danced.

When the formal dances were at an end the performers would sometimes individually or in twos and threes break into apparently impromptu steps on their own, with great *élan*. There would be a good deal of the distinctively woman's gesture in which a couple of women would spring towards each other, one arm upraised and touch hands at the top of their stretch in an access of *joie de vivre*. Again these flashes of vital energy and excitement struck one in the women's doings. They certainly seemed to find an outlet in their concerted activities from the unquestionably hard and often monotonous work of weeding, palm oil making and food preparing, that more than filled most of their days.

If there were any spectator who made a gift of money to the dancers it would be shared among them. The men accompanying them would not get the money. But such gifts were rare.

As for the learning of new dances, one of the women explained that if, in the dry season, they heard that the people of another place were doing a new dance, about ten of them would go off and learn it and they would then practice it in the moonlight.

In addition to these common activities of the wives of the village there were also times when they would take an oath together as a group for some reason or another. I did not see this done but I first heard of it one day at the beginning of the dry season from Nwa Ori Ego. She said that her daughter married in the Agbaja village of Umucagwa had been to see her and had told her that she and the other wives of Umucagwa were going to one of the big Agbaja deities to give it a fowl and to rejoice. A year previously they had gone to this deity and had sworn together by it that they would not poison people or steal or do other bad things, on pain of being killed by it. And now those who were still alive and were therefore free of the conditional doom were going to show their thankfulness. I asked if the women of Umueke ever swore thus. She said that they did, and also the men. They had not done it the previous year. They had talked about it but done nothing. But two years ago the men had sworn on a deity of a related village group, Umukabia, and the women had sworn on Iyi Amade, the guardian spirit of the next door Agbaja village. Later one of the old men of Umueke also told me about the women swearing by Iyi Amade and some of them fell ill or died. For, added he, is it not women as well as men who do bad things? Indeed, he continued, their knocking of *ofo* is what causes so much sickness. Their *ofo* is strong. Asked whether the women have real *ofo*, he said no, but they knock their hands on the ground instead.[1]

These were evidently cases of what might be called swearing on general principles. But the same device might

---

[1] See p. 175.

be resorted to for particular reasons. During my first stay in the village and about the beginning of the dry season, cows began mysteriously dying. The first I heard of it was from a stranger who asked me one day if I could suggest any way of preventing their cows dying. He had heard rumours that the white man could sometimes cure cattle and theirs were now dying quite unaccountably. Shortly after a friend of mine in Umuɛkɛ who owned several cows sent me the unusual present of a joint of meat. I then heard from one of his wives that his cows were dying suddenly from some unknown cause. The description of their death did not approximate to that occurring in any well-known cattle disease. But shortly after this one of the Umuɛkɛ women told me that the people of a village-group some miles away had said that as cow owners have a " meeting "[1] and subscribe money to take action in court against those who kill their cows with matchet or gun, they will go other ways to kill cows, by putting down things for them to eat that will cause them to die. And that is why cows are dying.

Evidently this was a new phase of the cow *versus* crops palaver, and I enquired whether only the people of that particular village group were killing cows. My informant replied indirectly that cows were dying everywhere, but in answer to my question said it was being done by men and not women. In view of other things which happened in this connection her answer may be regarded as cautious rather than correct.

An open clash occurred just at this time at the big market of Umuɛzɛala, the village-group next to Agbaja, and to which many Agbaja people were in the habit of going. The old widow, Nwa Ori Ɛgo, gave us an excited description of the scene. She said that the men and women of Umuduru Osu, another village-group near by, had made a law in their own place that cows should be restrained from eating the crops. They had then come to the market of Umuɛzɛala and had tried to impose a law there that anyone finding a cow in cultivated land should kill it. The people of Umuɛzɛala were indignant at this interference and a fight ensued, spears flying round the market and, as I afterwards heard, many people being arrested and taken to court. I asked

Nwa Ori Ɛgo if the Agbaja women were going to do anything about cows. She said yes, that next Oriɛ Ekpa, the Agbaja market day, and the Oriɛ four days after, they, supported by the men who do not possess cows, would take a drum and beat it in the market and make a law that any cows, sheep or goats found in farms would be killed. I asked how they would arrange about coming together to do this. She said that when something of this kind is in the air the women will talk to each other about it during one of the big markets to which most of them go. When they return home they will tell their fellow wives who did not go, and thus all will know and will come together. I left for England shortly after this and do not know what happened, but I am doubtful whether the degree of concerted action prophesied by Nwa Ori Ɛgo would in fact take place. The description was interesting though as illustrating again the tendency for " laws " to be proposals that more or less anyone could bring forward and that would only be recognised if they could win their way to general acceptance. It also again indicated the importance of markets as a channel of communication.

What was more interesting from the specific point of view of women's organisation was that Nwa Ori Ɛgo said that the wives of Umucagwa, one of the Agbaja villages where she had a married daughter, had already sworn on one of the big Agbaja deities that if any of their number were to kill a cow or other domestic animal in her farm the others would stand by her. She added that all the wives of Agbaja would swear thus and that the women of the *Osu* [_ _] village-group went and swore thus before making their law about cows. This swearing of mutual support in a common enterprise possibly throws light on the refusal of many women, after the Aba riots, to answer questions before the Commission of Enquiry.

The whole episode also gave point to a story that I had heard soon after my arrival in the village. Two people, a man and a woman, were chatting casually in my house and said, among other things, that a certain kind of cassava had only been introduced into these parts a few years previously. And they said that at that time the married women—of all Agbaja so far as I could gather—ran away to Oriɛ Ekpa, the central market place, and stayed there for eight days till their husbands came and begged them to return. They then said that the men must tie up their goats and sheep and cows, so that they, the women, might plant cassava. So the men agreed. And in return the women agreed to pay them ten shillings or a pound every year in return. They then returned home. And nowadays, if an animal eats crops the owner of the crop must report the matter to the owner of the animal. If the latter does not tie the creature up the crop owner kills it and puts it in a public place and tells the owner to come and take it. If he does not do so all the women of the village share it. They have this right because of their annual payment.

I did not hear about this annual payment at any other time and I doubt whether in fact it was made. But offending animals were sometimes killed by the women and the owner had to remove the bodies quickly if he did not want to lose them. As for the married women bringing collective pressure to bear on their husbands, a case had happened some years previously which had become famous. And I have no doubt that it was substantially true although it had probably been embellished and its scale magnified with the passage of years. I heard of it independently on three different occasions and in each case from a man, never from a woman. It was evidently with the men that the strong impression remained. In each case the story came spontaneously and each version bore out the others.

One of my informants was an old man of Umu Nwa Ebodim. He was talking about a dead half-brother. When asked how the brother had died he said that he killed himself. He stole, and *agbara*—supernatural beings—killed him. He then added that years ago—from his description it must have been between ten and twenty years previously—all the married women of Agbaja made all the Agbaja men swear for them and as a result of this swearing his brother, who was guilty of stealing domestic animals, died. The substance of the story, from three sources, was as follows.

Fifteen to twenty years before, judging by the internal evidence of the stories and by the fact that one informant placed the episode just before the severe influenza epidemic of 1919, the married women of Agbaja left their husbands villages and went either to Umunumu or to Oriɛ Ekpa taking their mats with them so that they could sleep where they were. They stayed away a month. When their husbands went to ask the reason for their withdrawal they said that too many women were dying. Either they would die when they were pregnant or when they were in child birth, or if a man passed behind their backs when they were pregnant they would miscarry. In the old days it was not like this. But nowadays men were going away to places like Onitsha and elsewhere and were bringing back bad medicine and were killing the women. Also things were being stolen.

So the elders went out to talk with the women. And it was arranged that at a certain time all the men of Agbaja should come to Oriɛ Ekpa and swear for the women on *Ala*— the earth—and the elders said that anyone failing to come would be killed. The wives of each village collected together the men of that village and they came in turn to Oriɛ Ekpa, the senior village coming first. The swearing took eight days, one village finishing before another began.

Oriɛ Ekpa, the central market place of all Agbaja, contains the shrine of one of its principal deities. And here the women dug a hole in the ground—*ala*—and poured into it water collected from the shrines of two of the most powerful Agbaja deities and made a kind of soup and put it in. And they killed a fowl and poured its blood into the hole. Women do not normally kill a sacrificial animal. But in answer to my question about this an old man explained that they did not take knife but pulled off the fowl's head with their hands. They also made fufu of pounded plantain and rolled it into small balls. The main body of women then stood back and the principal ones stood near the hole. And the men came up one by one and had to dip their hands in the hole and wash their faces in the liquid. Exact gestures illustrated this part of the story. Each man had then to eat a ball of the *ɵtara* [⁻ _ _]—fufu—and to swear on pain of death that he neither had killed nor would kill people or pregnant women or children. Nor had he stolen.

Each of the three narrators went on to say how many people had died during the two or three months after this swearing. One is at liberty to wonder how much the influenza epidemic helped. But in any case the whole thing had left a deep impression on the men. The hole was henceforward known as *ɔnɵ ala* [⁻ ⁻ _ _]—shrine of *ala*—and the fufu was always referred to as *ɵtara ala* [⁻ _ ⁻ _ _]—fufu of *ala*. The

ceremony had taken place just before the C.M.S. mission
came to Agbaja and had not been repeated since. But I
gathered that it could be revived at any time if need arose.

I asked one man how the women managed about food
during the time they stayed away from their husbands'
villages. He said their husbands cooked it for them. I asked
why and he said if a man saw other husbands cooking for
their wives would his wife be pleased if he did not do likewise ? When I asked why they did not leave the women
without any food in order to make them come home he
replied that they did so at first. And the women of each
village appointed ten of their number to go to the village and
procure food and cook it. This they did and carried the food
off for their companions, giving none to their husbands.
And when that consignment of food was finished another
ten women would come. So in order to get any food themselves the husbands cooked it for themselves and also for the
women and carried it to them. This description was given
with the animation of an eye witness. And when one remembers that in this society it is normally considered shameful
for a man to cook for himself the story of the husbands'
cooking acquires added poignancy.

It would probably be unwise to interpret too literally
the statement that " all the married women of Agbaja "
co-operated. But it certainly would seem that a certain
number of wives from all the eleven villages of Agbaja had
acted together. And rare though such occasions are they
are none the less of interest as throwing light on the poten-
tialities of women's organisation.

TITLES AND MISCELLANEOUS GROUPS

In Umuɛkɛ at the present day title-taking, as has been
pointed out already, does not seem to be of great importance.
Women as well as men can, in theory, take ɔʐɔ title though
in a different manner. But the only woman in the village
whom I heard of as having done so was Lɔlɔ of Umuɛkɛ-
owɛrɛ, and she was said not to have completed the process.
Such a woman has to observe certain conditions at the
time of the fourth month celebrations for Ajiɔkɵ Ji, the
yam spirit. I do not know whether or not this title was the
same as that of ɔʐɔ agwɵ nshi such as can be taken by a woman
in Mbieri.

These titled women will be called Lɔlɔ. But the name is not restricted to this usage. A man's first wife, for instance, may be referred to as his Lɔlɔ. And people may be called this simply because an ancestress of that designation has reincarnated in them. The name is, however, primarily a mark of honour. The female aspect of Ogbudi, the guardian spirit of Umuɛkɛ, was known as Lɔlɔ Ogbudi. The male aspect had the equivalent designation of Ɛzɛala Ogbudi.

As for special women's societies, the only one I heard of in the neighbourhood was that known as *eyɔrɔ* [_ _ _], of which nearly all the members were women. One of the initial qualifications of membership seemed to be the occurrence of hysterical symptoms. A certain amount of wealth was necessary for those who wished to proceed to full membership. No one in Umuɛkɛ belonged, as far as I know, and further details will therefore not be given here.

SIGNIFICANCE OF INTRA-VILLAGE GROUPING

In the whole of this section we have been discussing the grouping of women *qua* wives. The group which comes together to perform a common activity may be the wives of an extended family, or of a village half or of the whole village, or—in rare cases—a village-group like Agbaja. But in each and every case the women are there as the wives of their husbands and the group is based on the organisation of the husband's village. This grouping helps to strengthen cohesion and co-operation between the married women of a village, these women being all originally a collection of individuals born elsewhere. Some of them, of course, are inter-related, having come from the same stranger village or extended family. But as a group they are a heterogeneous collection bound together by the fact of having married into the same village in which they thereafter live. On this basis, as we have seen, communal action, common sentiments and common groupings arise, knitting together closely the one-time strangers, the married women, and stressing the unity of the village. But side by side with this principle of grouping runs another, whose importance is quite other but perhaps even greater. It is the principle of grouping, not according to the village into which the woman is married, but according to that into which she was born. And this system is so organised as to form a series of communicating links between the women scattered over a wide area. Whereas in their capacity of wives the women look inwards to the village where they are married, in their capacity of daughters they look outward in all directions to the innumerable villages in which they were respectively born. In the first case the unity of the village is emphasised. In the second case—that of the " meetings " between all the women born in the same village but scattered broadcast by marriage among the neighbouring villages—it is the links between the villages that are strengthened and institutionalised.

Chapter XVI. Groups based on Place of Birth

" Meetings " or, in the Ibo rendering, " *mikiri* " [⁻ _ _],
were a marked feature of Ibo social life in and around
Agbaja. A number of men or a mixture of men and women
from one or more villages would combine on a voluntary
basis to meet at intervals and to subscribe in money or,
sometimes, in kind for the benefit of each member in turn.[1]

But during my first stay in Umuɛkɛ there came into
being meetings whose basis of membership was new to this
village, though in the neighbourhood such meetings already
existed. The members of this new *mikiri* were to be the
women born in Umuɛkɛ and therefore married elsewhere.

It would, I think, be true to say that the basic factor of
the meeting in the eyes of its members was the economic
one. Many other considerations came in. At times it would
seem that the social or convivial aspect of the meetings
was uppermost. Now and then, if a serious offence was
toward, the judicial side was temporarily to the fore. Inter-
woven with the whole activity was a supernatural strand,
acting partly as sanction partly as safeguard. But if one
had asked a member what the meetings were for she would
probably have explained that on each occasion they all
subscribed a small sum of money, about threepence a head,
which was pocketed by the member who was acting as
hostess for that particular meeting. The gathering would
be held at her married home, that is to say in her husband's
village. The order in which the meetings were held was
therefore a matter of importance and in this the women
followed the sharing order of the men of their native village—
of the families, that is to say, in which they were born.

The woman who by family seniority had the right to
benefit by the first meeting was also the formal head of
the organisation and was usually referred to as Mama.
Various other officials were appointed and rules were drawn
up governing the conduct of the meeting members, who
killed a fowl and swore together to observe the rules. A pot of

---

1 See p. 44.

medicine or magic was sometimes bought out of the proceeds of fines for rule breaking. Its property was to keep peace between the members. It would be sprinkled on the floor of the meeting place and members would dip their fingers in it and lick them, dip them in again and touch their forehead, chest and toes.

Each meeting would last from the evening of one day, through the next day to the morning of the subsequent day. But some members would only come for the main day. And some would pay a visit to their husband's village during the progress of the meeting if it were necessary. But they would be fined if they were late getting back to the meeting. All the members would subscribe a small sum to be spent by the hostess on soup for them and they would each bring food with them. The hostess would supplement this according to her means. The soup would be scrutinised closely and one would sometimes hear complaints afterwards of its poor quality and suggestions that the hostess must have used the money for her own profit instead upon proper ingredients.

The main regular activities of the meetings, apart from the collection, were dancing, singing and much talking, and above everything was the dressing up. In ordinary life the women usually wore a short cloth folded round the hips and reaching to the knees, and some wore a headcloth. But for a meeting everyone would try to borrow, if she did not possess, some kind of a blouse or tunic, and all would wear a headcloth of some kind. The officials outshone everyone in fantastic uniform or fancy dress. There were policemen with miniature wooden rifles ; there was on one occasion a "D.C.", and every meeting had a *Nwa Bɛkɛ* [ˉ _ ˉ _]—white woman. She stands out in one's mind, sometimes for the ferocity of her expression, sometimes for her clothes—a pink silk dress with an orange Tam o'shanter on one occasion and horn-rimmed spectacles with a white blob on each lens. She gave one much food for thought.

In addition to their social activities the meeting members would sometimes try cases concerning one of their number. The offences might not have been committed against another member. The meeting could none the less act as a judicial body. It could also discuss matters of public concern to the women.

Such, in brief outline, were the essential features of the

women's *mikiri* or meeting series.[1] There might be about
fifty or more members and this considerable body of women,
living in the widely scattered villages of their husbands,
would thus come together every few weeks, each time in a
different place. When it is remembered that dozens of other
mikiri in the neighbourhood would be doing the same
thing it becomes possible to get some kind of picture of the
shuttle-like movement of women backwards and forwards
across the countryside. A woman would not only belong
to her own *mikiri* but would attend a certain number of
others held for instance by daughters or co-wives. In the
dry season of early 1937 when one returned to the village
from England there seemed to be a spate of meetings in
progress, so much so that later on, when rain was needed
for the crops, it was said to be later than usual because it
had been so persistently driven away by the rain drivers
in the interest of the meeting holders.

Since the women's *mikiri* seemed in the main to follow
the same general pattern, it will be enough to give some
account of the activities and vicissitudes—for the latter were
certainly not lacking—of the *mikiri* of the daughters of
Umuɛkɛ village.

Towards the end of the rainy season in 1935 the women
born in Umuɛkɛ gathered together several times in Umuɛkɛ
from their husbands villages to make the preliminary
arrangements for a *mikiri,* and the first of their series of
meetings was held in October in the next-door village of
Umuamɛkɛ, at the married home of one of their members.

At the outset an interesting hitch occurred. In theory the
first meeting should have been for the half-sister of the
man who took first share in all Umuɛkɛ since the women
followed the sharing order of their families. This man was,
of course, N.O., the holder of the village *afɔ*,[2] and the women
acknowledged that his half-sister ought to be the head of
their *mikiri* and also receive the first collection of money.
They therefore, at the preliminary gathering before their
first real meeting, each subscribed *ɛgo iri*—ten heads of

---

[1] The women themselves talked of their *mikiri* (Ibo pronunciation of
" meeting ") whether they meant a particular meeting or the whole
series of meetings and the body of members. It will, however, be clearer
if one uses " *mikiri* " for the organisation and meeting for a particular
gathering. [2] See p. 69.

cowries[1]—as was customary, and gave them to this woman to buy fish and other ingredients for soup for their first meeting. But this woman sent the money back. A member of the *mikiri,* talking to me about this on the day on which their first real meeting was held, explained that this woman's husband would not let her come. She also said that none of the Umuɛkɛ-owɛrɛ women were joining and that Umuɛkɛ-ama and Umu Nwa Ɛbodim were going ahead on their own. The first meeting, that very afternoon, was being held in the next-door village of Umuamɛkɛ, for the full sister of the man who took second share in all Umuɛkɛ—Nwa Onyɛ Okoro, of Umu Nwa Ɛbodim. This sister was married in Umuamɛkɛ and the meeting was taking her for head as being next in seniority to the real head woman.

In point of fact the Umuɛkɛ-owɛrɛ women did not for long stand aloof from the *mikiri.* Some, at any rate, of them joined in. Later I heard a fuller story about the woman who should have been head. Her half-brother, N.O., died shortly after this while I was in England. When I got back to Umuɛkɛ one of the men of the village told me that the *dibea* who was consulted about the cause of his death gave two reasons. The first, to which reference has already been made in an earlier chapter, was his refusal to become Court Member for Umuɛkɛ. His *ɔfɔ* killed him because he did not uphold its dignity in this matter. The second reason given for his death was that he had refused to allow his half-sister to become head of the *mikiri* of the women born in Umuɛkɛ. According to this version it was her half-brother, not her husband, who had prevented her. And my informant added that the women had then chosen the sister of Nwa Onyɛ Okoro to be their head and N.O.'s half-sister had joined as an ordinary member. But on the way to the meeting the money she had in her hand for her subscription vanished. So the women of the meeting went to a *dibea* to ask why, and he said it was because N.O. refused to let her be head. And the *dibea* told the women they must take a cock and sacrifice it on N.O.'s *ɔfɔ*, saying that it was not their doing but his that the woman was not their head. They therefore did this and the *ɔfɔ* killed N.O.

The story is interesting as showing the importance

---

[1] A head of cowries consists of six shells. This is the smallest cowry unit used. Ten heads was, at this time, worth rather less than ½*d.*

attached to the question of seniority. As in other spheres so in the women's meetings it did not appear that " Mama," the head—*onye ishi*—had any great executive power or importance. Ekutara Nene, the wife of Nwa Onyɛ Okoro, who belonged to a *mikiri* of the women of her native village, described their head as " no good." And at the first meeting I ever attended, before the formation of that of the daughters of Umuɛkɛ, I saw " Mama " fined by the *Nwa Bɛkɛ* [⁻ _ \ ]— white woman—for talking while she was eating, which the meeting had decided was against the rules for officials. But although Mama might not, particularly if she had an insignificant personality, wield much authority, it was none the less important that she be chosen with due regard to formal requirements and that the order of receiving the meeting collections be that of seniority.

The daughters of Umuɛkɛ had, however, no choice but to take as their head and as the hostess of their first meeting the woman who should really have come second. Henceforward she was known as Mama.

On the morning before this first meeting one of the members told me that some of their officials, including their *Nwa Bɛkɛ,* had already been chosen. One of their gun bearers was a tall, strong-looking daughter of old Nwa Ori Ɛgo. They had not yet chosen anyone for " policeman." Their head woman would choose her. Like the gun bearers she would be chosen for her size and strength.

One or two of the women married in Umuɛkɛ were joining this daughters' meeting for special reasons. For instance, there was a youngish widow called Mgbɔkwe in the village who was of Arɵ Cuku birth but who had married an Umuɛkɛ man and been brought back to the village by him. She could not join a meeting in her distant birthplace so she joined that of the Umuɛkɛ daughters. She lived near me and from the beginning was one of my best informants. Coming from far away she regarded the village with considerable detachment and was willing to give information in the early days while most of the women were standing aloof and wondering whether the white woman might perhaps not have come to tax them. It may also have been her Arɵ origin that gave her a certain cool independence. She was always standing up to the people who tried to do her out of her right to her dead husband's property. And it was not she who was going to be overawed by a strange white woman in the village. In any case she was a great help. And from her I learned many things about the *mikiri* of the daughters of Umuɛkɛ.

Just after the second meeting, at which I spent the afternoon, she told me that in the evening they had killed and eaten and sworn by a fowl. The blood was poured over the small table of the hostess, who brought the fowl, and the women put their hands on the table. The fowl was then cooked and eaten by all the women as a pledge that none of them would desert the *mikiri* and that if she died her brother or sister would continue her contributions. It is, of course, the great fear of the *mikiri* that a member will get her share of the subscriptions and will then try to get out of paying any more herself. Mgbɔkwe explained that the hostess for each of the first four meetings would buy a fowl to be killed thus. It would be bought with the money subscribed for buying soup. They had not yet got their pot of medicine to keep them from quarrelling. They would get that after killing the four fowls.

Later on she described other laws of the *mikiri*. The meeting day was Oriɛ Ajala and a good many of the members would go the evening before, on Ɛkɛ day, to sleep at the meeting place and some would sleep there the following night. Those with young babies would only go for the day, because of getting back to feed them. It was forbidden for a woman to have sexual intercourse with her husband or with any other man on the Nkwɔ night before the meeting— that is to say the night immediately before—and also at any time during the meeting. While they were staying at the meeting place several women would share a house for the night. When the *mikiri* members killed their fowls they swore to observe the laws of the *mikiri* and not to steal at the meetings nor " do any bad thing."

I asked what would happen if a woman broke the sex rule. Mgbɔkwe said that she had never heard of it happening, but that if it did the woman would have to bring a fine of sixpence or a shilling to the meeting and confess what she had done. She would make the man she had slept with produce the money. This account lacked conviction. But Mgbɔkwe then launched with great gusto into a story which was presumably to show the dangers of breaking the meeting laws about stealing—the classic Ibo crime. She described how, a short time before, a woman of another *mikiri* stole a plate of rice at a meeting and hid it in her box and took it home. Before the next meeting she had died, and when they carried her to the place where she was to be buried she became very heavy and the people put her down. She began to call to her husband saying that she was cold and let him bring fire. The people were frightened and ran away leaving her where she was. Since then many people had heard her calling, but Mgbɔkwe herself had been too frightened to go. But the woman's husband went to consult Igwɛ Ka Ala,[1] and when he got there he saw his dead wife crouching on the ground with her hands out in front of her. Igwɛ, the oracle, said the case must be judged between them and they must each say their part. The husband said he had never been party to her thefts. So Igwɛ tied the woman and since then she has not been calling out.

It was interesting that the women's meetings were supposed to entail abstention from sexual intercourse. It increased the impression one gained that the women did not consider themselves bound to bestow their favours on the men in season and out of season.

Beside its laws for important matters such as stealing, a *mikiri* had a number of petty regulations for the internal conduct of the meeting whose main object appeared to be the levying of fines, which the members could then use for communal purposes. Among such rules would be, for instance, the one forbidding officials to talk while they were eating.

The meetings of the daughters of Umuɛkɛ were all much alike except that the hospitality was more sumptuous in some than in others. The members themselves brought pounded food with them in the wooden box that also held their festive clothes and that formed part of the considerable luggage that they carried on their heads for these two-day visits to another village. The hostess had to supply soup to eat with this food and she had been provided by each woman at the previous meeting, as we have seen, with ten heads of cowries—rather less than a halfpenny—wherewith to buy the ingredients. But it seemed to be a point of

1 The well-known Umunɔha oracle, supposed to be no longer functioning but still used by Agbaja people.

honour that she should provide other food out of her own resources. If she had a son he would help her, perhaps by buying stockfish for her. Or a sister or half-sister would bring food to her. Other wives of her husband or wives in his extended family might help her, not of obligation but " if they had a good heart." Also if they hoped that she would help them in their turn. A woman's mother might give her money to help her. Nwa Ori Ɛgo, for instance, gave her daughter, married at Nzɛrɛm, a shilling when the daughter had a meeting. The member's husband and perhaps some of his male relations would bring palm wine. They would be given food in return. A hostess would acquire prestige by entertaining generously. In some cases she must have spent all the money due to her at her benefit meeting, if not more. Ekutara Nene, the wife in Umuɛkɛ who took second share in the village, belonged to the *mikiri* of her native village. She said that when they were due to come to her her son went to Umuahia, the nearest European centre, with ten shillings to buy food. They borrowed the money against what she was expecting to receive at the meeting. She also killed a fowl, not for swearing on, but " for boasting," because she was a big woman both in her husband's village and her own. Incidentally she said that the head of her meeting was no good and had not even produced a fowl for them to swear on. They had had to use something else.

Food would be of various different kinds, a certain amount of rice, which was something of a luxury, usually being produced by the hostess. When one of the daughters of Nwa Ori Ɛgo had her meeting she entertained on a fairly lavish scale. She produced a good deal of food which appeared to be mainly cassava and banana, for the members. And to the men and women who came from her father's extended family she gave rice and stockfish and *ihɛ agwɵgwɔ*.[1] She also gave food to the kinsmen of her husband who had brought palm wine. But in this region, where wealth was rare, even the more sumptuous of the meetings was none the less on a modest scale.

The meeting members would eat their food sitting in groups of three or four at the little tables which were a

[1] A mixture, usually of sliced oil bean, oil and beans.

constant feature at these gatherings, and on which their contributions were also placed when the moment arrived. This moment would be towards the end of the afternoon after dancing. The normal subscription for a member was threepence and those who failed to turn up had to pay fourpence. But a member married in the same village as the hostess might give her fourpence. And an official might give sixpence to another official when she was hostess.

At the second meeting of the daughters of Umuɛkɛ, held in the next door village of Umuamɛkɛ, several of the elders of Umuɛkɛ, dressed up for the occasion, dropped in at one stage. Some of them were from different extended families from that of the hostess. They made a money contribution and then went and sat apart from the women and drank together. We were told that they contributed because some days before the hostess had brought food to Umuɛkɛ and called them to eat. Mama, on the contrary, had not done this before her own meeting, the first of the series, and only two men of her own extended family had gone. She was therefore feeling cross at this other woman's meeting.

Several of the young men of Umuɛkɛ, kinsmen, of course, of the meeting members, used to go to each meeting to act as masters of the ceremony for the dancing, cut up stockfish and otherwise make themselves useful. They were known as the *nde dɛdɛ* [¯ ¯ \ _]. At one meeting they certainly gave the hostess threepence each and presumably this was usual. Whether they got anything more than food in return I do not know.

Thus, although these meetings of women married in the same village were their own organisation and concern, they had not the exclusively feminine character of the women's annual religious rites or their nocturnal judging of cases. Some of the meetings even admitted men members, but the daughters of Umuɛkɛ, though they discussed the matter, did not, so far as I know, go to this length.

Dancing and singing took place at intervals during the meeting and particularly in the afternoon. It was then that the women went and put on their festive cloths or their meeting uniform. Most of them were painted with beautiful *uri* patterns in addition to bringing an unwonted amount of clothing, part European, part indigenous. Mama would usually have a hat of some kind, sometimes a man's Homburg. *Nwa Bɛkɛ,* who, among the Umuɛkɛ daughters, was quite a mild young woman, would have European garments of some kind or another. She would address the stranger white woman as *ago*—namesake—to the entertainment of the meeting. But the most resplendent, and also the hottest, of the costumes were those worn by four or five gun bearers or policewomen. Over long cloths reaching almost to the ground they had thick dark blue blouses looking as though they were made of serge. A big scarf went over one shoulder and a miniature wooden rifle was slung at their backs. They had black headcloths and usually a pink and green pill-box hat of the Boys' Brigade shape perched rakishly on the side of the headcloth.

Dancing took place under the palm leaf shelter always erected as a protection from the sun in the yard of a house-group where a meeting was to be held. The space was sometimes extremely restricted and there were often about fifty members present. Some of the older ones, instead of dancing, sat at some of the little tables like dowagers at a ball and one would see them with their heads together revelling in the chance of a really good gossip.

The dancers formed a circle in the middle of which the hostess and Mama would sometimes sit with one or two women soloists to whom the dancers replied in chorus as they moved round and round at a walking pace, sometimes growling in the way peculiar to the women's dances. The *nde dɛdɛ*—the young men from Umuɛkɛ— stood in customary fashion in the middle of the circle holding sticks and sometimes blowing whistles. Because of the heat the women did what they called playing —*ɛgwu*—instead of real dancing—*uri*. Certainly they dripped. And usually either a man or a woman in the middle of the circle would stand holding a cloth and mopping each face that went past. The dust would rise in clouds from under the moving feet, and altogether, before long, the dancers would be glad to subside once more beside their small tables and chat or make their contributions. The payments were apt, as one would expect, to evoke a certain amount of quick-tongued argument, just as the food would at times provoke comment and criticism. This added spice to the occasion. But on the whole the meetings seemed to be amiable and convivial, not only in intention, but to a considerable extent in fact.

Occasionally, however, they got into heavy weather

through no fault of their own. One husband, in a village-group notorious for its uncouth behaviour—it had eaten its mission teacher a year or two before we arrived—had had a quarrel with his wife and had told her that she must hold her meeting at her father's place. This, of course, was not customary except for the young unmarried members of the *mikiri,* and the woman decided to carry on at her married home. But when, on a wet day, the meeting members arrived the husband refused to allow them to enter his house and pulled down their palm leaf shelter. Mgbɔkwe gave a scandalised description of the incident and said that she had never seen anything like it. It was indeed exceptional.

A women's *mikiri* was, however, not only a benefit society and a convivial gathering. If occasion arose it could try women's cases or discuss public matters with a view to taking action. Nwa Ori Ɛgo explained that it would be shameful for a case between two people of the same household to be put before a meeting and so published abroad. But other cases would go. One of the elders of Umuɛkɛ-owɛrɛ, she said, had repeatedly brought before the *mikiri* of the Umuɛkɛ daughters the case of his daughter who had left her husband and refused to go back to him. But the *mikiri* had so far come to no decision against the daughter. They thought that perhaps the fault was on the side of the men in the case.

A few weeks later one of Nwa Ori Ɛgo's two daughters became involved in judicial proceedings herself. Salome and I, knowing nothing of this, went along to see the old lady and found her in the greatest agitation. *" A hɵ ihe ka ubi ɛ rɛ ɔba "*—" If you see a thing which is greater than farm you will sell your barn "—said she as we entered her house, meaning that whatever we had come to talk about she had news of far greater importance. Then, with flashing eyes and waving arms, her foot tapping the floor and her body making dance movements as she sat, she told us how her eldest daughter, a widow, was being accused of the abhorred crime of stealing—her daughter whose father had looked after her so well that people had said he would not let any one come and marry her. But he had said he would. He had fed her on meat and on snake, so well did he look after her. Never from her childhood up had her daughter stolen and was she going to begin now that she was old ?

She then recounted how a fowl had been stolen from a

woman married in the same village as her daughter. The thief had been discovered because she refused to give a piece to her child, saying he would inform the owner, and he had retaliated by going and giving the information. The women of the village had judged the case and fined the thief £1 which they shared among themselves. And now, a woman born in Umuɛkɛ, in the extended family of Umu Nwa Ɛbodim, had been spreading rumours at recent meetings that the real thief was the daughter of Nwa Ori Ɛgo. And about eight days ago, at the last meeting, this rumour had come to the ears of the daughter. I asked Nwa Ori Ɛgo why her daughter had been accused and she said perhaps because both she and her daughter were poor and had no husbands to look after them.

The case was to be judged at a forthcoming meeting of the daughters of Umuɛkɛ which was being held in the village itself, since it was for an unmarried member. This was an opportunity for the trial. It was not considered correct to advertise the shortcomings of members by trying them at meetings held in villages other than the native one of Umuɛkɛ. The patriotism of birth took precedence, apparently, of that of marriage.

The hostess of this meeting being one of the unmarried girls of Umuɛkɛ and her father being dead, the meeting was held in the yard of a male kinsman of the same extended family, that of Umu Nwa Ɛbodim. In the afternoon the members adjourned to the open space of this part of the village and under the big tree in the middle of it they judged the case of Nwa Ori Ɛgo's daughter. By the tree sat Mama and another oldish woman on chairs, and near them the meeting member to whom the rumour about Nwa Ori Ɛgo's daughter had been whispered. A number of the older men of the village joined the gathering and the young *nde dɛdɛ* were there. One of them, a mild youth, remarked gently at one point that he would flog anyone who made any noise. No one appeared to pay any attention to him. But in fact proceedings were fairly orderly and speakers got quite a good hearing.

Nwa Ori Ɛgo's daughter spoke first, putting her case and saying how she had heard that people had been whispering behind her back that she was a thief. A number of other women, including Mama, spoke in her favour and when the accuser spoke she did so very feebly. It transpired that weeks before, when she was not a member of the meeting, she had made the accusation to one of the members, who had told her that she must on no account say this thing to anyone else and that she herself would not repeat it. After this, about sixteen days before the present meeting, the accuser had joined the *mikiri*. It was customary to explain the meeting rules to new members. Amongst other things they were told they must not steal. And they were told that if they saw any of their co-members involved in a dispute at market they should draw near and listen, and if she had been stealing they were to inform the other *mikiri* members. When these rules were explained to the accuser she brought forward the name of Nwa Ori Ego's daughter and repeated the rumour she had already whispered. Hence the trying of this case.

Nwa Ori Ego's daughter was unanimously acquitted, the main gist of the argument being that she had never in all her life been known to steal and she was not likely to begin now. Her accuser was told to pay her five shillings, of which she would probably hand on one shilling to the meeting members for palm wine. A fine of £1 was suggested but the guilty woman was said to have no money.

A man and woman had come from the village of Nwa Ori Ego's daughter's late husband to speak for her. They and her mother were angry at the small amount of the fine. They said that if the acquitted woman had been found guilty she would have had to pay more.

One of the comments of the meeting on the whole episode was that members must be careful not to do things to make the *mikiri* " scatter." People must not, in fact, lightly accuse one another of wrong doing. This fear of *mikiri* being broken up by internal discord was an ever present one both among the women and the men. Hence such remedies as magical pots of medicine against quarrelling and the discouragement of damaging rumours. The quick Ibo temper and the readiness to dispute always meant difficulty in maintaining stable communal activity. But the danger was realised and efforts were made, as has been seen, to guard against it. And certainly the women's *mikiri* seemed to surmount its obstacles and flourish in spite of them.

As to the actual payment of the fine there was the almost

invariable delay which attended fines other tnan those seized on the spot under threat of distraining upon the culprit's property. Some months later the five shillings had still not been paid. The guilty party had offered three shillings. But Nwa Ori Ɛgo's daughter had refused it, knowing that if she took it it would be doubly hard to extract the remaining two shillings. Her mother told us that one of the young men, the *nde dɛdɛ* of the *mikiri* was urging the culprit to pay the fine, saying that it was already much in arrears and that if the *mikiri* had to take up the matter again she would not get off so lightly as before. What happened I do not know as I left the village shortly after.

Over and above the trying of cases the women's *mikiri* might discuss matters of public importance that concerned them. In looking at the implications of exogamy it was seen that certain crimes between men of the same village— betwcen " brothers " that is to say—were the special concern of their " sisters," the women born in the village. A grave case of this kind occurred not long after the formation of the *mikiri* of the daughters of Umuɛkɛ. While I was away in England the young half-brother of Em., of Umuɛkɛ, died. His kinsfolk went to several *nde dibea* to ask the cause of his death and one and all said that Em. had killed him. When I got back to the village I found a widespread belief in the truth of this verdict. We heard rumours that the people of Agbaja were coming to seize property from Umuɛkɛ because Em. had done a thing forbidden—*nsɔ* [‾ ‾]—in killing his half-brother. In the local words he had used *nshi uyo* [‾ ‾ ‾ _]—poison of the house. It was also said that because of the breaking of this taboo the women born in Umuɛkɛ and married elsewhere were also coming to seize property from Umuɛkɛ.

Rather later, however, one of the young men of Umuɛkɛ told me that the *mikiri* of the daughters of Umuɛkɛ had discussed the matter, since it is at their meetings that they talk over such things, and had wanted to go and seize Em.'s property, as it is customary—or had been before the coming of the white man—that they should do. But he and the other men of the meeting had dissuaded them, saying that if they did so all Agbaja would come to seize Umuɛkɛ's property. There was evidently a complicated balancing of pros and cons and, in this case, apparently, the women were restrained. What in fact happened was that the holder of the big ɔfɔ of each of the eleven villages came to Em. who swore his innocence on their eleven ɔfɔ. A year then had to elapse in which ɔfɔ would either kill or vindicate him.

It is, I think, clear how important a feature of women's organisation these *mikiri* of the women born in one village present. The rules of exogamy decree that such women shall, at marriage, be dispersed over the neighbouring countryside. The social regulations concerning birth, death, marriage, sickness, religious festivals and other landmarks of existence decree, in their turn, that there shall be constant goings and comings between the natal villages of husband and wife. But this linkage is given institutionalised form and the women born in a village are connected not only to it but to each other in their *mikiri*. In this series of meetings, held every few weeks at different points over a considerable area, the women have a constant opportunity of hearing and discussing matters of common interest and of disseminating news of concern to them all. If such meetings were in being at the time of the Aba riots their relevance to the situation needs no comment. That they are in being at the present time is a fact that it would be unfortunate to ignore. It would be to overlook a ready means for getting in touch with organised women's opinion.

Looking back from the point we have now reached it is possible to state briefly a few salient points.

From a political point of view it appears that in part, at any rate, of Ibo country the village is the largest social unit with any claim to be a unit of government. The village-group may be considered as a whole in certain respects. But it is the village which, for most practical purposes, manages its own affairs. Within the village authority is dispersed among groups rather than centralised in any one individual or body. And the spirit of rivalry institutionalised in the dual division of the village is one of the sources of executive action and one of the mainsprings of communal activity. This pluralistic organisation, the tendency to balance two halves against each other rather than to unify them into a whole, would appear to be a characteristic of village government of a different order from the fact that the extended families composing the village themselves paddle their own canoe in many matters. The organisation

referred to here and described in the first section is that
which deals with matters of concern to the whole village
and not merely to an extended family. And though the whole
village considers itself theoretically a kinship unit, in fact
the sentiment of kinship wears thin outside the bonds of the
extended family and merges into a feeling which has more
of a local or political character.

But if it is essential to realise the small scale of Ibo political
organisation it is none the less vital to understand something
of the intricate social strands that weave together the
politically independent but socially inter-dependent village
cells. It has long been realised that the Ibo people, for all
their lack of political unity, have none the less a widespread
similarity of customs and language in spite of many local
variations. It is recognised that their markets are potent
economic and social links and that powerful oracles have
spread their tentacles of intercommunication over wide
areas. But it seems to be less generally grasped that the
Ibo system of exogamy works like a cement binding the
villages together, or like a consolidating network which
has to some extent, among other things, made trading
between the village units possible. It has certainly made
for the mitigation of inter-village fighting. And in all this
the leading part has fallen to the women.

A consideration of exogamy leads on to the third part of
our subject which deals with women's organisation. In
Ibo society men are organised on the basis of the village
in which they are born and live. But women, from the fact
that they marry into a different village from the one in
which they are born, are citizens, so to speak, of two cities
and their organisation has thus two territorial bases instead
of one. Inside the village the wives have their own organisation side by side with that of the men and due cognisance
must be taken of both if the running of the village is to
be understood. But the women, as daughters of their native
village, have also their far-flung inter-village organisation
which has no parallel in that of the men and which has
thus a special interest and importance as an inter-village
system of links. The series of contacts set up between the
villages by the rules and implications of exogamy becomes
thus, through the women's meetings, an organised network
of intercommunication.

APPENDIX

Temperament

I. THE TEMPERAMENT FACTOR

IT is usual in books of social anthropology to pass over the question of temperament in a few pàragraphs. The reason for this is given by Dr. Richards in her book, *Land, Labour and Diet in N. Rhodesia.* She stresses the importance of temperamental characteristics and then says : " But, unfortunately, it is just these temperamental traits that are so difficult to describe objectively. Until some more scientific criteria have been evolved the observer is bound to rely on his personal judgment and impressions."[1]

It is true that until lately, social anthropology has lacked adequate guidance from psychology in this matter. But in the last few years there has been an advance from the side of medical psychology in the scientific handling of temperament. This has been the work of Dr. Murdo Mackenzie and more specifically in his book, *The Human Mind.*[2]

I only came upon it after my return from Ibo country, but I have found it of great use in reflecting upon the material I gathered there. No one can stay in that country without being aware of the element of psychological tension that exists between English and Ibo. Nor can anyone fail to be interested in the temperamental factor in Ibo society, even though he may not be able to analyse it. For this reason, therefore, it seems worth devoting more space than is usual to the matter. But I believe, further, that a study of temperament is of basic importance to the theory of culture.[3] There has been a tendency to regard man's social heritage as the result of the cultural elaboration of the biological urges. This would appear, however, to beg the question by explaining culture in terms of cultural elaboration. Animals have biological urges but they do not have culture. If, however, a mental factor is recognised there is no need to beg the

---

[1] A. I. Richards : *Land, Labour and Diet in Northern Rhodesia.* 1939, p. 28.
[2] M. Mackenzie : *The Human Mind.* Churchill, London, 1940. See also by the same author : *When Temperaments Clash.* Murby, 1937.
[3] I am here using the word " culture " to include " social structure."

question. If mind has supervened to complicate biology, it must be reckoned with in any theory of culture, however unfashionable such a reckoning may, at the moment, be.

The scientific treatment of the temperamental aspect of mind with which we shall be concerned suggests, moreover, that any view of man as an undifferentiated lump of jelly which can be poured into a cultural or environmental mould is untenable. It would appear that there are varieties of temperament and that these varieties are among what Linton calls the constants in the anthropological situation. This clearly has a bearing on the question of patterns of culture.

For all these reasons it seems worth while to consider what light the work of Mackenzie throws upon our Ibo material and, incidentally, on certain general questions of social anthropology. As his work is still unfamiliar to many people we must start by looking at its main thesis.

In *The Human Mind* Mackenzie advances the theory that there are four basic types of temperament. This view is founded, in the first instance, on his observations as a medical psychologist of the mind in defence or in faulty functioning. In such conditions the automatic forces driving the mind are clearly open to observation. They are, so to speak, crystallised in defence. And it is for this reason that medical psychology has been able to throw light on the problem of temperament. To say that the study of the pathological functioning of mind is not valid for the normal or healthy mind is to ignore the fact that the mental forces revealed in the mental defences, or neuroses, are also found to be those of the healthy mind. In the one case they are functioning pathologically, in the other normally, but the forces themselves are the same.

It is on the observational basis of the mental defences that Mackenzie's study of temperament rests. It is therefore necessary to understand something of the nature of these defences if one is to grasp his hypothesis about temperamental differences. Here we can only attempt to condense the salient points of what is already a condensed presentation of the subject in his book. In his Preface he says :

" In its early days Psychology was the study of man's behaviour and emphasised his sensations, emotions and instincts rather than his organ of thought. The notion of man's mind as a discrete organ with a specific function, working in rhythm in space and time and driven by strictly mental forces is, I think, new and elaborated for the first time in this book."[1]

He goes on to point out that every mind is driven by two temperamental forces each of which is one of a pair of opposites. There are what he calls the time forces, to which he gives the names immediacy and deliberation and there are the space forces which he calls amplification and simplification. Every mind is driven by a combination of two of these forces, either immediacy or deliberation plus either amplification or simplification. Thus there are basically four types of temperament.

Immediacy and deliberation are opposites in the sense that the immediate thinks in terms of the present, seeks to raise the intensity of the actual moment, functions best in a crisis, whereas the deliberate's mind works best in terms of the past and future, resents being forced into the present, seeks to diminish the intensity of the actual moment, and needs an atmosphere of peace for its best functioning. The immediate works in terms of the actual, the deliberate of the potential. The former rejoices in society and makes quick social contacts, the latter tends to like a good deal of solitude and to make fewer and slower social contacts than the immediate. When immediacy and deliberation clash instead of combining and the mental forces are thrown into defence, there is in one case an aggressive response and in the other a pacific one.

" It is important to understand the difference between immediates and deliberates without any prejudice in favour of one or the other. When they are being complimented, immediates are commonly called brilliant, and when they are blamed they are called superficial. There is nothing in this judgment save the recognising of spectacular success or failure. On the other hand, successful deliberates are often called sound, and, if they fail, are described as dull. This, again, is little more than the description of a dignified success or failure. The two, immediacy and deliberation, subserve different activities. Immediates are by nature opportunists in the best sense of that word, just as deliberates are naturally wise. Deliberation has the capacity for attention to a few objects, and, as such, is more concerned with changing,

---

[1] Mackenzie : *The Human Mind,* p.v.

perfecting and altering these objects than with a wide range of activity.

"Individual effort is the keynote of deliberation; it works at its best at peace and on its own, perfecting a technique rather than attracting notice. Immediacy, on the other hand, arrests attention, and does so by its capacity for rapid passing from one object to another. The intensiveness of deliberation, however, precludes this wide canvas and its need for quiet removes the capacity for arresting attention."[1]

It is not difficult to think of examples of these contrasting attitudes of mind. Mr. Churchill and Neville Chamberlain will probably occur to everyone, or perhaps Lloyd George in contrast to Asquith. The "Wait and see" which popular fancy coined for the latter statesman might almost have been designed as the motto of deliberation.

The mind, then, is driven by one or other of the two forces of immediacy or deliberation, the forces in terms of which it makes contact with things. But it is also driven by one or other of the space forces, in terms of which it apprehends things. These forces have been given the names of simplification and amplification, since "simplification suggests the process of contracting the facts into a unifying principle, and amplification, the process of ordering the facts into a chain of evidence."[2] "The one method works in terms of a unifying principle, the other in terms of a chain of evidence; truth or error can be reached by either method, for they merely demonstrate contrasting ways of dealing with the same problems."[3]

"The comparison of Newton with Einstein illustrates this. Newton postulated his Law of Gravitation, and deduced the motions of the worlds around. Einstein, from the evidence of the world around him, arrived at the theory of Relativity. The former great physicist passed from cause to effect, the latter from evidence to probability; the first method being known as the Law of Causation, the second the Law of Probability ... This clash or contrast in the way of apprehending the universe—on the one hand in terms of a unifying principle or Causation, and on the other hand in terms of evidence or Probability—started with the history of thought, and there is reason to believe that it will survive as long as

---

[1] Mackenzie : *The Human Mind,* pp. 21-22.   [2] *Ibid.,* p. 32.   [3] *Ibid.,* p. 24.

that thinking animal, man. It can be traced in pre-scientific times, from the contrast between the Christian Fathers, Origen and Tertullian, to the clash of Reformation and counter-Reformation in John Calvin and Ignatius Loyola. The contrasts exemplify the fact that some minds work essentially in terms of a unifying principle, others in terms of evidence."[1]

" Between John Calvin, the Puritan, and Ignatius Loyola the Jesuit, there was an insuperable barrier ; the former abolished the concrete symbol, and exhorted man to find and know God by a direct mental act of faith ; the latter worked out his system in terms of the evidential symbol and the tangible presence, and passed from these to faith."[2]

This raises the question, fundamental for sociology, as to the extent to which society can mould the mentality of its component individuals. That it can to a great extent condition the expression of this mentality, is undoubted. But if it is dealing with well-defined and differentiated mental forces, it is evidently working within certain limits. Light is thus thrown on the important problems raised by Dr. Benedict[3] and Dr. Mead,[4] and on the whole question of typology in culture.

It is on this point that the evidence of medical psychology is particularly illuminating. In certain conditions of strain the mind goes into defence, a condition of secondary nervousness which in its pronounced form is known as a neurosis. It is in the defences that the mental forces are clearly open to observation, and they are there seen to be constant and consistent in any individual. Before looking at Mackenzie's description of the defences it is necessary to follow his account of primary nervousness, or anxiety, not only as a help to understanding the way in which the defences arise, but because certain points of importance for sociology are involved in this concept.

When the mind is thrown into conflict by stresses in the environment such as a leopard in the bush or a bomb in the next street, its normal rhythm is speeded up and it is thus enabled to deal with the emergency. This speeding up is known medically as anxiety and this state of over-running

---

[1] Mackenzie : *The Human Mind*, pp. 30-31.   [2] *Ibid.*, p. 126.
[3] R. Benedict : *Patterns of Culture*, 1934.
[4] M. Mead : *Sex and Temperament*, 1935.

is ultimately succeeded by a condition of under-running or apathy, before the mind returns to its normal rhythm.

If anxiety is prolonged this state of primary nervousness may be succeeded by the condition of secondary nervousness in which the mind goes into defence. The mental forces shift from the contemplation of an unbearable reality. If the anxiety is due to external causes the secondary reaction eases mental tension for the time being and allows the mind to go over from defence to release when the crisis is over. But the chief cause of persisting anxiety is conflict within the mind arising from the clash of innate mental forces with their contrasting opposites. This dynamic quality of mind upon which Freud insisted, finds its full recognition here. The word " force " is used for this reason and must be borne in mind.

It is, of course, in the early formative years of life that internal mental conflict is set up. If a child with the innate force of immediacy is blocked by an innately deliberate parent, it is thrown into a state of conflict and therefore of persisting anxiety. If its innate force is amplification and it finds itself in an educational system based on simplification, the result again is conflict and anxiety, the conflict being on the unconscious or automatic level. In such a state the child over-values the mental forces that are the opposite of its own, and loses confidence in its own way of doing things without being able to find satisfaction in the opposite way. Loss of confidence and persisting anxiety ensue, and when these become intolerable the mind swings over into defence.

If in the course of time external circumstances add their strain to the internal burden, the defence may develop into neurosis. In defence the innate forces of the mind insist upon finding expression, but they do so at the cost of pinning down mental activity, and isolating it from reality. The mind shifts from the real to the tolerable.[1] The neurosis is a sub-stitute for the anxiety, but at the heavy price of stagnation. The mind automatically removes itself from the situation which has become unbearable, from the effort which has become too great.

Mackenzie shows how the mind whose innate force is amplification combined with immediacy produces the

---

[1] Mackenzie : *The Human Mind*, p. 84.

hysterical neurosis. On the other hand, if the amplifier is a deliberate, it is an obsessional neurosis that will occur.

" In both these reations there appears a demonstration rather than a plea. That is, evidence rather than the unifying principle."[1]

The hysteric with a palsy or a functional paralysis—the loss of the idea of a function described by Pierre Janet—says " Look at my arm or leg, how can I work when these are not functioning ? " He produced concrete evidence for his inability to meet the demands of the situation.

" Hysteria, with its dramatic symptomatology, shows also all the force of immediacy. With the hysterical patient, scenes are common."[2] There is also the marked suggestibility of this reaction.

In the obsessional neurosis the dramatic element of immediacy is absent. " As Freud has pointed out it is less noisy and boisterous than hysteria." But like hysteria it is an example of evidential thinking. " This reaction may reveal itself as an obvious concrete act or it may be confined to the mental sphere alone. It consists of a ritual of some kind, which may be performed in fact, or only thought about ; the nature of the observance varies, from the contemplation of a series of numbers to the performance of some harmless but useless ritual."[3] Or the mind may focus itself upon the supposed disease of some vital organ of the body. In either case, there is a specific withdrawal from the limelight, with the insistence that evidence points to the inadequacy of the organs or to some other untoward circumstance.[4] " The mind shifts to the contemplation of some organised obstruction or to the contemplation or actual performance of an interfering ritual by the individual."[5]

Janet and Freud described and treated hysteria and obsession which are the neuroses of amplification.[6] But Mackenzie has isolated the mental forces underlying them, and has gone on to describe the defences of simplification, which he calls depression and assertion. In both there is a unifying principle. When the simplifier is a deliberate he makes a specific withdrawal based on the principle or plea of his inadequacy. In this defence or neurosis of depression he contemplates his own inadequacy instead of contemplating

[1] Mackenzie : *The Human Mind*, p. 24.   [2] *Ibid.*, p. 24.
[3] *Ibid.*, p. 26.   [4] *Ibid.*, p. 29.   [5] *Ibid.*, p. 89.   [6] *Ibid.*, p. 87.

the intolerable situation. The depressive, whose wife goes off with another man, takes the onus on himself instead of making a fuss and says : " I'm a rotter. I did not deserve her." When, on the other hand, simplification is combined with immediacy, the defence is an assertive instead of a pacific one. The unifying principle is one of super-adequacy instead of inadequacy. The assertive whose wife goes off with someone else declares dramatically that he was too good for her and he will show her what she has lost, whatever it may cost him. He contemplates his super-adequacy rather than his intolerable loss.

It has been suggested that the defences of simplification might be called the " I am " defences, whereas those of amplification might equally well be labelled the " There is " defences. The depressive says : " I am inadequate, I am a rotter." The assertive says : " I am superior." But the hysteric and the obsessive both say : " There is " something preventing me from coping with the situation.

The constancy and consistency of these mental defences indicate clearly that the mental forces which drive the mind are constant in the individual and not interchangeable. A mind that goes periodically into defence does not oscillate between one defence and another but swings consistently into the same one. And the fact that these secondary reactions can only be treated each by its own method points in the same direction. " To face the obsessive with argument or the depressive with evidence only increases the intensity of their reactions."[1] Moreover, when the mind is in release and functioning normally, the same forces are seen to be driving it.

The identification of the four temperamental forces by the psychologist is of great service to the sociologist. But he gets a further clarification. Dr. Bateson explains that among the Iatmul he found a psychological type which he believed to be that described by Kretschmer as cyclorhyme except that the individual did not exhibit the " circular " tendency spoken of by Kretschmer, the tendency to alternate between excitability and stupor.[2] Mackenzie throws light on this point by showing that this alternating rhythm which, in its acute form, is known as the manic-depressive disorder,

[1] Mackenzie : *The Human Mind*, p. 30.
[2] Bateson : *Naven*, 1936, p. 161.

is something quite different from temperamental type. It is, in fact, simply the anxiety-apathy cycle, to which all minds are subject in certain circumstances. The confusion between attitude of mind, which is a question of the temperamental forces, and the anxiety-apathy cycle which is a question of mental rhythm, has come about because anxiety has been confused with immediacy and apathy with deliberation. The over-running of anxiety has been equated with the extensiveness of immediacy and its excitability in the assertive defence. The under-running of apathy has been equated with the intensiveness of deliberation and its depressive defence.[1] There is the same confusion when sociologists describe as mass hysteria what really is mass anxiety. The implications of the two states, if indeed the former exists, obviously are very different.

The great importance of distinguishing in any individual, the two temperamental forces and the factor of mental rhythm is more fully brought out in an examination of Jung's clinical work by Mackenzie.[2] There he shows how extravert and introvert are blanket terms beneath which Jung has not discriminated between temperamental type and mental rhythm and has not identified the two distinct temperamental forces which are present in each individual temperament.

---

[1] Mackenzie : *The Human Mind,* p. 87.
[2] " Jungs Contribution to Clinical Psychiatry," *Proc. of Royal Society of Medicine,* June, 1935, Vol. XXVIII (Section of Psychiatry, pp. 23-36).

II. Temperament and Social Groups

The theory of mind that we have been examining is based on the study of individuals. My own experience in applying it to Ibo problems suggests that it is a working hypothesis full of possibilities for the study of social groups. Clearly the transference from one to the other must be handled with great care. The complexities of the situation increase so markedly when the study of the group replaces that of the individual that the greatest caution is needed. One cannot insist too strongly on the fact that the psychological factor is always one among many others, and that any attempt to use it as a master key to solve all problems merely makes confusion worse confounded. But to refuse to handle it at all because of the risks involved is a counsel of despair.

It will be best first to see what lead, if any, Mackenzie has given in the matter of social groups and then, very tentatively, to see what light is thus thrown on our Ibo material. In his discussion of individual cases he makes certain more or less incidental, but none the less clear, references to group characteristics. He considers, for instance, that in Great Britain it is simplification rather than amplification which is the natural way of thinking of the majority.[1] He also suggests that during the last fifty years the impact of certain currents of Continental thought has set up an over-valuation of amplification which has largely stunted English creative thought and produced a sense of inadequacy.[2]

---

[1] Mackenzie : *The Human Mind,* p. 126, p. 144.

[2] " This contrast between the evidential symbol and the unifying principle—between the mind, which by its very constitution must apprehend in terms of evidence, and the mind which must apprehend in terms of a unifying principle—has had curious repercussions ; since, for some fifty years or more, evidence has been confused with facts. The great British thinkers, with few exceptions, made use of the unifying principle : John Milton, Isaac Newton, John Locke, Adam Smith and a host of others show the way in which the British community apprehend the universe. Charles Darwin, a supreme simplifier, was one of the last of the great British thinkers and, although there have been many clever and erudite English-speaking scholars since his day, there has been an absence of creative thought. This is due to a current tyranny of amplification, in which the evidential method claims the monopoly

This is an interesting suggestion from the point of view of culture contact and we shall return to it. But in the meantime it suggests for investigation the possibility that certain groups or peoples may tend predominantly either to simplification or to amplification.

The two modes of thought or of mental expression described by these terms are so strongly contrasted, so incompatible except on a basis of great mutual tolerance, that it may be that a people can only achieve group stability by standardising one or the other as the normal attitude. Certainly one sees how some of the more stable political units in Europe, for instance, seem on the whole to tend one way or the other. And one also sees the bitter clashes in Central Europe, in Palestine, in India, where the temperamental factor enters in on the unconscious or automatic level and makes irreconcilable, because unrecognised, a conflict that has already enough other elements of disagreement.

It may be that only a people far advanced in stability and security can tolerate the riches and the risk of stamping both attitudes with its social approval.

In any case the larger, inclusive group such as a nation may have predominantly one or other mental outlook, but room may be found for the other in sub-groups such as minority religions or denominations. Examples of this will easily occur to the mind of any Englishman.

If it is found that a people has, on the whole, either a simplifying or an amplifying mentality, the factors both of education and of selection must be considered as contributing to or maintaining the situation. If the admired quality is, for instance, amplification, education will normally speaking emphasise this method and it will be encouraged by general social approval. Simplifiers will find difficulty in adapting

---

over facts. Facts can be arranged and used, either to form a chain of evidence or to build up a unifying principle or theory ; and creative thought will not return to these islands, until the identification of an observable fact with the use of evidence as a method of thinking is dispelled. So long as evidence is identified with fact and called scientific, and the use of the unifying principle is identified with fiction and called speculative, just so long will the method which characterised British science, from Newton to Faraday, be described as obsolete, and the method which characterises anything but British thinking be called clever." *The Human Mind,* p. 126-127.

themselves to this society unless there is tolerance for minority points of view and means for their expression. If there is not, the deviants will constitute a problem.

It may be though, that the factor of selection will operate for the elimination of deviants. It may work in the direction of breeding them out. Data on this point are lacking, so far as I know.

History suggests, however, that selection may work also by a system of purges in societies that have not yet achieved the maturity and stability which make for tolerance and for diversity in unity. Louis XIV of France, when he revoked the Edict of Nantes and drove out the Huguenots, probably eliminated a large element of simplification from France. England, on the other hand, at about the same time, was eliminating the amplifying Stuarts from the body politic. Germany, later in the day, would seem to have reacted violently against amplification, as expressed by the Jewish people.

Turning to the second pair of temperamental opposites, those of immediacy and deliberation, it is clear from the whole tenor of *The Human Mind* that both these forces must co-exist in any social group such as a nation or tribe. They are the poles of mutual attraction on whose interplay the life of society largely depends. Marriage, at any rate in Britain, is normally between these contrasting types. So entirely are they complementary that social life without both is hardly conceivable. That they may and do conflict is the reverse side of the medal.

Although both forces are present, it may be, however, that a community will select one or other as its " admired " or predominant type.

An Englishman who had married a French woman told me one day, apropos of no psychological theories at all, that for him the difference between the French and the English temperament was indicated by the difference between their traffic lights. In Paris green changed instantaneously to red, thereby precipitating one of those crises in which the normal life of that city flourishes. In London, as he pointed out, green passes to amber and the pedestrian, duly warned, makes a dignified passage to the opposite pavement. Each has found the method best suited to him. And the recognition that in each case a different mental force is at work does something to clarify the situation. The contrast between the French and British attitudes to empire will at once come to the mind of anyone interested in such matters.

It may be, also, that the role for which men are cast in any particular culture approximates rather to one type and that of women to the other. In England, it is not hard to see how the strong silent man and the more voluble and expressive woman of public imagination are cast for their respective parts. And when Punch depicts two dogcarts driven by two pacific Englishmen meeting in an impassably narrow road, it is the wife of one who says to her spouse, " Go on, drive him off the road ! " while the other replies to his male opponent : " Don't worry old chap, I've got one like that at home myself ! "

In such a situation a more subtle form of maladjustment will arise than in the case of, say, an amplifier in a predominantly simplifying social group because in the eyes of society a particular form of temperament has been identified with sex. Those, therefore, whose innate temperament is the opposite of that expected of their sex have the double disadvantage of being out of gear not only with what is expected of a member of that society, but with what is considered " natural " to a member of that sex.[1]

Such a brief statement of the question of temperamental forces and types is perhaps enough to suggest the relevance that it may have to sociological investigation in general. But it is also clear that in studying a community the investigator must consider not only the temperamental forces but also the question of anxiety and apathy. Apart from the ups and downs of circumstance to which any society may, in whole or in part, be subject, the investigator has to consider whether, generally speaking, his community is functioning in terms of confidence and mental release or in terms of anxiety and mental defence. This may be particularly important in a situation of culture contact, where opposite temperamental forces may have clashed and produced conflict and hence anxiety and defence.

Contact problems, such, for instance, as the relative ease or difficulty with which one culture will assimilate elements of another, might well repay investigation in the light of the psychological factors we have been considering.

---

[1] Psychological observation on this point is supplemented by the sociological data in Mead, *Sex and Temperament*.

That all such situations are enormously complex will be recognised either by a historian or a sociologist. But the presence of a psychological factor, though only as one of many, is certainly suggested by the facts.[1] And its importance in any situation is that it operates on the unconscious, or automatic, level and tends to generate a bitterness of which the source is unrecognised and which is therefore not accessible to reason. The general principles of individual therapy suggestd in *The Human Mind* would also seem to be relevant to a situation of culture conflict. They consist largely in making the maladjusted individual understand the existence of contrasting temperamental forces and the dynamics involved, and thus giving him control over the situation through understanding. This, however, is the concern of the citizen rather than of the scientific investigator.

---

[1] It should be unnecessary to point out that the temperamental factor, important though it may be in the social equation, is none the less only one factor and as such is only one key, and not the only one, to the understanding of a society. It is not the short cut to understanding of which Malinowski was so rightly sceptical. See Firth : *We, the Tikopia,* 1936. Preface by Malinowski, p. vii.

III. Temperament and Ibo Society

One cannot, I think, doubt that of amplication and simplification it is the former which is culturally standardised among the Ibo described in this book. Concrete or evidential symbolism is the very marrow of their thought. Their religion is full of it. A shrine in *ihu agbara* [¯ ¯ ¯ _ _]—the face of the supernatural being—or *ono agbara* [¯ ¯ ¯ _ _]—the mouth—in other words, the place where *agbara* comes to receive food in sacrifice. Prayer is assisted by the use of a concrete symbol. Of *ofo* people say : " We take it to pray with." Any religious ceremony consists largely in the manipulation of sacred objects.

Every feature of daily activity of any importance seems to crystallise, as with the ancient Romans, into a deity or sub-deity with a material representation. *Mbatake* [_ ¯ _ _] —literally the entering in of wealth is a carved wooden object to which sacrifices are offered and which is to ensure the success of the owner in trade.

Ci, the creating deity, is referred to less as a universal, all pervading spirit than as a multitude of localised *Ci*—your *Ci*, my *Ci*—having each their shrine or sacred symbol.

In the same way ritual, formalised patterns of behaviour regulate innumerable situations, and have certain common elements running through many of them. Of these the use of definite numbers, and particularly of the sacred number four and its multiples, is specially marked. At childbirth the umbilical cord must be touched four times by the midwife, and at each time the mother must refuse to have it cut until the fourth. It is then severed with the piece of sharpened stick used on this occasion.

When an *ofo* holder dies and his *ofo* is ceremonially handed over to his successor, it must be offered to him four times and only at the fourth time must he accept. Otherwise people would say that he had wanted the death of the former holder. Such a ceremony did not take place while I was in Umueke but it was described to me.

249

When the widow or widows of a man are being ritually set free from their period of mourning, they must, among many other observances, go to the central Agbaja market place and certain specified women must take them by the hand and pull them four times into the market.

The number four occurs time and agáin in the offerings brought for sacrifice to a deity, in the gifts specified for certain occasions such as those from the husband to his wife's mother after the birth of a child, in the rites performed by a *dibea,* in the number of days in the week.

And even when the number four is not involved, any account of food presented or exchanged tends to be given in numerical terms. One does not hear that many yams and much palm wine were brought. One is told that there were sixty yams and eight gourds of palm wine.

Ritual, usually with this motif of four or multiples of four, accompanies almost every important occasion. What has sometimes been called the sacralisation of the crises of life, such as birth, initiation at puberty, marriage, death is, of course, a widely spread social phenomenon. But sacralisation does not necessarily imply an elaborate ritual. Here, however, in Ibo culture there is ritualisation of one occasion after another, sometimes fairly simple though still quite formal as at the circumcision or clitoridectory of a baby, sometimes elaborate as at death and second burial ceremonies, or again when a baby, soon after birth, is carried by its mother and both are led by the family elder to the ancestral shrines. The regulation of life by formal rules, which we have described earlier, is closely related to this ritualising tendency.

We have not yet referred to the ritual of magic as practised by the *nde dibea.* Ibo magic is full of ritual and symbolism, and magic is a very common feature of Ibo life. There are certain occasions such as the boys' initiation rites for which it is socially prescribed. But usually it is performed at the demand of an individual to meet some need of the moment, such as sickness, or to protect his family and property against enemies and thieves. There is, therefore, all this occasional ritual in addition to what might be called the regular ritual accompanying the successive phases of existence.

And here the absence of witchcraft belief among the inland Ibo is an interesting point. Is it possible that this absence can be correlated with their mentality ? Typically, witchcraft would seem to be the possession of an inherent quality rather than the performance of a traditional ritual. An individual is a witch, whereas an individual makes or possesses magic. And there would seem to be two opposite attitudes that a witch may take up. Sometimes he or she may confess with horror and self-abasement to the harm she has wrought. Sometimes the witch may boast of his or her superior powers and use them to obtain a dominant social position. Not having lived with a people possessing witchcraft beliefs I suggest these characteristics very tentatively. But if they are at all correct, they sound very much like the attitudes of depression and assertion. These, it will be remembered, are the mental defences of simplification and one would not, therefore, expect to find them, at any rate in an institutionalised form, in an amplifying culture like that of the inland Ibo. The witchcraft beliefs of places like Onitsha and Arǝ Cuku, towards the fringes of Ibo country, might presumably be intrusive. If so, and if they have come into an amplifying culture, it would be interesting to see how far the forms of witchcraft can be modified by an amplifying mentality. I have no data on this point. And I raise this whole question of the absence of witchcraft beliefs among the people I lived with, not in order to dogmatise about it, but to suggest it as one of the many points that might be investigated in the light of the theory of mind we have been discussing.

A further tendency to ritualistic, formal behaviour among the Ibo appears in their constant resort to a formal oath in one type of relationship after another. Two friends, not content with a general reliance on the principles of friendship, will swear together. A stranger who comes and settles in the village will swear repeatedly with his host. I was told that the elder of the two strangers who had settled in Umuɛkɛ had sworn many times with N.Ɛ., the oldest man in this division of the village, and looked up to as its leader. A husband will swear with the lover he has recognised and approved for his wife. A *dibea* making medicine for a patient will swear with the patient and will accompany the oath with a ritual rich in concrete symbolism.

I myself experienced the difficulty that arises between Ibo and British when each expresses himself according to his own mentality. The elders of the village, in spite of the fact that some of them were nervous lest the white woman might have designs upon their land and palm trees, were none the less convinced that if she decided to decamp they would be ridiculed by the surrounding villages. They were therefore always urging me to swear with them that I would not go away. I, on the other hand, assured them, whenever these requests were made, that I was actuated only by friendly motives towards them, and that there was no need to resort to formal oaths, which I should certainly not consider any more binding than my informal assurances. We each remained outwardly polite, but inwardly unconvinced and a little irritated. This is typical of what tends to happen, though not always with politeness, when minds working in terms of general principles meet those working in terms of demonstrable evidence and neither side realises where the source of the difficulty lies.

When we turn to consider the other pair of mental forces, those of immediacy and deliberation, it is again clear which of them has been standardised on the dominant attitudes of the community we have been considering. There is a tempo of crisis, drama, excitement, sociability, to say nothing of noise, which is apt to leave the English participant a little stunned. No one could doubt the tendency to heighten the intensity of the moment, who has listened to an argument or seen the squall that suddenly breaks over a group discussing some matter or trying a case. The wave of excitement rises momentarily so high that one is left breathless.

And the quick comeback of word or action which promotes a vivid social intercourse also, on its reverse side, constitutes a social danger which, as we have seen, the community tries to avert by making false accusation a penal offence.

Also symptomatic of immediacy, with its tendency to live in the present, is the ready Ibo adaptability to new ideas, the adoption, both for better and worse, of new standards, the eagerness to be in with the stream of progress.

One sees, too, the interplay of the dramatic volubility of the orator with the suggestibility of his audience. And, indeed, it has been institutionalised as one of the methods by which public business such as the judging of cases is transacted.

If one asks what are the qualifications required of a leader in practical affairs, it is not wisdom or dignity that will be mentioned, though this does not mean that they will not be valued. But the individual required must be one who " gets mouth." He must also get sense and be able to " free one from the case." And " strong eye " is also referred to. But getting mouth, being able to speak, is important. And it is one of the complaints against the British that they will not listen, " they just cut the case." Oratory and volubility do not appeal to the strong silent Briton, whose paucity of words is disconcerting. He must be plotting something, in his cunning way, under this mask of silence.

The suggestibility that is so responsive to the orator comes out in many other ways. It helps to account for the comfort that people get from their diviners and magicians. It explains the speed and volume of the rumours that sweep through the bush. It is part of the quick sympathy for certain kinds of suffering that is so noticeable among these people.

It is connected, too, with their sociability, their need for many and continuous human contacts. " The more we are together, the better we shall be " might be their slogan. The seething crowd of an Ibo market with its chattering and its gossip—and its transaction of business withal—epitomises much of Ibo life. The constant *mikiri*—meetings—too, are social occasions *par excellence*. The system of living in house groups and the fact that most activities—pounding palm nuts, cracking kernels, making palm oil—are carried on out of doors, means that even when an individual is engaged alone on a job, he or she is not solitary. Often work such as hoeing is done by teams. And team work may be accompanied by singing, with a consequent heightening of a sense of solidarity which also finds expression in the dancing of the men on market days, and of the women in the market place on other days. Solitude is held to be a mark of wickedness, as we saw in the case of Awazie. An Ibo friend of mine in London tells me how the absence of this general passion for sociability is one of the things that depresses him most. It is not merely that he misses his family, but that life is lived on a different basis. When I tell him that, after a day's work, I enjoy a quiet evening alone, he is appalled and then incredulous. " The English—are they human ? " one hears him thinking——.

With Ibo sociability goes that pleasant convention of

hospitality which prompts every woman to ask the passing caller " Shall I cook for you ? " and which means that the host will bring out *ɔje* [‾ ‾]—kola or a substitute—and palm wine to pass the time of day.

There is, too, a demonstrative element in human relationships that one sees when the men play with the babies or when a small boy covers the arm of his baby brother with kisses. There is a constant tendency towards a dramatic form of behaviour.

An individual who is forcibly prevented, probably for tactical reasons by his or her own side, from having a say in a case, will take refuge in some form or other of expression, as though incapable of remaining quiet. I have seen the mother of S., unable to contain her feelings any longer while a case was being tried, burst into a strange, prowling dance on the fringe of the crowd, with her whole body swaying and gesticulating. A woman will express her pleasure at a gift by graceful dance movements of her arms and body.

The shooting of guns is a normal method of celebrating a notable event either individual or communal. When Agbaja obtained permission to have a school, they went to their central market, the *ama* half on one occasion and *owɛrɛ* on the other, dressed up in any gala clothes they possessed or could borrow and shot their Dane guns to express their pride and satisfaction. I missed this celebration by a few days through being on leave, but was given vivid accounts of it. There is no doubt that the natural medium of these people is of the twopence coloured and not of the penny plain variety.

One sees, too, the element of boasting that appears again and again both in individual and in communal affairs. A " big " woman will kill a fowl for her co-meeting members when they come to her house, not because it is obligatory but to boast with, as she will explain. In the modest scale of Agbaja living the gesture is considerable.

At one point the people of Umuɛkɛ begged me not to leave them, adding, lest I should take merit to myself, that they used me to boast with. But when they tried also to get the Agbaja school established in their village, the rest of Agbaja protested, on the ground that a school and a white woman were too much for any village. Evidently they wanted to do some boasting on their own.

In a somewhat different context, boasting appears to be one element in the cannibalism practised by these people. To kill an enemy is one thing, but to eat him is to establish ones contempt and superiority beyond a peradventure.

This spirit of open rivalry is again a recurrent feature of their life. It has been institutionalised in their social organisation, as we have seen, in their system of dual division and is one of the driving forces of the community. It appears again when the village goes to the Agbaja market place after the annual path clearing, and " we count ourselves to show how many we are." And how often does one hear : " We want to make our place—or our market—get up."

In the same way, among individuals, it is the go-getter that is admired, the man who has wives and children and bestirs himself and makes money. A man who just sits quiet is not respected. The general rite we have described which is performed to make the dead man " smart," in the sense of being a pusher, is an indication of these admired qualities. A man whose *ɔba* is not full of yams will, as we have seen, feel shame if anyone goes into it and sees his small stock.

When one suggests that immediacy is the dominant note in Ibo society, it is in fact the men that one is mainly thinking of. The role for which they are cast would seem to be epitomised in the boys initiation rites of which the chief feature, it will be remembered, is the acquiring of aggressive medicine. It is not *nnyiε ɔgwθ*—female or cooling or defensive medicine—that they acquire on this notable occasion but *okε ɔgwθ*—aggressive medicine—to be used against strangers or women or anyone who has not participated in these rites. It is characteristic of the whole attitude to life marked out as befitting men in this culture. Theirs is, in some sense, the dominant social mode of expression. But it is interesting to consider the position of the women. Looking back on the facts, which one observed in ignorance of any theories of temperament, one sees that the social role of the women is, to a large extent, that of deliberation. It is suggested by the terminology of medicine in which female medicine is the cooling defensive antidote of male or aggressive medicine. And it is confirmed by one situation after another in which the emphasis is either on the peace-making function associated with women or on the particular techniques that they employ either individually or communally.

In actual fighting, particularly between two villages, one of the recognised means of re-establishing peace is for the women, the " sisters " of the fighters, to put ɔkɔrɔ leaf between them to stop them fighting.

If a man kills his " brother " it is customary that the women born in the village should come from the places where they are married to deal either ritually or practically with this forbidden act of violence. It suggests that they are to some extent looked on as guardians of the peace. Nwa Onyɛ Okoro pointed out that in trying a case it would be well to have one or two good women who would help to put peace between the parties to the case.

Women seem, moreover, to be expected on the whole to behave quietly and circumspectly vis-a-vis the men. As between men and women born in the same village or exogamous unit of villages, there is Ekutera Nene's remark that she will not speak freely in the presence of her brother but will just keep quiet. As to the behaviour of women in a case where both men and women are concerned, there is Abraham's comment that the women will not speak much if men are present.

We have seen that the women take the line that they sit quietly at home and obey their husbands. And we have seen how, when a woman is displeased with her husband she reacts, not aggressively, but by withholding his food from him. And when the women are collectively displeased with the men, their technique of mass withdrawal until the men are brought to their knees strikes one as a pacific retreat par excellence.

As for the greater conservatism of the women than of the men in adopting new ways and in advancing to meet European culture, there are many factors, occupational and social, which must be given due weight. But it may be that a culturally standardised attitude of deliberation is one factor in the situation.

There are occasions when the women seem to adopt the methods of immediacy, as when they pounce on and rub with mud the defaulting women at the time of their annual religious rites. There is also the excitement and swift tempo of their midnight judging of a woman's case. But one notices that both these examples are exclusively women's occasions. The men withdraw and leave the field to feminine occupation.

Whether or not this is relevant I do not know. It is a point
for future investigation.[1] But one must also notice that in
the midnight judging there seems to be a certain balance
between the two opposite attitudes of immediacy and
deliberation. Even though there is great and voluble excitement on the one hand, there is none the less the indirect
method of bringing pressure to bear on the guilty woman
by " dancing for her," instead of the direct method of the
men of seizing the victim's property if he defaults in his
rightful payment of fine or subscription.

As to the question of deviants in a culture where society
has assigned the role of immediacy to the men and, on the
whole, that of deliberation to the women, we cannot go into
the matter here. But I look back and realise that in the uneasy
atmosphere of N.E.'s compound and also that of his sons,
where there were always troubles and grievances of one
kind and another, the element of deviance was clearly present.
The old man, with his quiet, shrewd, dignified behaviour,
his wife, S's mother, with her dramatic outbursts and her
quick temper, were both the opposites of what society
required them to be. In the same way S., with his tendency
to morose manners and his feeling that all the world had a
down on him, and his wife, R., who could storm and scream
and curse through a long, hot afternoon, were also deviants
from the social norm and were no doubt further exasperated
by the tension in the paternal circle.

A discussion of the temperamental forces observable in
any particular culture or community should include a description of the pathological types most commonly found
there. Since it is in the neuroses that the temperamental
forces can be most clearly observed it would be of great
value to have details about any neurotic or unstable individuals found in the community. This would require
special training in the observer and the point is raised here
not in the hope of dealing with it but in order to stress its
importance in the study of temperament in culture.

There are certain facts which one noted in a somewhat
desultory fashion, not realising their significance at the time,
but which indicate the need for expert investigation. There
is, for instance, the belief that an individual who shows signs

---

[1] It may have a bearing on the question of the Aba riots.

of mental instability may be troubled by *Agwọ Nshi,* the spirit which presides over divination and magic. Such an individual will be taken by his relatives to a diviner—*dibea*—and if it is confirmed that *Agwọ Nshi* is troubling him—*na-awa ya* [_ _ ̄ ̄]—and wants him to become a diviner, he will, if he can afford it, embark upon the necessary initiation. As a diviner he is believed to have the power of seeing the supernatural world. Part of his technique is the beating with a deafening noise of a tortoise shell, which might well produce a state of conditioned trance in those trained to it. His job is then to answer the questions of his clients and there is no doubt that extreme suggestibility would be very serviceable to him in picking up information from them about the very problems they are laying before him. There is enough to raise the question whether divination in this society does not make use of the hysterical type of instability associated with amplification and immediacy.

In the same way some of the accounts one was given of *amọma,* a force said to drive some people, were suggestive of hysteria.

These are only straws in the wind, but they point in the same direction as the normal phenomena we have been discussing. Amplification and immediacy would seem to be the dominant attitudes of Ibo culture in the area here described.[1] When one reflects that these are the opposites of the English cultural norm it is clear that a culture contact situation leading to anxiety may easily arise. And when, in addition, there is everything in Ibo economic conditions to promote anxiety, even without psychological friction, it is again clear that a stable social equilibrium will be hard to achieve unless understanding contributes to its establishment.

---

[1] A man from the Mbiɛri area at present in London says that his people look with distrust on the people of Arọ Cuku as being cunning and indirect, and as never saying what they are really thinking. This suggests that possibly in Arọ deliberation may be the norm.

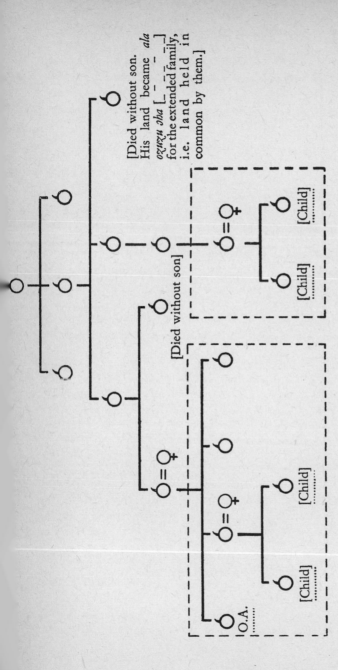

[Died without son.
His land became *ala*
oʒuʒu oha [– –]
for the extended family,
i.e. land held in
common by them.]

[Died without son]

[Child]

[Child]

[Child]

O.A.

[Child]

[Child]

GENEALOGICAL TABLE OF MALES OF KINDRED OF UMU NWACUKU

The dotted lines show the different land owning groups.

♂ denotes male.   ♀ denotes female.

ROUGH SKETCH MAP OF THE VILLAGE OF UMUƐKƐ AGBAJA

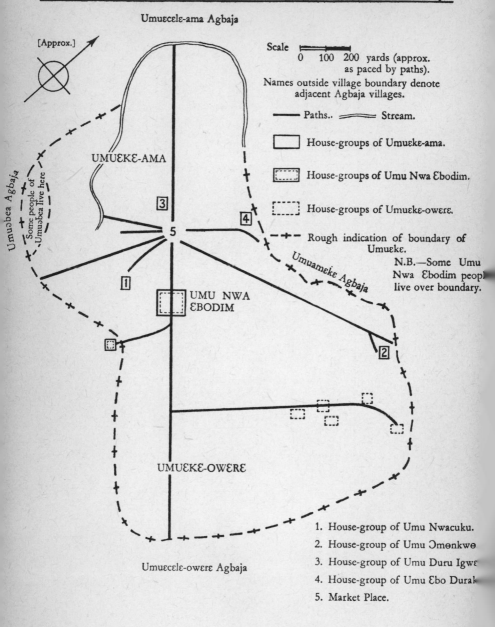

Umuɛcɛlɛ-ama Agbaja

[Approx.]

UMUƐKƐ-AMA

Umuɔbɛa Agbaja

Some people of Umuɔbɛa live here

Umuameke Agbaja

UMU NWA ƐBODIM

UMUƐKƐ-OWERƐ

Umuɛcɛlɛ-owerɛ Agbaja

Scale

0   100   200   yards (approx.
                 as paced by paths).

Names outside village boundary denote
      adjacent Agbaja villages.

———— Paths.. ≈≈≈≈ Stream.

☐ House-groups of Umuɛkɛ-ama.

⬚ House-groups of Umu Nwa Ɛbodim.

⬚ House-groups of Umuɛkɛ-owerɛ.

–+– Rough indication of boundary of
      Umuɛkɛ.

      N.B.—Some Umu
      Nwa Ɛbodim peopl
      live over boundary.

1. House-group of Umu Nwacuku.
2. House-group of Umu Ɔmɛnkwɛ
3. House-group of Umu Duru Igwɛ
4. House-group of Umu Ɛbo Durak
5. Market Place.

260

INDEX